INTRODUCTORY ECONOMETRICS
FOR UNDERGRADUATES

Introductory Econometrics for Undergraduates
A Student's Guide to the Basics

Elia Kacapyr

Routledge
Taylor & Francis Group

LONDON AND NEW YORK

First published 2011 by M.E. Sharpe.Inc

Published 2016 by Routledge
2 Park Square, Milton Park, Abingdon, Oxon OX14 4RN
711 Third Avenue, New York, NY 10017, USA

Routledge is an imprint of the Taylor & Francis Group, an informa business

Library of Congress Cataloging-in-Publication Data

Kacapyr, Elia, 1956–
  Introductory econometrics for undergraduates : a student's guide to the basics / Elia Kacapyr.
      p. cm.
  Includes bibliographical references and index.
  ISBN 978-0-7656-2792-6 (pbk. : alk. paper)
  1. Econometrics. I. Title.
  HB139.K26 2011
  330.01'5195—dc22   2010041814

ISBN 13: 978-0-76562-792-6 (pbk)

Contents

Preface

It is amazing how much ground is covered in some undergraduate econometrics courses. A working knowledge of statistics is required to understand econometrics and some courses present or review this prerequisite knowledge. By the end of the semester, students may be grappling with vector autoregressions or instrumental variable techniques.

I believe it better to go slower, cover less ground, and give students a solid intuitive understanding of the fundamental concepts. "Intuitive" does not mean "easy" or "skip the proofs." Just the opposite – having econometric intuition means you understand the concepts so well that you can guess how a proof will turn out.

It takes me two semesters to cover the material in this book. The material is presented concisely and students learn by doing. The problems at the end of each chapter require students to apply the concepts they have learned. Downloading the data, wrestling with statistical software, and interpreting the output takes time.

Econometrics can be a real eye-opener for some students. They come to understand that some of the theories they have learned can be questioned and subjected to tests using real-world data. The data sets for all of the end-of-chapter problems in this text are available online at www.mesharpe-student.com. In addition, instructors should challenge students to develop their own hypotheses and test them with data the students have gathered. I always tell students that grubbing the data will take you at least four times as long as you think it will.

Students may want to use this text to supplement the one required for their course. The solutions to the odd-numbered problems are presented in the back of the book, and there are six sample exams with solutions so that students can gauge their abilities.

A course with terms like "heteroskedasticity," "first-order Markov scheme," and "pseudoautocorrelation" can seem intimidating, but it doesn't have to be. In fact, my hope is that the typical junior or senior economics major could pick up all of these topics and much more from reading this text and working on the problems at the end of each chapter.

EK
Ithaca, NY

Chapter 1

The Nature of Econometrics

What is Econometrics?

The Econometric Methodology

Many Applications

Terms

Chapter 1 Problems

1.1 What is Econometrics?

Literally, econometrics means "economic measurement." Therefore, national income accounting and other forms of economic data such as consumer confidence indexes and the like could be considered econometrics. However, in practice econometrics is about testing economic hypotheses with statistical techniques. Respected econometricians have given us a variety of definitions. One favorite, perhaps because of its brevity, is from Henri Theil: "Econometrics is concerned with the empirical determination of economic laws." (Theil 1971, p.1).

1.2 The Econometric Methodology

You might remember the "scientific method" from a middle school science class. Econometric methodology is a specific form of that. Let's work through an example: Keynes's law of consumption:

> The fundamental psychological law, upon which we are entitled to depend with great confidence both *a priori* from our knowledge of human nature and from the detailed facts of experience, is that men are disposed, as a rule and on average, to increase their consumption as their income increases, but not by as much as the increase in income. (Keynes 1936, p. 96)

The steps of the econometric methodology can be applied to this law.

1) State the theory, law, or hypothesis

It is impossible to state Keynes's law more eloquently than the master economist himself. However, it may be stated more succinctly: When income goes up, consumer spending goes up, but not by as much.

2) Specify the econometric model

This step requires writing the idea in mathematical form. One of the simplest forms is slope-intercept. Again, from middle school you may remember $y = mx + b$. We shall replace the "y" with CONS (consumer spending) and the "x" with DPI (consumer disposable income):

$$CONS = m\,(DPI) + b$$

The tradition in econometrics is to write the same equation this way:

$$CONS = \beta_0 + \beta_1\,DPI + u$$

Where "m" is represented by β_1 and "b" is represented by β_0. The "u" is known as the error term, disturbance, or residual. (You will soon come to see that everything in econometrics has at least two names.) This formulation assumes the relationship between CONS and DPI is linear (in slope-intercept form). The error term is explicit recognition that the relationship is not exact.

Notice that Keynes's law implies that $0 < \beta_1 < 1$. That way if DPI increases by \$1, CONS will increase by \$$\beta_1$.

3) Collect the data

Now we need data on CONS and DPI so that we can see if CONS does indeed go up when DPI increases, but not by as much. Several alternatives present themselves. The Bureau of Labor Statistics annually surveys households concerning their income and expenditures. We could get CONS and DPI for each household in 2009. This is cross-sectional data.

HOUSEHOLD	CONS	DPI
1	\$76,234	\$83,234
2	\$22,346	\$23,457
3	\$56,873	\$57,876
4	\$44,829	\$35,987
...	...	...

Another possibility is to use the macroeconomic data in the National Income and Product Accounts. Here we have CONS and DPI for the entire nation over the years. This is time-series data.

YEAR	CONS billions of \$ per capita	DPI billions of \$ per capita
2002	24630	26236
2003	25101	26596
2004	25816	27230
2005	26476	27340
...	...	...

Finally, we could pool both cross-sectional and time-series data. If we surveyed the households in the Consumer Expenditure Survey over the years, then we would have panel data.

YEAR	Household	CONS	DPI
2002	1	\$76,234	\$83,234
2003	1	\$77,703	\$82,316
2002	2	\$22,346	\$23,457
2003	2	\$29,294	\$34,970
...	...	...	...

In any case, we would have a vector of data on CONS and a vector of data on DPI. Using the macro time-series data from 1929 to 2009, we can graph the numbers.

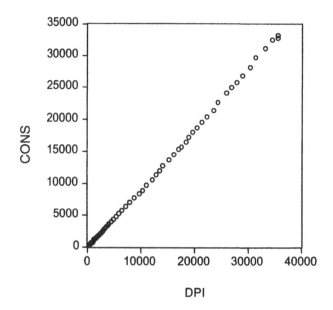

Each dot on the scattergram represents the CONS/DPI combination for a particular year.

4) Estimate the parameters of the model

In this step we find values for β_0 and β_1. There are many possibilities. The "eyeball" technique involves drawing a straight line freehand in the scattergram above. If we use graph paper we can read off β_0 – it is the vertical intercept. β_1 is the slope of the line.

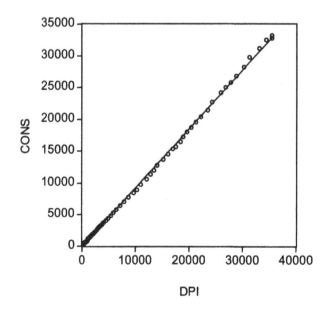

If we extend the line back to the vertical axis, it appears as if it may intersect at around (0,0). The slope of this line, as calculated from the graph, is about one. Therefore, we have CONS = 0.0 + 1.0 DPI + u.

One problem with the eyeball technique is that different people may estimate different lines. We need a more scientific approach. Indeed, much of the next chapter will be concerned with developing such a technique – ordinary least-squares.

5) Test the theory, law, or hypothesis

If we use ordinary least-squares to estimate β_0 and β_1, we get:

$$CONS = -161.47 + 0.93 \, DPI + u$$

These results verify Keynes's law of consumption because $\beta_1 = 0.93$, which is greater than zero but less than 1. The equation above makes it clear that if DPI increased by \$1, then CONS would be expected to increase by \$0.93. Indeed, the 0.93 is an estimate of the marginal propensity to consume in the United States. Given an extra dollar, the typical American will increase consumption by 93 cents.

Statisticians are very loath to "accept" theories. In this case, we are not willing to say that our analysis has verified Keynes' law of consumption. Instead, we say our analysis has "not rejected" the theory. If we were to conduct the analysis with data from another country or time period, or if we used cross-sectional data instead of time-series data, we would obtain different results. The new results could produce a β_1 that is greater than one or less than zero, which would reject Keynes' theory.

6) Forecast with the model

We can use our results to make predictions. For example, in 2009 DPI = \$35,505. We would expect CONS = \$32,858 (= -161.47 + .93 × \$35,505). This forecast is almost perfect given that CONS = \$32,812 in 2009.

1.3 Many Applications

The econometric methodology outlined above has been applied to an incredible array of theories and hypotheses. The popular book *Freakonomics: A Rogue Economist Explores the Hidden Side of Everything* (Levitt and Dubner 2009) details some of the more exotic applications: Did legalization of abortion lower the crime rate? Is a backyard swimming pool more dangerous to little children than a gun? Do street level drug dealers make less than the minimum wage?

Some of these issues do not appear to be within the realm of economics, but they are. Remember, economics is about how people make choices to maximize their satisfaction. All of the applications in *Freakonomics* concern the choices people make in order to get the most out of life.

Many disciplines have their own versions of the econometric methodology. Thus we have biometrics, psychometrics, and sociometrics. Sabermetrics is the analysis of baseball with this very same methodology. No matter what field we are investigating, the object is to test hypotheses with statistical techniques.

Terms

Cross-sectional data – Observations on multiple entities at one point in time.

Econometrics – Testing economic hypotheses with statistical techniques.

Econometric model – A mathematical expression of the relationship between variables.

Ordinary least-squares – A technique for fitting lines to scattergrams.

Panel data – Observations on multiple entities over time.

Scattergram – A graph showing corresponding pairs of values for two variables.

Time-series data – Observations on an entity over time.

Chapter 1 Problems

1. The hours of study (per weekday) and GPA of three students are given below:

hours	GPA
2	2
4	3
2	3

A) Draw a line through these dots so that the sum of the vertical distances from the dots to the line equals zero. When the dot lies above the line the distance is positive. When the dot lies below the line the distance is negative. Can you draw another line that meets this criterion?

B) Now draw two lines through the dots so that the sum of the absolute value of the vertical distances between the dots and the line is minimized.

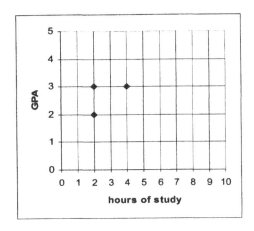

2. The SAT scores and GPA of three students are given below:

SAT	GPA
800	2
1000	2
1000	3

A) Draw a line through these dots so that the sum of the vertical distances from the dots to the line equals zero. When the dot lies above the line the distance is positive. When the dot lies below the line the distance is negative. Can you draw another line that meets this criterion?

B) Now draw two lines through the dots so that the sum of the absolute value of the vertical distances between the dots and the line is minimized.

SAT	GPA
800	2
1000	2
1000	3

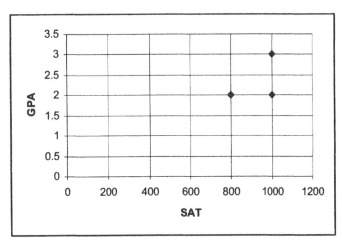

3. Suppose we estimate the following regression: CONS $= -1218 + 0.97$ DPI $+ u$

   A) What is the predicted value of CONS in 1960 given DPI $= \$9,735$ in 1960?

   B) Actual CONS in 1960 equals $8,837. Give several reasons why the forecast may be off from the actual.

4. Suppose we estimate the following regression: CONS $= -1218 + 0.97$ DPI $+ u$

   A) What is the predicted value of CONS in 2005 given DPI $= \$27,340$ in 2005?

   B) Actual CONS in 2005 equals $26,476. Give several reasons why the forecast may be off from the actual.

5. A) Specify an econometric model to test the theory that an increase in the money supply has no effect on real GDP.

   B) What does this theory imply about the value of β_1?

6. A) Specify an econometric model to test the theory that an increase in the interest rate on automobile loans will lower car sales.

   B) What does this theory imply about the value of β_1?

Chapter 2

Simple Regression Analysis

The Basic Idea

Notation

The Ordinary Least-Squares Technique

Deriving the Ordinary Least-Squares Estimators

An Example of Regression Analysis

The Stochastic Error Term

Example: Economic Performance and Corruption

Terms

Chapter 2 Problems

Appendix: Algebra of Summation Signs

2.1 The Basic Idea

Suppose we have a hypothesis that X affects Y negatively. That is, whenever X increases, this causes Y to decrease. The econometric model to test this hypothesis might be: $Y = \beta_0 + \beta_1 X + u$. If the hypothesis is true, then β_1 should be negative.

Now we collect data on Y and X. Here are the data and a scattergram of them:

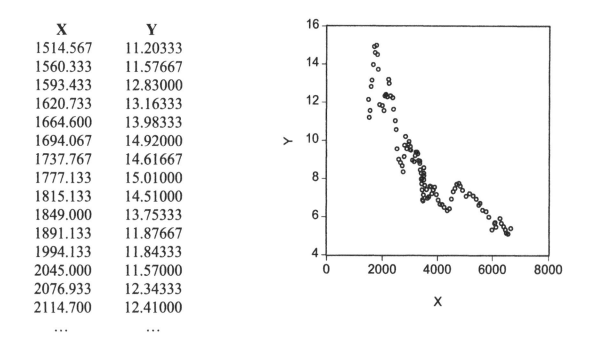

X	Y
1514.567	11.20333
1560.333	11.57667
1593.433	12.83000
1620.733	13.16333
1664.600	13.98333
1694.067	14.92000
1737.767	14.61667
1777.133	15.01000
1815.133	14.51000
1849.000	13.75333
1891.133	11.87667
1994.133	11.84333
2045.000	11.57000
2076.933	12.34333
2114.700	12.41000
...	...

We need to fit a straight line through the points on the scattergram. We discussed the "eyeball" technique in Chapter 1. Another possibility is to take the point furthest to the left and the point furthest to the right and draw a line connecting them, ignoring all the other points. Both of these techniques are simple and easy to apply, but lack rigor.

The preferred technique is to fit a line so that the sum of the vertical distances from the points to the line squared is minimized. That is, fit a line such that Σu^2 is minimized. Later we will be in a position to see why this technique is preferred.

2.2 Notation

Even though it may appear fussy, notation is important in econometrics. All of the subscripts, carets, and bars we will use symbolize concepts. If your notation is incorrect it implies that your understanding of the underlying concepts may be faulty.

To test the notion that X affects Y negatively, we have written the following econometric model: $Y = \beta_0 + \beta_1 X + u$. Nothing is wrong with this notation. However, we may add subscripts to indicate that this is the "i*th*" of n observations on X and Y:

$$Y_i = \beta_0 + \beta_1 X_i + u_i$$

The term u_i indicates that there will be n error terms. Y_i is known as the "dependent variable" or "y-variable." X_i is called the "independent variable" or the "x-variable." β_0 and β_1 are referred to as "estimators" or "structural parameters." We do not know their values, but can estimate them. The entire equation is called the "econometric model," "structural equation," or "regression function." Again, everything in econometrics goes by at least two names.

If we obtain all the data on Y_i and X_i, error-free, then we can use some technique, such as the "eyeball" technique, to estimate β_0 and β_1. However, in most instances we will only be able to obtain a sample of the observations on Y_i and X_i, and those numbers will undoubtedly have some errors in them. Since we only have an error-ridden sample of the true Y_i and X_i, we will not obtain the true values of β_0 and β_1. To indicate this situation we place carets (^) over the values that are mere estimates of the true values.

$$Y_i = \hat{\beta}_0 + \hat{\beta}_1 X_i + e_i$$

In addition, the u_i's turn into e_i's because we will not obtain the true error terms without the true β_0 and β_1. $Y_i = \beta_0 + \beta_1 X_i + u_i$ is called the "population regression function." Only the gods know the true values of β_0 and β_1 because only they have access to the all the error-free data on Y_i and X_i.

$Y_i = \hat{\beta}_0 + \hat{\beta}_1 X_i + e_i$ is known as the "sample regression function" because we mortals are working with a sample of the entire population of data on X_i and Y_i. We put carets (sometimes called hats) over β_0 and β_1 to indicate that these are merely estimates of their true values. The e_i's are estimates of the u_i's.

Another notational complication arises when we want to refer to the predicted value of Y. To obtain this value for any given i, we plug in for X_i:

$$E(Yi|Xi) = \hat{Y}_i = \hat{\beta}_0 + \hat{\beta}_1 X_i$$

We no longer add on the e_i because that would give the actual value of Y_i and we want the predicted value ($\hat{Y}_i$). The caret appears over the Y_i because it is an estimated value, not the actual value. $\hat{Y}_i$ can be written E(Yi|Xi). This latter notation is read "the expected value of Y_i given X_i."

2.3 The Ordinary Least-Squares Technique

We want to obtain values of $\hat{\beta}_0$ and $\hat{\beta}_1$ such that Σe_i^2 is minimized. Another way to envision this task is that we want to fit a line between the observations on a scattergram so that the distances from the points to the line squared is minimized. This technique has many advantages over the "eyeball" technique and "first dot/last dot" method of fitting a line. $\hat{\beta}_0$ is the vertical intercept of our line and $\hat{\beta}_1$ is its slope. When we fit a line with this criterion in mind we are utilizing the ordinary least-squares technique.

There are many reasons for choosing to calculate $\hat{\beta}_0$ and $\hat{\beta}_1$ so that Σe_i^2 is minimized. Certainly this criterion is more rigorous than the "eyeball" technique and does not waste as much data as the first dot/last dot method. Later we will see that the estimators that result from ordinary least-squares have many desirable qualities. At this point one or two advantages will be mentioned.

The ordinary least-squares line is unique. Only one line will minimize Σe_i^2. This is not true of some other criteria such as calculating $\hat{\beta}_0$ and $\hat{\beta}_1$ so that $\Sigma e_i = 0$. It turns out that there are an infinite number of lines that would fit this latter criterion in any given situation. The ordinary least-squares line not only minimizes Σe_i^2, but also is one of the infinite lines that have $\Sigma e_i = 0$.

Another possibility is to fit the line so that $\Sigma |e_i|$ is minimized. In most cases this will yield a unique line. Unfortunately, the resulting estimates of $\hat{\beta}_0$ and $\hat{\beta}_1$ will not have the desirable statistical properties of the ordinary least-squares estimates.

The ordinary least-squares technique is easy to implement. In order to fit a line such that Σe_i^2 is minimized, all one needs to do is calculate

$$\hat{\beta}_0 = \overline{Y} - \hat{\beta}_1 \overline{X}$$

and

$$\hat{\beta}_1 = \frac{\Sigma (X_i - \overline{X}) Y_i}{\Sigma (X_i - \overline{X})^2}$$

In these formulas $\overline{Y}$ and $\overline{X}$ refer to the means of Y and X, respectively. $\hat{\beta}_0$ is the vertical intercept and $\hat{\beta}_1$ is the slope of a line that minimizes Σe_i^2. The formulas for each of these estimators are derived below. First let's do an example.

Suppose we want to test the hypothesis that grade point average (GPA) is affected by the amount of time a student spends studying (HOURS). An econometric model of this hypothesis would be:

$$GPA_i = \hat{\beta}_0 + \hat{\beta}_1 \, HOURS_i + e_i$$

To keep the calculations to a minimum we consider only three students:

Student	GPA	HOURS
1	2	2
2	3	4
3	3	2

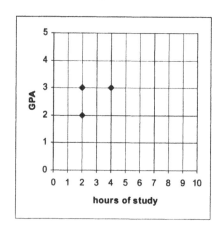

First calculate the numerator of equation $\hat{\beta}_1 = \dfrac{\Sigma(X_i - \overline{X})Y_i}{\Sigma(X_i - \overline{X})^2}$:

$$\Sigma(X_i - \overline{X})Y_i = (2 - 2.667)(2) + (4 - 2.667)(3) + (2 - 2.667)(3) = 0.667$$

Now the denominator of the equation:

$$\Sigma(X_i - \overline{X})^2 = (2 - 2.667)^2 + (4 - 2.667)^2 + (2 - 2.667)^2 = 2.667$$

So that we have:

$$\hat{\beta}_1 = \frac{\Sigma(X_i - \overline{X})Y_i}{\Sigma(X_i - \overline{X})^2} = \frac{0.667}{2.667} = 0.25$$

Now we can plug into the equation $\hat{\beta}_0 = \overline{Y} - \hat{\beta}_1\overline{X}$:

$$\hat{\beta}_0 = \overline{Y} - \hat{\beta}_1\overline{X} = 2.667 - 0.25(2.667) = 2.0$$

And we may report the regression results as:

$$GPA_i = 2.0 + 0.25\ HOURS_i + e_i$$

The structural parameters can be interpreted as follows:

$\hat{\beta}_0 = 2.0$ – a student who reports 0 study hours is expected to have a GPA equal to 2.0.

$\hat{\beta}_1 = 0.25$ – If HOURS increases by 1 unit, then GPA is expected to increase by 0.25 units.

$\hat{\beta}_0$ is the vertical intercept and $\hat{\beta}_1$ is the slope of our regression line:

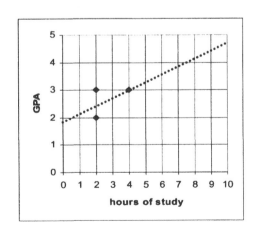

The three error terms can be calculated by rewriting our results:

$$GPA_i = 2.0 + 0.25 \text{ HOURS}_i + e_i \quad \text{as:}$$

$$e_i = GPA_i - 2.0 - 0.25 \text{ HOURS}_i$$

$$
\begin{aligned}
\text{Then } e_1 &= 2 - 2.0 - 0.25(2) = -0.5 \\
e_2 &= 4 - 2.0 - 0.25(3) = 0.0 \\
e_3 &= 2 - 2.0 - 0.25(3) = 0.5
\end{aligned}
$$

As mentioned previously, $\Sigma e_i = 0$. The $\Sigma e_i^2 = -0.5^2 + 0.0^2 + 0.5^2 = 0.5$. How do we know that there is not another line that yields a lower Σe_i^2? Because $\hat{\beta}_0$ and $\hat{\beta}_1$ were derived so that they would minimize Σe_i^2. The derivation makes it clear that our line is unique.

2.4 Deriving the Ordinary Least-Squares Estimators

We have $Y_i = \hat{\beta}_0 + \hat{\beta}_1 X_i + e_i$.

We want to minimize $\sum e_i^2$; that is, minimize $\sum (Y_i - \hat{\beta}_0 - \hat{\beta}_1 X_i)^2$

To find the equations for $\hat{\beta}_0$ and $\hat{\beta}_1$ that minimize this expression, take the partial derivative with respect to $\hat{\beta}_0$ and set it equal to zero:

$$\frac{\partial \Sigma (Y_i - \hat{\beta}_0 - \hat{\beta}_1 X_i)^2}{\partial \hat{\beta}_0} = 2\Sigma (Y_i - \hat{\beta}_0 - \hat{\beta}_1 X_i)(-1) = 0$$

Dividing both sides of this equation by –2 leaves $\Sigma (Y_i - \hat{\beta}_0 - \hat{\beta}_1 X_i) = 0$

Now distribute the summation sign: $\Sigma Y_i - n\hat{\beta}_0 - \hat{\beta}_1 \Sigma X_i = 0$; n is number of observations i.

Moving the second and third terms to the other side gives: $\Sigma Y_i = n\hat{\beta}_0 + \hat{\beta}_1 \Sigma X_i$

The result is known as a "normal equation."

We repeat the process only this time with respect to $\hat{\beta}_1$. Begin by taking the partial derivative of the expression we wish to minimize with respect to $\hat{\beta}_1$ and set it equal to zero:

$$\frac{\partial \Sigma (Y_i - \hat{\beta}_0 - \hat{\beta}_1 X_i)^2}{\partial \hat{\beta}_1} = 2\Sigma (Y_i - \hat{\beta}_0 - \hat{\beta}_1 X_i)(-X_i) = 0$$

Dividing both sides of this equation by –2 leaves $\Sigma(Y_i - \hat{\beta}_0 - \hat{\beta}_1 X_i)(X_i) = 0$

Now distribute X_i and the summation sign: $\Sigma Y_i X_i - \hat{\beta}_0 \Sigma X_i - \hat{\beta}_1 \Sigma X_i^2 = 0$

Moving the second and third terms to the other side gives: $\Sigma Y_i X_i = \hat{\beta}_0 \Sigma X_i + \hat{\beta}_1 \Sigma X_i^2$

The result is known as a "normal equation."

We have two normal equations and two unknowns, $\hat{\beta}_0$ and $\hat{\beta}_1$. The first normal equation can be solved for $\hat{\beta}_0$:

$$\Sigma Y_i = n\hat{\beta}_0 + \hat{\beta}_1 \Sigma X_i$$
$$n\hat{\beta}_0 = \Sigma Y_i - \hat{\beta}_1 \Sigma X_i$$

$$\hat{\beta}_0 = \frac{\Sigma Y_i - \hat{\beta}_1 \Sigma X_i}{n} = \bar{Y} - \hat{\beta}_1 \bar{X}$$

This result can be substituted into the second normal equation which is then solved for $\hat{\beta}_1$:

$$\Sigma Y_i X_i = \hat{\beta}_0 \Sigma X_i + \hat{\beta}_1 \Sigma X_i^2$$

$$\Sigma Y_i X_i = (\bar{Y} - \hat{\beta}_1 \bar{X})\Sigma X_i + \hat{\beta}_1 \Sigma X_i^2$$

Distribute the ΣX_i: $\Sigma Y_i X_i = \bar{Y}\Sigma X_i - \hat{\beta}_1 \bar{X}\Sigma X_i + \hat{\beta}_1 \Sigma X_i^2$

Now factor the last two terms on the right: $\Sigma Y_i X_i = \bar{Y}\Sigma X_i + \hat{\beta}_1(\Sigma X_i^2 - \bar{X}\Sigma X_i)$

Rearrange the terms: $\hat{\beta}_1(\Sigma X_i^2 - \bar{X}\Sigma X_i) = \Sigma Y_i X_i - \bar{Y}\Sigma X_i$

To isolate $\hat{\beta}_1$, divide both sides by $(\Sigma X_i^2 - \bar{X}\Sigma X_i)$: $\hat{\beta}_1 = \dfrac{\Sigma Y_i X_i - \bar{Y}\Sigma X_i}{\Sigma X_i^2 - \bar{X}\Sigma X_i}$

A more convenient expression for $\hat{\beta}_1$ is:

$$\hat{\beta}_1 = \frac{\Sigma(X_i - \bar{X})Y_i}{\Sigma(X_i - \bar{X})^2} \quad \text{which is equivalent to} \quad \hat{\beta}_1 = \frac{\Sigma Y_i X_i - \bar{Y}\Sigma X_i}{\Sigma X_i^2 - \bar{X}\Sigma X_i}$$

The proof of this equivalence comes up in the problems at the end of this chapter. More importantly, any time we want to fit a line so that $\sum e_i^2$ is minimized, we only need calculate the intercept and slope of that line with our two formulas.

2.5 An Example of Regression Analysis

Let's do an example. Given the data below on Y and X calculate $\hat{\beta}_0$ and $\hat{\beta}_1$ in:

$$Y_i = \hat{\beta}_0 + \hat{\beta}_1 X_i + e_i$$

Y	X
11.20	5.40
–27.10	6.70
33.40	7.10
0.02	8.80

First calculate $\hat{\beta}_1 = \dfrac{\Sigma(X_i - \overline{X})Y_i}{\Sigma(X_i - \overline{X})^2}$. Begin with the numerator.

Subtract $\overline{X}$ from the first X_i : $5.40 - 7.00 = -1.60$
Subtract $\overline{X}$ from the second X_i : $6.70 - 7.00 = -0.30$
Subtract $\overline{X}$ from the third X_i : $7.10 - 7.00 = 0.10$
Subtract $\overline{X}$ from the fourth X_i : $8.80 - 7.00 = 1.80$

Now multiply each of these results by the respective Y_i:

$$
\begin{array}{rrrrr}
-1.60 & \times & 11.20 & = & -17.92 \\
-0.30 & \times & -27.10 & = & 8.13 \\
0.10 & \times & 33.40 & = & 3.34 \\
1.80 & \times & 0.02 & = & 0.04
\end{array}
$$

The last operation in the numerator is to sum up these four products to get –6.41.

$$\hat{\beta}_1 = \frac{-6.41}{\Sigma(X_i - \overline{X})^2}$$

In the denominator, we once again subtract each $\overline{X}$ from X_i. This time each result is squared:

$$
\begin{array}{rrr}
-1.60^2 & = & 2.56 \\
-0.03^2 & = & 0.09 \\
0.10^2 & = & 0.01 \\
1.80^2 & = & 3.24
\end{array}
$$

The last operation in the denominator is to sum up these four squares to get 5.90.

$$\hat{\beta}_1 = \frac{-6.41}{5.90} = -1.09$$

Once we calculate $\hat{\beta}_1$ to equal -1.09 it is a simple matter to obtain

$$\hat{\beta}_0 = \overline{Y} - \hat{\beta}_1 \overline{X} = 4.38 - (-1.09)(7.00) = 11.99$$

The slope of our regression is -1.09 and the vertical intercept is 11.99.

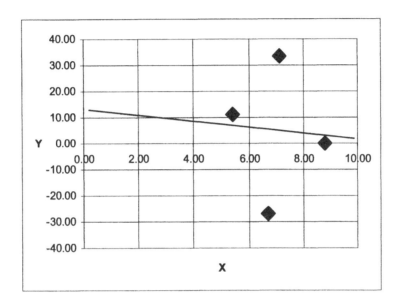

2.6 The Stochastic Error Term

Notice that our regression line does not pass through any of the four observations. The distance of each observation from the regression line is the error term or e_i.

$$e_i = Y_i - \hat{Y}_i = Y_i - (\hat{\beta}_0 + \hat{\beta}_1 X_i) = 11.20 - (11.99 + (-1.09 \times 5.40)) = 5.08$$

The first observation lies 5.08 units above the regression line. The other error terms are calculated in a similar manner.

$$e_i = Y_i - \hat{Y}_i = Y_i - (\hat{\beta}_0 + \hat{\beta}_1 X_i) = -27.10 - (11.99 + (-1.09 \times 6.70)) = -31.81$$

$$e_i = Y_i - \hat{Y}_i = Y_i - (\hat{\beta}_0 + \hat{\beta}_1 X_i) = 33.40 - (11.99 + (-1.09 \times 7.10)) = 29.13$$

$$e_i = Y_i - \hat{Y}_i = Y_i - (\hat{\beta}_0 + \hat{\beta}_1 X_i) = 0.02 - (11.99 + (-1.09 \times 8.80)) = -2.40$$

Notice that the four error terms sum to zero. The distances of the error terms above the line exactly equal the distances of the error terms below the line. Although we fit our line such that Σe_i^2 is minimized, it turns out that $\Sigma e_i = 0$ as well.

Also notice that the regression line passes through $(\overline{Y}, \overline{X}) = (4.38, 7.00)$. If we plug 7.00 into the regression line we get: $\hat{Y}_i = 11.99 + (-1.09)(7.00) = 4.38$

2.7 Example: Economic Performance and Corruption

To test the hypothesis that corruption negatively affects a nation's economic performance we propose the following econometric model:

$$GDP_i = \hat{\beta}_0 + \hat{\beta}_1 COR_i + e_i$$

COR measures corruption in a nation on a scale of 0 (least) to 10 (most) and GDP measures output in dollars per capita. We have cross-sectional data from four nations:

Nation	COR	GDP
Brazil	5.9	6100
Bulgaria	6.7	4100
Chile	3.1	12500
China	6.6	3600

Applying our formulas we obtain:

$$\hat{\beta}_1 = \frac{\Sigma(X_i - \overline{X})Y_i}{\Sigma(X_i - \overline{X})^2} = \frac{-20652.5}{8.55} = -2416.20$$

$$\hat{\beta}_0 = \overline{Y} - \hat{\beta}_1\overline{X} = 6575.00 - (-2416.20)(5.58) = 20045.33$$

We do indeed obtain a negative value for $\hat{\beta}_1$ indicating that COR and GDP are negatively related. More specifically, $\hat{\beta}_1 = -2416.20$ may be interpreted as follows: When COR increases by 1 unit, GDP is expected to decrease by 2416.20 units.

$\hat{\beta}_0 = 20045.33$ is interpreted as follows: When COR = 0, GDP is expected to equal 20045.33 units. This strict interpretation of $\hat{\beta}_0$ often results in nonsense, as we shall see going forward.

The four error terms of this model are calculated to be:

$$e_i = Y_i - \hat{Y}_i = Y_i - (\hat{\beta}_0 + \hat{\beta}_1 X_i) = \quad 6100 - (20045.33 + (-2416.20 \times 5.9)) = \quad 310.27$$

$$e_i = Y_i - \hat{Y}_i = Y_i - (\hat{\beta}_0 + \hat{\beta}_1 X_i) = \quad 4100 - (20045.33 + (-2416.20 \times 6.7)) = \quad 243.23$$

$$e_i = Y_i - \hat{Y}_i = Y_i - (\hat{\beta}_0 + \hat{\beta}_1 X_i) = 012500 - (20045.33 + (-2416.20 \times 3.1)) = \quad -55.10$$

$$e_i = Y_i - \hat{Y}_i = Y_i - (\hat{\beta}_0 + \hat{\beta}_1 X_i) = \quad 3600 - (20045.33 + (-2416.20 \times 6.6)) = \quad -498.39$$

Proportionally speaking, these errors are rather small. What causes the errors to be large or small? The error term is the result of four categories of factors:

1) Important variables excluded – There are many variables that affect GDP per capita in a given nation. Money supply and fiscal policy come to mind. Leaving these important factors out of our econometric analysis results in larger errors.

2) Randomness – Even if no important variables are omitted from consideration, we can still make large errors when the dependent variable is erratic. For example, it is extremely difficult to predict daily changes in stock prices. They have a large random component. This will lead to larger errors in a regression analysis.

3) Measurement error – If errors were made when measuring COR or GDP, then larger errors will result. COR and GDP are figures that are estimated. To the extent that these estimates are poor, we can expect larger error terms.

4) Minor variables excluded – Undoubtedly, many minor factors impact GDP in a given nation. Hopefully, these often immeasurable forces will cancel each other out. To the extent that they do not, larger regression errors will result.

Terms

Dependent variable (Y-variable) – In an econometric model, this variable appears to the left of the equality sign. It is affected by the independent variable.

Econometric model (structural equation or regression equation) – A mathematical expression that captures the essence of the cause-and-effect relationship between two variables.

Error term (residual or disturbance) – This variable is attached to the end of an econometric model. It captures the difference between the observed value of the Y-variable and the value predicted by the econometric model.

Independent variable (X-variable) – In an econometric model, this variable appears to the right of the equality sign. It is affects by the dependent variable.

Normal equation – An equation that comes up in the derivation of the formulas for the ordinary least-squares estimators.

Ordinary least-squares – A technique for estimating the structural parameters of an econometric model. This technique minimizes Σe_i^2.

Population regression function – An econometric model estimated with error-free data that includes the entire population of interest.

Sample regression function – An econometric model estimated from sample data.

Stochastic variable – A variable that can take on different values depending on the sample data. $\hat{\beta}_0$ and $\hat{\beta}_1$ are stochastic variables, as are the e_i's.

Structural parameter – In an econometric model, $\hat{\beta}_0$ and $\hat{\beta}_1$ are the structural parameters.

Chapter 2   Problems

1. Which of the following is (are) NOT correct?

   A) $Y_i = \beta_0 + \beta_1 X_i + e_i$ D) $Y_i = \hat{\beta}_0 + \hat{\beta}_1 X_i + e_i$ G) $Y_i = \beta_0 + \beta_1 X_i$

   B) $\hat{Y}_i = \beta_0 + \beta_1 X_i + e_i$ E) $\hat{Y}_i = \hat{\beta}_0 + \hat{\beta}_1 X_i + e_i$ H) $\hat{Y}_i = \beta_0 + \beta_1 X_i + u_i$

   C) $Y_i = \beta_0 + \beta_1 X_i + u_i$ F) $Y_i = \hat{\beta}_0 + \hat{\beta}_1 X_i + u_i$ I) $E(Yi|Xi) = \hat{\beta}_0 + \hat{\beta}_1 X_i + e_i$

2. Which of the following is (are) NOT correct?

   A) $Y_i = \beta_0 + \beta_1 X_i + u_i$ D) $Y_i = \hat{\beta}_0 + \hat{\beta}_1 X_i + u_i$ G) $Y_i = \beta_0 + \beta_1 X_i$

   B) $\hat{Y}_i = \beta_0 + \beta_1 X_i + u_i$ E) $\hat{Y}_i = \hat{\beta}_0 + \hat{\beta}_1 X_i + u_i$ H) $\hat{Y}_i = \beta_0 + \beta_1 X_i + e_i$

   C) $Y_i = \beta_0 + \beta_1 X_i + e_i$ F) $Y_i = \hat{\beta}_0 + \hat{\beta}_1 X_i + e_i$ I) $E(Yi|Xi) = \beta_0 + \beta_1 X_i + u_i$

3. The savings and number of children of four families are given below:

sav	child
0.03	2
0.874	2
0.374	0
1.2	1

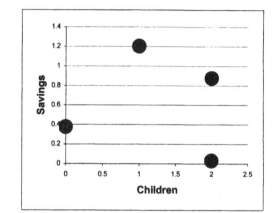

   A) Calculate the values of $\hat{\beta}_0$ and $\hat{\beta}_1$ so that Σe_i^2 is minimized for

   $$sav_i = \hat{\beta}_0 + \hat{\beta}_1\ child_i + e_i$$

   B) Interpret the values you obtained.

   C) Sketch your line in the graph.

4. The hours of preparation and math SAT scores of four students are given below:

prep	SAT
1	300
3	400
1	400
3	500

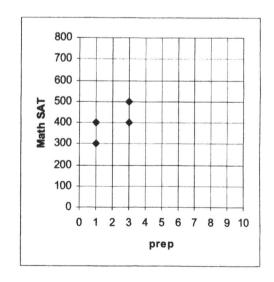

   A) Calculate the values of $\hat{\beta}_0$ and $\hat{\beta}_1$ so that Σe_i^2 is minimized for

   $$Math\ SAT_i = \hat{\beta}_0 + \hat{\beta}_1\ prep_i + e_i$$

   B) Interpret the values you obtained.

   C) Sketch your line in the graph.

5. A) Calculate the values of the structural parameters for a regression of X on Y given:

Y	X
1.8	2
1.7	5
1.5	–2
0.6	5
25.4	6

B) Show that the $\Sigma e_i = 0$ in this case.

6. C) Calculate the values of the structural parameters for a regression of X on Y given:

Y	X
1.8	1.2
1.7	–8.4
1.5	4.8
0.6	3.5
25.4	2.2

B) Show that the $\Sigma e_i = 0$ in this case.

7. Prove $\dfrac{\Sigma Y_i X_i - \bar{Y}\Sigma X_i}{\Sigma X_i^2 - \bar{X}\Sigma X_i} = \dfrac{\Sigma(X_i - \bar{X})(Y_i - \bar{Y})}{\Sigma(X_i - \bar{X})^2}$

8. Prove $\dfrac{\Sigma(X_i - \bar{X})(Y_i - \bar{Y})}{\Sigma(X_i - \bar{X})^2} = \dfrac{\Sigma(X_i - \bar{X})Y_i}{\Sigma(X_i - \bar{X})^2}$

9. Prove that $\Sigma e_i X_i = 0$ for the ordinary least-squares regression line.

10. Prove that $\Sigma e_i = 0$ for the ordinary least-squares regression line.

Most students have had little experience doing algebra when summation signs (Σ) are involved. It turns out that only a few rules are required to get through all the derivations and proofs in this book.

FOILing: Suppose we want to expand the following expression: $\Sigma(X_i - \overline{X})(Y_i - \overline{Y})$. We can FOIL it out. FOIL stands for First; Outer; Inner; Last.

$$\Sigma(X_i - \overline{X})(Y_i - \overline{Y}) = \Sigma(X_i Y_i - X_i \overline{Y} - \overline{X}Y_i + \overline{XY})$$

Distribution: Suppose we wish to distribute the summation sign through the parentheses in the following expression:

$$\Sigma(X_i Y_i - X_i \overline{Y} - \overline{X}Y_i + \overline{XY})$$

Just bring the summation sign before each of the four terms:

$$\Sigma X_i Y_i - \Sigma X_i \overline{Y} - \Sigma \overline{X}Y_i + \Sigma \overline{XY}$$

The first term ($\Sigma X_i Y_i$) cannot be simplified further. It instructs us to take each X_i and multiply it by the corresponding Y_i and then sum up those i products.

The second term ($\Sigma X_i \overline{Y}$) may be rewritten as $\overline{Y}\Sigma X_i$. This is because a constant ($\overline{Y}$ is the mean of the Y_i's) can be pulled out and placed before the summation sign.

Similarly, the third term ($\Sigma \overline{X}Y_i$) becomes $\overline{X}\Sigma Y_i$.

The fourth term ($\Sigma \overline{XY}$) makes no sense. It asks us to sum up the product of two constants ($\overline{XY}$). There is nothing to sum up. In cases like this, when the summation sign is placed before a constant or constants alone, it turns into an 'n.' So the fourth term becomes $n\overline{XY}$.

In summary, the summation sign may be distributed through the parentheses in $\Sigma(X_i Y_i - X_i \overline{Y} - \overline{X}Y_i + \overline{XY})$ to obtain $\Sigma X_i Y_i - \overline{Y}\Sigma X_i - \overline{X}\Sigma Y_i + n\overline{XY}$.

Substitution: The expression $\Sigma X_i Y_i - \overline{Y}\Sigma X_i - \overline{X}\Sigma Y_i + n\overline{XY}$ can be simplified further by making some substitutions. ΣX_i is equal to $n\overline{X}$. Using this substitution, the second term in our expression becomes $\overline{Y}n\overline{X}$. The third term becomes $\overline{X}n\overline{Y}$. So now we have:

$$\Sigma X_i Y_i - \overline{Y}n\overline{X} - \overline{X}n\overline{Y} + n\overline{XY}$$

Cancellation: Notice that the last three terms in the expression $\Sigma X_i Y_i - \overline{Y}n\overline{X} - \overline{X}n\overline{Y} + n\overline{XY}$ are equivalent. One of the two negative terms will cancel the fourth term which is positive and we are left with $\Sigma X_i Y_i - \overline{Y}n\overline{X}$.

Chapter 3

Residual Statistics

Measures of Goodness-of-Fit

The Standard Errors of $\hat{\beta}_0$ and $\hat{\beta}_1$

Repeated Sampling

Terms

Chapter 3 Problems

Test Yourself on Chapters 1, 2, and 3

3.1 Measures of Goodness-of-Fit

The regression from the last example in Chapter 2 appears to have rather small error terms.

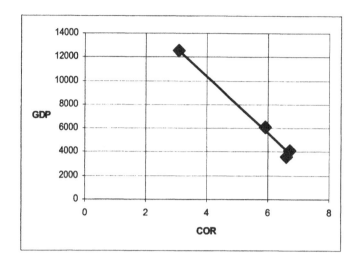

However the example from section 2.5 appears to have larger errors.

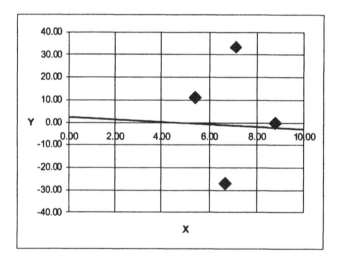

But these diagrams can be deceptive because of the scaling. Indeed the largest error in the second diagram is –31.81, while the smallest error in the top diagram is –55.10. But proportionally, the errors in the first diagram are smaller.

It would be useful to have a statistic that would help us discern when we have small errors (a good fit) or large errors (a poor fit). There are several popular statistics for this purpose. We will discuss two of them.

$$\textbf{Standard Error of the Regression (SER)} = \hat{\sigma} = \sqrt{\frac{\Sigma e_i^{\,2}}{n-2}}$$

This statistic represents the typical distance of an observation from the regression line. The SER is useful only when compared to the dependent variable. If the SER of a given regression equals 0.487, we have no way of assessing if this is large or small. A good rule of thumb is if the SER is less than half of the mean of the absolute value of the dependent variable, then the fit is adequate.

For the first diagram, the SER = 451.03; for the second, SER = 30.75. Even though it doesn't look like it when comparing the graphs, the errors in the first diagram are larger. However, relative to the magnitude of the dependent variable, the errors in the first diagram are proportionally smaller.

The first diagram represents an adequate fit since the SER < ½ the absolute value of the mean of GDP, which is 6575.00. The interpretation here is that the typical distance of an observation from the regression line is 451.03. This is a rather small error given that the dependent variable has a mean of 6575.00.

The second diagram represents a poor fit since the SER > ½ the absolute value of the mean of Y, which is 4.38. The interpretation in this case is that the typical distance of an observation from the regression line is 30.75. However, 30.75 is a rather large error given that the dependent variable is centered on 4.38.

The second measure of goodness-of-fit is the coefficient of determination.

$$\textbf{Coefficient of Determination } (\textbf{r}^2) \quad = 1 - \frac{\Sigma e_i^2}{\Sigma (Y_i - \bar{Y})^2}$$

The coefficient of determination (or r-squared) is the most popular measure of goodness-of-fit. It ranges between 0 and 1, where 1 is a perfect fit and zero is a horizontal regression through random observations.

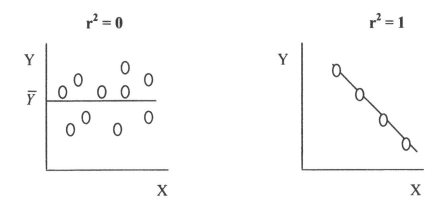

Going back to the two drawings at the beginning of this section, the first has an $r^2 = 0.99$. The interpretation is 99 percent of the variation in GDP is explained by COR. The second drawing has an $r^2 = 0.004$; only 0.4 percent of the variation in Y is explained by X.

Both the SER and r^2 indicate the same results: The regression between COR and GDP has an adequate or very good fit, while the regression of Y on X has a poor fit.

3.2 The Standard Errors of $\hat{\beta}_0$ and $\hat{\beta}_1$

$\hat{\beta}_0$ and $\hat{\beta}_1$ vary in repeated sampling. If we were to get data on Y and X and run a regression, we would obtain estimates of $\hat{\beta}_0$ and $\hat{\beta}_1$. If we were to obtain a new sample of data on Y and X and re-run the regression, it would be highly unlikely that we would obtain the exact same values for $\hat{\beta}_0$ and $\hat{\beta}_1$. Can we expect the new values of $\hat{\beta}_0$ and $\hat{\beta}_1$ to be close to the original estimates? That depends. The standard error of $\hat{\beta}_0$ is an estimate of how much $\hat{\beta}_0$ typically varies in repeated sampling.

$$\text{Standard Error of } \hat{\beta}_0 = \text{SE}(\hat{\beta}_0) = \sqrt{\frac{\hat{\sigma}^2 \Sigma X_i^2}{n \Sigma (X_i - \overline{X})^2}} \quad ; \text{ where } \hat{\sigma}^2 = \frac{\Sigma ei^2}{n-2} = \text{SER}^2$$

Similarly, the standard error of $\hat{\beta}_1$ is an estimate of how much $\hat{\beta}_1$ typically varies in repeated sampling.

$$\text{Standard Error of } \hat{\beta}_1 = \text{SE}(\hat{\beta}_1) = \sqrt{\frac{\hat{\sigma}^2}{\sum (X_i - \overline{X})^2}}$$

Going back to our example of corruption's impact on economic growth, we can now more fully report the results:

GDP$_i$ = 20045.33 − 2416.20 COR$_i$ + e$_i$
    (889.14)   (154.27)   ← standard errors

SER = 451.03 $\overline{\text{GDP}}$ = 6575.00 r^2 = 0.99   n = 4

COR measures corruption in a nation on a scale of 0 (least) to 10 (most)
GDP measures output in dollars per capita.

These results indicate that $\hat{\beta}_0$ is estimated to be 20045.33. However, if we ran the regression repeatedly with new data each time, we would expect $\hat{\beta}_0$ to vary by 889.14 on average. This does not mean that $\hat{\beta}_0$ cannot come out to be zero in one of the regressions, but that would surprise us since $\hat{\beta}_0$ typically varies by 889.14 in repeated sampling and its estimated value is 20,045.33.

$\hat{\beta}_1$ is estimated to be –2416.20 with a standard error of 154.27. The regression has an SER equal to 451.03 indicating an adequate fit since the SER < ½ the mean of GDP. r^2 is equal to 0.99, which means 99 percent of the variation in GDP is explained by COR. Finally, n = 4 says four data points were used to estimate all these statistics.

3.3 Repeated Sampling

The concept of repeated sampling will be used extensively going forward. It is the hypothetical notion that the structural parameters, $\hat{\beta}_0$ and $\hat{\beta}_1$, could be estimated tens of thousands of times using fresh data each time. The values obtained each time would be different. That's what is meant by the term "stochastic": $\hat{\beta}_0$ and $\hat{\beta}_1$ vary in repeated sampling.

Terms

Coefficient of determination (r^2) – A statistic that measures how well a regression line fits the data.

Repeated sampling –Estimating the structural parameters of a regression over and over with fresh data each time.

Standard error of an estimator – A statistic that estimates the amount a structural parameter will vary on average in repeated sampling.

Standard error of the regression (SER) – A statistic that represents the typical distance of an observation from the regression line.

Chapter 3   Problems

1.A) Calculate the values of the structural parameters for a regression of X on Y given:

Y	X
1.8	2
1.7	5
1.5	–2
0.6	5
25.4	6

   B) Interpret the value you obtained for the intercept.
   C) Interpret the value you obtained for the slope coefficient.
   D) Calculate r^2 for this regression.
   E) Interpret the value of r^2 for this regression.
   F) Calculate the SER for this regression.
   G) Interpret the value of the SER for this regression.

H) Calculate the standard error of the intercept term.
I) Interpret the standard error of the intercept term.
J) Calculate the standard error of the slope coefficient.
K) Interpret the standard error of the slope coefficient.

2. A) Calculate the values of the structural parameters for a regression of X on Y given:

Y	X
1.8	1.2
1.7	-8.4
1.5	4.8
0.6	3.5
25.4	2.2

B) Interpret the value you obtained for the intercept.
C) Interpret the value you obtained for the slope coefficient.
D) Calculate r^2 for this regression.
E) Interpret the value of r^2 for this regression.
F) Calculate the SER for this regression.
G) Interpret the value of the SER for this regression.
H) Calculate the standard error of the intercept term.
I) Interpret the standard error of the intercept term.
J) Calculate the standard error of the slope coefficient.
K) Interpret the standard error of the slope coefficient.

3. Given the following: $GDP_i = \hat{\beta}_0 + \hat{\beta}_1 COR_i + e_i$

Nation	COR	GDP
Ukraine	7.4	2200
UK	1.4	21200
USA	2.5	31500
Vietnam	7.4	1770

Where COR measures corruption in a nation on a scale of 0 (least) to 10 (most) and GDP measures output in dollars per capita.

A) Calculate the values of the structural parameters for the regression above.
B) Interpret the values of the structural parameters.
C) Calculate r^2 for this regression.
D) Interpret the value of r^2 for this regression.
E) Calculate the SER for this regression.
F) Interpret the value of the SER for this regression.
G) Does this regression have a good fit? Explain.
H) Calculate the standard error of the intercept term.
I) Interpret the standard error of the intercept term.
J) Would you be surprised if the intercept term equaled 26776.70 if you re-ran this regression with data on four different countries? Explain.

4. Given the following: $GDP_i = \hat{\beta}_0 + \hat{\beta}_1 COR_i + e_i$

Nation	COR	GDP
Bulgaria	6.7	4100
Canada	0.8	22400
Chile	3.1	12500
China	6.6	3600

Where COR measures corruption in a nation on a scale of 0 (least) to 10 (most) and GDP measures output in dollars per capita.

A) Calculate the values of the structural parameters for the regression above.
B) Interpret the values of the structural parameters.
C) Calculate r^2 for this regression.
D) Interpret the value of r^2 for this regression.
E) Calculate the SER for this regression.
F) Interpret the value of the SER for this regression.
G) Does this regression have a good fit? Explain.
H) Calculate the standard error of the slope coefficient.
I) Interpret the standard error of the slope coefficient.
J) Would you be surprised if the slope coefficient equaled –3342.80 if you re-ran this regression with data on four different countries? Explain.

Test Yourself on Chapters 1, 2, and 3

1. Given

Yi	Xi
11.2	5.4
–27.1	6.7
33.4	7.1
0.02	–8.8

A) Calculate the values for the structural parameters of $Y_i = \hat{\beta}_0 + \hat{\beta}_1 X_i + e_i$
   (Show your work, making the details of your calculations apparent.)
B) Interpret the values you obtained for $\hat{\beta}_0$ and $\hat{\beta}_1$ above.
C) According to the SER, is the fit of the regression adequate? Explain.
D) What percent of the variation in Y is explained by X in this regression?
E) Suppose we ran this regression again with a new set of observations on Y and X. Would you be surprised if $\hat{\beta}_1$ turned out to be –2.0? Explain why or why not.

2. Answer the following questions:

A) Distinguish between the population regression function and the sample regression function.
B) Distinguish between cross-sectional and time-series data.
C) What is a normal equation?
D) Explain why a perfectly vertical regression line is impossible.

3. Which of the following is (are) NOT correct?

A) $Y_i = \beta_0 + \beta_1 X_i$

B) $\hat{Y}_i = \beta_0 + \beta_1 X_i$

C) $Y_i = \beta_0 + \beta_1 X_i + u_i$

D) $Y_i = \hat{\beta}_0 + \hat{\beta}_1 X_i + e_i$

E) $\hat{Y}_i = \hat{\beta}_0 + \hat{\beta}_1 X_i + e_i$

F) $Y_i = \hat{\beta}_0 + \hat{\beta}_1 X_i + u_i$

G) $E(Y_i|X_i) = \beta_0 + \beta_1 X_i$

H) $\hat{Y}_i = \beta_0 + \beta_1 X_i + u_i$

I) $E(Y_i|X_i) = \hat{\beta}_0 + \hat{\beta}_1 X_i + e_i$

4. Answer True or False:

A) Sabermetrics is the application of statistical analysis to war.

B) Unless all the observations lie on a straight line, it is impossible to fit a line such that $\Sigma|e_i| = 0$.

C) When a line is fit to observations on a scattergram so that Σe_i^2 is minimized, then $\Sigma e_i = 0$.

D) When a line is fit to observations on a scattergram so that Σe_i^2 is minimized, then sometimes more than one line meets this criteria.

E) $\Sigma(X_i - \bar{X})(Y_i - \bar{Y}) = \bar{X}\Sigma Y_i - \bar{Y}\Sigma X_i$

F) $\Sigma(X_i - \bar{X}) = 0$

G) A large SER and low r^2 can be the result of the Y- variable being very random.

H) If $r^2 = 0$, then β_1 must $= 0$.

I) If $r^2 = 1$, then β_1 must $= 1$.

J) If SER $= 0$, then r^2 must $= 1$.

Chapter 4

Hypothesis Testing

4.1 Hypothesis Testing

Once we calculate $\hat{\beta}_0$ and $\hat{\beta}_1$, we will want to test various hypotheses about them. For instance, suppose we calculate $\hat{\beta}_0 = 0.12$. Is that close enough to call $\hat{\beta}_0$ zero? The answer depends on the standard error of $\hat{\beta}_0$. Suppose the $SE(\hat{\beta}_0) = 0.03$. Then we know that if we run the regression many times with different samples it is unlikely that $\hat{\beta}_0$ will turn out to be zero or negative in many instances. Therefore, even though $\hat{\beta}_0 = 0.12$ seems quite close to zero, it is probably too far away to say that it is no different than zero.

However, we cannot say with certainty that $\hat{\beta}_0 \neq 0$. No one knows for certain. Instead, we will use a hypothesis testing procedure that allows us to be specific about how certain we are that $\hat{\beta}_0 = 0$. That procedure is outlined in the box below.

The 5-step hypothesis testing procedure
1. State the null and alternative hypotheses
2. Choose the level of significance
3. State the decision rule
4. Get the numbers
5. Reject or do not reject the null hypothesis

We will use the regression results below to demonstrate various hypothesis tests. Thirty students in an econometrics class were asked about their grade point average (GPA) and study time (ST).

$GPA_i = 2.87 - 0.02\, ST_i + e_i$
    (0.21) (0.06) ← standard errors

$SER = 0.45$ $\overline{GPA} = 2.81$ $r^2 = 0.004$ $n = 30$

GPA_i is grade point average of the ith student
ST_i is average daily study time of the ith student

Here is a strict interpretation of the regression results:

$\hat{\beta}_0 = 2.87$ A student with zero study time is expected to have a GPA of 2.87.
$\hat{\beta}_1 = -0.02$ A 1 unit increase in study time is expected to lower GPA by 0.02 units.

SER = 0.45   The typical distance of an observation from the regression line is 0.45 units.

$\overline{GPA}$ = 2.81   The average GPA of the 30 students is 2.81. The fit of the model is adequate since SER < ½ $\overline{GPA}$.

r^2 = 0.004   0.4 percent of the variation in GPA is explained by study time.

n = 30   The regression was estimated with a sample of 30 students.

4.2 Test of Significance

A test of significance is used to determine if an estimator is probably equal to zero or not. Let's perform a test of significance on $\hat{\beta}_1$ = –0.02 using the 5-step procedure:

1. State the null and alternative hypotheses

The hypothesis we wish to test is the null hypothesis. The alternative hypothesis is the implication if the null hypothesis is rejected.

$$Ho: \beta_1 = 0 \quad Ha: \beta_1 \neq 0$$

2. Choose the level of significance

The level of significance is sometimes called the "critical level" of the test. It represents the probability that the test will result in a TYPE I error. A TYPE I error is when a true null hypothesis is rejected. The tradition in econometrics is to use 5 or 10 percent for the critical level. Let's make it our tradition to use 5 percent.

$$5\%$$

To demonstrate the difference between TYPE I and TYPE II errors, consider the judicial system in the United States. Any defendant is considered innocent until proven guilty. That is, the null hypothesis is that the defendant is not guilty.

$$Ho: \text{Defendant Is Not Guilty} \quad Ha: \text{Defendant Is Guilty}$$

Suppose the defendant is in truth innocent and the jury finds her guilty. This would be a TYPE I error since a true null is rejected. If a guilty defendant is found innocent by the jury, this is a TYPE II error. Here, a false null hypothesis is not being rejected.

In Truth →	Defendant Is Guilty	Defendant Is Not Guilty
Jury Finds ↓		
Defendant Guilty	**Proper Verdict**	**TYPE I Error**
Defendant Not Guilty	**TYPE II Error**	**Proper Verdict**

Econometricians, like jurists, abhor TYPE I errors. Our judicial process has all sorts of mechanisms to ensure that an innocent defendant will be found not guilty. Miranda rights and the right to an attorney are two examples of these mechanisms.

Econometricians prevent against TYPE I errors by setting very low critical levels for hypothesis tests. A 5 percent chance of committing a TYPE I error is the norm and 10 percent is typically the highest most econometricians are willing to risk in hypothesis testing.

Unfortunately, there is only one way to ensure that no TYPE I errors will occur: Do not reject any null hypotheses. Declare every defendant not guilty. But then we would make the maximum number of TYPE II errors. There is an inverse relationship between the probability of TYPE I and TYPE II errors.

In econometrics we set the critical level of hypothesis tests at 5 percent because we want to protect against the possibility of making a TYPE I error. This means we will be making more TYPE II errors than if we had set the critical level higher. However, like jurists who are unsure in a particular case, we would rather let a guilty defendant go free than convict an innocent person.

3. State the decision rule

The decision rule is used to test the hypothesis. You simply must know which rule to use for each test. After we do a few tests it will become apparent which rules should be used in which circumstances. For a test of significance the decision rule is:

$$\text{If } |\text{t-ratio}| > t^c, \text{ then reject Ho}$$

The t-ratio is defined as:

$$t\text{-ratio} = \frac{\hat{\beta}_1 - \beta_{Ho}}{SE(\hat{\beta}_1)} \text{ ; where } \beta_{Ho} \text{ is the value of } \hat{\beta}_1 \text{ stated in the null hypothesis.}$$

t^c is the critical t-ratio found in a t-table such as the one in the back of this book. To look up t^c, three pieces of information are needed:

> 1) The degrees of freedom of the test $= n - k = 30 - 2 = 28$
> 2) The critical level of the test $= 5\%$
> 3) The fact that a test of significance is 2-sided

This last bit of information is referring to the fact that the alternate hypothesis is $\hat{\beta}_1 \neq 0$. $\hat{\beta}_1$ may differ from zero in two ways – by being greater than zero or by being less than zero. The ability to distinguish between 1-sided and 2-sided tests will become apparent as we do more examples.

4. Get the numbers

Here we calculate the t-ratio and look up t^c.

$$t\text{-}ratio = \frac{\hat{\beta}_1 - \beta_{Ho}}{SE(\hat{\beta}_1)} = \frac{-0.02 - 0}{0.06} = -0.33$$

From the table in the back of the book, $t^c = 2.048$

5. *Reject or do not reject the null hypothesis*

Since $|\,t\text{-}ratio\,| < t^c$, we cannot reject Ho. This implies that β_1 is not significantly different than zero. Let's think about that for a second. If $\beta_1 = 0$ then no matter how much study time (ST) increases, GPA will not be affected. In other words, study time is an insignificant factor in determining a student's GPA. Do you believe this result? Why or why not?

Do Not Reject Ho: β_1 is not statistically different than zero.

Here is the summary of the entire 5-step procedure for this particular test of significance.

Test of significance
1. Ho: $\beta_1 = 0$ Ha: $\beta_1 \neq 0$
2. 5%
3. If $|\,t\text{-}ratio\,| > t^c$, then reject Ho
4. $0.33 < 2.048$ (d.f. = n - k = 30 – 2 = 28)
5. Do Not Reject Ho ; β_1 is not statistically different than zero.

4.3 Confidence Intervals

A confidence interval is a range of values within which the true value of an estimated parameter is likely to fall. To form a 95 percent confidence interval around the coefficient on ST ($\hat{\beta}_1 = -0.02$) in our example:

$$95\% \text{ CI for } \hat{\beta}_1 = -0.02:\ \hat{\beta}_1 +/- se(\hat{\beta}_1)(t^c)$$

$$-0.02 +/- 0.06\,(2.048) \quad \rightarrow \quad -0.14 \text{ to } 0.10$$

If we construct an infinite number of such intervals, 95 percent of them will contain the true β_1. Notice that the interval spans zero. This corresponds with our test of significance at the 5 percent critical level that indicated that $\hat{\beta}_1$ is not statistically different than zero.

$$90\% \text{ CI for } \hat{\beta}_1: \quad -0.02 +/- 0.06\,(\mathbf{1.701}) \quad \rightarrow \quad -0.12 \text{ to } 0.08$$

If we construct an infinite number of such intervals, 90 percent of them will contain the true β_1. Notice that the 90% confidence interval is smaller than the 95% confidence interval. This makes sense. To be more confident, we need a wider interval. A 100% confidence interval would run from negative infinity to positive infinity.

4.4 Negative Sign Test

A negative sign test is different than a test of significance in that we are solely interested in the estimator being less than zero. A negative sign test is more specific in that Ha is $\beta_1 > 0$, not $\beta_1 \neq 0$. $\hat{\beta}_1 = -0.02$ in our example. Let's test if this is significantly less than zero.

1) Ho: $\beta_1 = 0$ Ha: $\beta_1 < 0$
2) 5%
3) If t-ratio $< -t^c$, then reject Ho
4) $-.33 > -1.701$ (d.f. $= n - k = 30 - 2 = 28$)
5) Do Not Reject Ho $\rightarrow \beta_1$ is not significantly negative

Notice the differences between this test and the test of significance:

1) Ha is now $\beta_1 < 0$, not $\beta_1 \neq 0$.
2) The decision rule is, If t-ratio $< -t^c$, then reject Ho, not If $|$ t-ratio $| > t_c$, then reject Ho. Still, the t-ratio is calculated with the same formula.
3) The degrees of freedom are the same, however, this is a one tailed test, so we obtain a different t^c.

The conclusion of our negative sign test is that β_1 is not significantly negative.

4.5 Positive Sign Test

A positive sign test is different than a test of significance in that we are not interested in the estimator being different than zero, but greater than zero. $\hat{\beta}_0 = 2.87$ in our example. Let's test if this is significantly greater than zero. Here is the 5-step procedure:

1) Ho: $\beta_0 = 0$ Ha: $\beta_0 > 0$
2) 5%
3) If t-ratio $> t^c$, then reject Ho
4) $13.67 > 1.701$ (d.f. $= n - k = 30 - 2 = 28$)
5) Reject Ho $\rightarrow \beta_0$ is significantly positive
   We reject Ho which implies that β_0 is significantly positive.

4.6 A Review of the Decision Rules

After doing a test of significance and two sign tests, you have learned three decision rules. It is easy to remember which decision rule to use in each instance because the rules are aligned with the alternate hypotheses.

Review of decision rules

If Ha has a ≠: if $|\text{t-ratio}| > t^c$, reject Ho
If Ha has a >: if $\text{t-ratio} > t^c$, reject Ho
If Ha has a <: if $\text{t-ratio} < -t^c$, reject Ho
(The latter two are one-tailed tests.)

4.7 Specific Value Test

A specific value test is used to determine if an estimator equals some prespecified value, not zero. Specific value tests can be one- or two-tailed. It depends on how they are set up. For instance, we might ask if $\hat{\beta}_0$, which equals 2.87 in our example, is significantly less than 3. This is a one-tailed test since the alternate hypothesis is Ha: $\hat{\beta}_0 < 3$.

Be careful in calculating the t-ratio since $\beta_{Ho} \neq 0$ in this test:

$$t\text{-}ratio = \frac{\hat{\beta}_0 - \beta_{Ho}}{SE(\hat{\beta}_0)} = \frac{2.87 - 3}{0.21} = -0.62$$

Here is the entire test:

1) Ho: $\beta_0 = 3$ Ha: $\beta_0 < 3$
2) 5%
3) If t-ratio $< -t^c$, then reject Ho
4) $-0.62 > -1.701$ (d.f. = n − k = 30 − 2 = 28)
5) Do Not Reject Ho → β_0 is not significantly less than 3

We do not reject Ho which implies β_0 is not significantly less than 3.

4.8 Test for r = 0

r is the correlation coefficient between two variables. It ranges between plus and minus 1.

$$r = \frac{\Sigma(X_i - \bar{X})(Y_i - \bar{Y})}{\sqrt{\Sigma(X_i - \bar{X})^2(Y_i - \bar{Y})^2}}$$

When r = 1, it implies that the two variables are perfectly linearly correlated. For instance, every time X increases by 7, Y increases by 3. When r = –1, the two variables are perfectly inversely correlated. Every time X increases by 7, Y decreases by 3. When r = 0 it implies that the variables are not linearly related.

The correlation coefficient between GPA and ST in our example equals –0.061. Is this value close enough to zero to say that there is no correlation between GPA and ST?

The t-ratio for this test is calculated as follows:

$$t\text{-}ratio = \frac{r\sqrt{n-2}}{\sqrt{(1-r^2)}} = \frac{-.061\sqrt{30-2}}{\sqrt{1-.0037}} = \frac{-.323}{.998} = -.324$$

1. Ho: r = 0   Ha: r ≠ 0
2. 5%
3. If | t-ratio | > t^c, then reject Ho
4. 0.324 < 2.048 (d.f. = n – 2 = 30 – 2 = 28)
5. Do Not Reject Ho; r is not statistically different than zero.

We do not reject Ho, which implies that r is not statistically different than zero. Notice that all of the hypothesis tests we have learned to this point include a statistic called "t-ratio," sometimes referred to as "t-statistic." Also notice that this statistic is calculated differently for some of the tests. This can be confusing. The test of significance, positive sign test, and negative sign test all use the same formula to calculate the t-ratio. However, the specific value test and the test for r = 0 use different formulas for the t-ratio.

The next hypothesis test uses an F-statistic.

4.9 Test for $r^2 = 0$

If the coefficient of determination (r^2) equals zero it implies that the explanatory variable explains none of the variation in the dependent variable. In our example, $r^2 = 0.004$. Is this close enough to be called zero?

This is the first hypothesis test we have encountered where the test statistic is distributed as an F-statistic. F-statistics can only be positive so they are always one-sided tests. Here is the 5-step procedure:

1. Ho: $r^2 = 0$ Ha: $r^2 > 0$
2. 5%
3. If F > F^c, then reject Ho
4. 0.104 < 4.20 (d.f. = k – 1 in the numerator and n – k in the denominator)
5. Do Not Reject Ho; r^2 is not statistically greater than zero.

The F is calculated with either of the formulas below:

$$F = \frac{\Sigma(Y_i - \bar{Y})^2/(k-1)}{\Sigma e_i^2/(n-k)} \quad \text{or} \quad F = \frac{r^2/(k-1)}{1-r^2/(n-k)}$$

F^c is found in a table such as the one in the back of this book. To look up F^c, find where the degrees of freedom in the numerator (k – 1 = 1) intersect with the degrees of freedom in the denominator (n – k = 30 – 2 = 28).

In this example we do not reject Ho – r^2 is not statistically greater than zero. Study time does not account for any of the variation in GPA across these 30 students.

4.10 Probability Values

A probability value is the lowest level of significance that can be used in a hypothesis test while still rejecting Ho. As such, P-values (as they are commonly known) provide a quick method for determining the results of a hypothesis test: If the P-value is less than .05, then the result of the hypothesis test will be to reject Ho.

Consider the GPA regression we have used throughout this chapter. The P-value on the coefficient on ST for a test of significance is equal to 0.73. Since this is greater than the critical level of the test (0.05), the test of significance will result in "do not reject Ho." That is, we can immediately see that ST is insignificant at the 5 percent critical level since the P-value is greater than 0.05.

Indeed, even if we set the critical level of this test of significance at 72 percent, we would still say reject Ho. Only when the critical level surpasses 73 percent would we conclude that ST is significant.

Terms

Confidence interval – A range of values within which the true value of an estimated parameter is likely to fall.

Correlation coefficient (r) – A statistic ranging between –1 and 1 that measures the degree to which two variables are linearly related.

Critical level (level of significance) – The probability of making a TYPE I error in a hypothesis test.

Probability value – The lowest level of significance that can be used in a hypothesis test while still rejecting Ho.

t-ratio (t-statistic) – Any statistic that follows the t-distribution.

F-ratio (F-statistic) – Any statistic that follows the F-distribution.

TYPE I error – When a true null hypothesis is rejected.

TYPE II error – A false null hypothesis is not rejected.

Chapter 4   Problems

1. A professor has polled 25 students and asked them about their seat belt use (Do you wear your seat belt regularly?) and smoking (Do you smoke cigarettes?).

   A) The correlation coefficient (r) between seat belt use and cigarette smoking is –.034. Are you surprised that the correlation is negative? Explain.

   B) Do a test to determine if r is different than zero. Show the 5-step procedure.

   C) Do a test to determine if r is less than zero. Show the 5-step procedure.

   D) Explain why seat belt use and smoking may be correlated despite the tests above.

2. A professor has polled 30 students and asked them about their job situation (Do you have a full or part-time job this semester?) and their overall GPA (What is your overall GPA?).

   A) The correlation coefficient (r) between having a job and GPA is 0.21. Are you surprised that the correlation is positive? Explain.

   B) Do a test to determine if r is different than zero. Show the 5-step procedure.

   C) Do a test to determine if r is greater than zero. Show the 5-step procedure.

   D) What is the probability that a TYPE I error is being made in the test above?

3. Given the following regression results:

$$CORUPT_i = 5.47 - 0.05\ MIL_i + e_i$$

             (0.49) (0.05) ← standard errors

             (0.00) (0.36) ← P-values

    $SER = 2.35$ $\overline{CORUPT} = 5.14$ $r^2 = 0.02$ $n = 48$

    $CORUPT_i$ is the corruption level of the country

(1 is low; 10 is high)

MIL_i is military presence in the country

(military personnel per 1000 citizens)

   A) Do a test of significance on the coefficient on MIL. Show the 5-step procedure.

B) Would the results of your test turn out differently if the critical level of the test was 40% instead of 5%? Explain.

C) Is the constant term significant at the 1% critical level? Answer this question without doing a test of significance. Just explain.

D) Form a 90% confidence interval around the coefficient on MIL.

E) Determine if $r^2 = 0$ for this regression. (The F-statistic = 0.95.) Show the 5-step procedure.

F) Would your results for E) be different if the critical level of test was 33%? Explain. (P-value for this test is 0.34.)

G) Do a test to determine if the coefficient on MIL equals zero or if it is greater than zero. Show the 5-step procedure.

H) Do a test to determine if the coefficient on MIL equals -0.1 or not. Show the 5-step procedure.

4. Given the following regression results:

$$CORUPT_i = 7.54 - 0.25\ OVER65_i + e_i$$
$$\quad\quad (0.62)\ (0.06) \quad \leftarrow \text{standard errors}$$
$$\quad\quad (0.00)\ (0.02) \quad \leftarrow \text{P-values}$$

$$SER = 1.99 \quad \overline{CORUPT} = 5.14 \quad r^2 = 0.29 \quad n = 32$$

$CORUPT_i$ is the corruption level of the country
(1 is low; 10 is high)
$OVER65_i$ is percentage of the population 65 or older

A) Do a test of significance on the coefficient on OVER65. Show the 5-step procedure.

B) Would the results of your test turn out differently if the critical level of the test was 1% instead of 5%? Explain.

C) Is the constant term significant at the 1% critical level? Answer this question without doing a test of significance. Just explain.

D) Form a 90% confidence interval around the coefficient on OVER65.

E) Determine if $r^2 = 0$ for this regression. (The F-statistic = 12.25.) Show the 5-step procedure.

F) Would your results for E) be different if the critical level of test was 3%? Explain. (P-value for this test is 0.01.)

G) Do a test to determine if the coefficient on OVER65 equals zero or if it is greater than zero. Show the 5-step procedure.

H) Do a test to determine if the coefficient on OVER65 equals –1.00 or not. Show the 5-step procedure.

Chapter 5

Multiple Regression

5.1 Parameter Estimation in Multiple Regression

In a multiple regression there are two or more explanatory variables. Consider the case of two explanatory variables: $Y_i = \hat{\beta}_0 + \hat{\beta}_1 X1_i + \hat{\beta}2 X2_i + e_i$.

We still want to min Σe_i^2 or min $\Sigma(Y_i - \hat{\beta}_0 - \hat{\beta}_1 X1_i - \hat{\beta}2 X2_i)^2$. That requires taking three partial derivatives and setting the resulting equations equal to zero. The three normal equations can then be solved for $\hat{\beta}_0, \hat{\beta}_1$, and $\hat{\beta}_2$:

Take the partial derivative with respect to $\hat{\beta}_0$:

$$\frac{\partial \Sigma(Y_i - \hat{\beta}_0 - \hat{\beta}_1 X1_i - \hat{\beta}_2 X2_i)^2}{\partial \hat{\beta}_0} = 2\Sigma(Y_i - \hat{\beta}_0 - \hat{\beta}_1 X1_i - \hat{\beta}_2 X2_i)(-1) = 0$$

Divide both sides of the above by -2 and distribute the sum sign:

$$\Sigma Y_i - n\hat{\beta}_0 - \hat{\beta}_1 \Sigma X1_i - \hat{\beta}_2 \Sigma X2_i = 0$$

Solve for $\hat{\beta}_0$:

$$\Sigma Y_i = n\hat{\beta}_0 + \hat{\beta}_1 \Sigma X1_i + \hat{\beta}_2 \Sigma X2_i \quad \text{(normal equation)}$$

$$\hat{\beta}_0 = \frac{\Sigma Y_i - \hat{\beta}_1 \Sigma X1_i - \hat{\beta}_2 \Sigma X2_i}{n} = \overline{Y} - \hat{\beta}_1 \overline{X}1_i - \hat{\beta}_2 \overline{X}2_i$$

Take the partial derivative with respect to $\hat{\beta}_1$:

$$\frac{\partial \Sigma(Y_i - \hat{\beta}_0 - \hat{\beta}_1 X1_i - \hat{\beta}_2 X2_i)^2}{\partial \hat{\beta}_1} = 2\Sigma(Y_i - \hat{\beta}_0 - \hat{\beta}_1 X1_i - \hat{\beta}_2 X2_i)(-X1_i) = 0$$

Divide both sides of the above by -2 and distribute the sum sign:

$$\Sigma Y_i X1_i - \hat{\beta}_0 \Sigma X1_i - \hat{\beta}_1 \Sigma X1_i X1_i - \hat{\beta}_2 \Sigma X2_i X1_i = 0$$

Solve for $\hat{\beta}_1$:

$$\Sigma Y_i X1_i = \hat{\beta}_0 \Sigma X1_i + \hat{\beta}_1 \Sigma X1_i X1_i + \hat{\beta}_2 \Sigma X2_i X1_i \quad \text{(normal equation)}$$

.

.

.

$$\hat{\beta}_1 = \frac{(\Sigma y_i x_{1i})(\Sigma x_{2i}^2) - (\Sigma y_i x_{2i})(\Sigma x_{1i} x_{2i})}{(\Sigma x_{1i}^2)(\Sigma x_{2i}^2) - (\Sigma x_{1i} x_{2i})^2} \; ; \text{ where } y_i = Y_i - \overline{Y} \, ; \, x_{1i} = X1_i - \overline{X}1 \, ; \, x_{2i} = X2_i - \overline{X}2$$

Take the partial derivative with respect to $\hat{\beta}_2$:

$$\frac{\partial \Sigma (Y_i - \hat{\beta}_0 - \hat{\beta}_1 X1_i - \hat{\beta}_2 X2_i)^2}{\partial \hat{\beta}_2} = 2\Sigma (Y_i - \hat{\beta}_0 - \hat{\beta}_1 X1_i - \hat{\beta}_2 X2_i)(-X2_i) = 0$$

Divide both sides of the above by –2 and distribute the sum sign:

$$\Sigma Y_i X2_i - \hat{\beta}_0 \Sigma X2_i - \hat{\beta}_1 \Sigma X1_i X2_i - \hat{\beta}_2 \Sigma X2_i X2_i = 0$$

Solve for $\hat{\beta}_2$:

$$\Sigma Y_i X2_i = \hat{\beta}_0 \Sigma X2_i + \hat{\beta}_1 \Sigma X1_i X2_i + \hat{\beta}_2 \Sigma X2_i X2_i \quad \text{(normal equation)}$$

$$\vdots$$

$$\hat{\beta}_2 = \frac{(\Sigma y_i x_{2i})(\Sigma x_{2i}^2) - (\Sigma y_i x_{1i})(\Sigma x_{1i} x_{2i})}{(\Sigma x_{1i}^2)(\Sigma x_{2i}^2) - (\Sigma x_{1i} x_{2i})^2} \; ; \text{ where } y_i = Y_i - \overline{Y} \, ; \, x_{1i} = X1_i - \overline{X}1 \, ; \, x_{2i} = X2_i - \overline{X}2$$

The formulas for $\hat{\beta}_1$ and $\hat{\beta}_2$ are too cumbersome to calculate by hand. We are grateful to have computers to do this sort of thing for us. Here is the formula for $\hat{\beta}_1$ written out in all its glory:

$$\hat{\beta}_1 = \frac{(\Sigma (Y_i - \overline{Y})(X1_i - \overline{X}1)(\Sigma X2_i - \overline{X}2)^2 - (\Sigma (Y_i - \overline{Y})(X2_i - \overline{X}2)(\Sigma (X1_i - \overline{X}1)(X2_i - \overline{X}2))}{(\Sigma X1_i - \overline{X}1)^2 (\Sigma X2_i - \overline{X}2)^2 - (\Sigma (X1_i - \overline{X}1)(X2_i - \overline{X}2))^2}$$

The problems at the end of this chapter and beyond require you to use a statistical software package to perform cumbersome calculations such as the one above. Eviews by Quantitative Micro Software was used to solve the problems in this book, but any package will do. EXCEL by Microsoft can be used to run regressions, but it does not calculate all the residual statistics you will need in later chapters. Free shareware is available (such as gretl) that can do all the problems in this text. All of the input data required for any problems in this textbook are available at www.mesharpe-student.com. The data files are in EXCEL format which allows them to be imported into a variety of statistical packages including Eviews and gretl.

5.2 The Variance and Standard Errors of the Estimators

As we move to multiple regression from simple regression, our formulas for the standard errors of the structural parameters are changed.

$$\text{var}(\hat{\beta}_0) = \left[\frac{1}{n} + \frac{\overline{X}1^2 \Sigma x_{2i}^2 + \overline{X}2^2 \Sigma x_{1i}^2 - 2\overline{X}1\overline{X}2 \Sigma x_{1i}x_{2i}}{(\Sigma x_{1i}^2)(\Sigma x_{2i}^2) - (\Sigma x_{1i}x_{2i})^2} \right] \bullet \hat{\sigma}^2$$

$$se(\hat{\beta}_0) = \sqrt{\text{var}(\hat{\beta}_0)}$$

$$\text{var}(\hat{\beta}_1) = \frac{\Sigma x_{2i}^2}{(\Sigma x_{1i}^2)(\Sigma x_{2i}^2) - (\Sigma x_{1i}x_{2i})^2} \bullet \hat{\sigma}^2$$

$$se(\hat{\beta}_1) = \sqrt{\text{var}(\hat{\beta}_1)}$$

$$\text{var}(\hat{\beta}_2) = \frac{\Sigma x_{1i}^2}{(\Sigma x_{1i}^2)(\Sigma x_{2i}^2) - (\Sigma x_{1i}x_{2i})^2} \bullet \hat{\sigma}^2$$

$$se(\hat{\beta}_2) = \sqrt{\text{var}(\hat{\beta}_2)}$$

The interpretation of these standard errors is still the same. If we calculate $se(\hat{\beta}_2) = 1.23$, it means that $\hat{\beta}_2$ is expected to vary by 1.23 on average in repeated sampling.

5.3 Goodness-of-Fit in Multiple Regression

The measures of goodness-of-fit that we developed for simple regressions are slightly altered when we move to multiple regressions.

The SER is still interpreted and (almost) calculated the same way $\hat{\sigma} = \sqrt{\dfrac{\Sigma e_i^2}{n-2}}$

For multiple regression $\hat{\sigma} = \sqrt{\dfrac{\Sigma e_i^2}{n-k}}$; where k is the number of structural parameters.

Interpretation: 0.487   The typical distance of an observation from the regression line is 0.487.

The coefficient of determination is now denoted by R^2 (as opposed to r^2), but it is still calculated with the same formula:

$$R^2 = 1 - \frac{\Sigma e_i^2}{\Sigma (Y_i - \overline{Y})^2}$$

Interpretation: .001 – 0.1 percent of the variation in Y is explained by the X variables.

R^2 is monotonically increasing with respect to k. Hence, it is inappropriate to compare R^2 from regressions with a different number of explanatory variables. Instead, use adjusted R^2 $(\overline{R}^2)$:

$$\overline{R}^2 = 1 - \frac{\Sigma e_i^2 / (n-k)}{\Sigma (Y_i - \overline{Y})^2 / (n-1)}$$

$\overline{R}^2$ will decrease if the additional explanatory variable has little or no impact on the dependent variable. Indeed, it can be shown that $\overline{R}^2$ will decrease if the added explanatory variable has a t-ratio < 1 in absolute value.

5.4 An Illustrative Example with Hypothesis Testing

Let's consider a classic econometric study as an example of multiple regression (Andersen and Jordan, 1969). In this study, Andersen and Jordan hypothesized that changes in nominal GDP would depend on changes in monetary and fiscal policy. They measured monetary and fiscal policy in a variety of ways using quarterly data from the first quarter of 1952 through the second quarter of 1968. Here we replicate the study using annual data from 1964 through 2005.

$$NGDP_t = 127.35 + 1.06\ M2_{t-1} - 0.29\ FP_{t-1} + e_t$$
$$(3.75)\quad (5.55)\quad\quad (-0.71)\quad \leftarrow \text{t-ratios}$$

SER = 132.65 $\overline{NGDP}$ = 282.42 R^2 = 0.47   n = 42

NGDP is the change in nominal GDP
M2 is the change in the M2 money supply
FP is the change in standardized federal budget deficit

Notice that M2 and FP are lagged one period (t–1). This is because monetary and fiscal policy actions last year impact this year's nominal GDP. Our replication confirms Andersen and Jordan's original results – monetary policy has an impact on nominal GDP but fiscal policy is statistically insignificant.

Before doing any hypothesis testing, let's interpret the regression results noticing how the interpretations differ from those in a simple regression.

Interpretations:

$\hat{\beta}_0$ = 127.35: If $M2_{t-1}$ and $FP_{t-1} = 0$, then $NGDP_t = 127.35$

$\hat{\beta}_1$ = 1.06: If $M2_{t-1}$ increases one unit, then NGDP increases 1.06 units, holding FP_{t-1} constant

$\hat{\beta}_2$ = –0.29: FP_{t-1} increases one unit, then NGDP decreases 0.29 units, holding $M2_{t-1}$ constant

R^2 = 0.47: 47 percent of the variation in NGDP is explained by $M2_{t-1}$ and FP_{t-1}

SER = 132.65: the typical regression error is 132.65

Hypothesis Testing

Notice that the coefficient on FP_{t-1} has the correct sign: an increase in the standardized federal budget deficit is expected to contract the economy and decrease nominal GDP. However, the coefficient is not statistically different than zero.

Test of significance on $\hat{\beta}_2$

1) Ho: $\beta = 0$ Ha: $\beta_2 \neq 0$
2) 5%
3) If |t-ratio| > t^c, then reject Ho
4) 0.71 < 2.042 (d.f. = n – k = 42 – 3 = 39; but using 30 because of our t-table)
5) Do Not Reject Ho → $\hat{\beta}_2$ is not statistically significant

Changes in the money supply, however, have a positive impact on nominal GDP according to a positive sign test:

Positive Sign Test on $\hat{\beta}_1$

1) Ho: $\beta_1 = 0$ Ha: $\beta_1 > 0$
2) 5%
3) If t-ratio > t^c, then reject Ho
4) 5.55 > 1.697 (d.f. = n – k = 42 – 3 = 39; but using 30 because of our t-table)
5) Reject Ho → $\hat{\beta}_1$ is significantly positive

These results suggest that monetary policy is an effective macroeconomic policy while fiscal policy is not.

5.5 The Intuition of Multiple Regression

Geometrically, simple regression can be represented by fitting a line between observations in two-dimensional space.

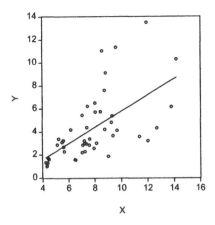

A regression with two explanatory variables is akin to fitting a plane in three-dimensional space.

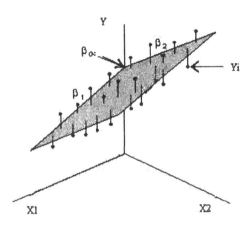

A regression with three explanatory variables would be fitting a three-dimensional object into observations in four-dimensional space. We leave it to the reader to visualize this case.

5.6 Model Specification

Whether or not to include a particular variable in a given regression is not something that can be taught. However, there are some general rules to help researchers decide about model specification. Before we consider those rules it should be understood that the process of model selection is crucial.

It is completely inappropriate, and unethical, to run regression after regression, slightly altering the set of explanatory variables each time, and then stop when the results conform to your premonitions. Hypothesis testing in this situation is invalid since the researcher has actively worked to ensure that the results would support preconceived notions.

The proper approach to model specification is to thoroughly research which explanatory variables belong in a particular regression. Theory is the best guide. It is important to include every explanatory variable that has a substantial impact on the dependent variable. Re-running the regression with more variables is not a crime, but it begins to look like fishing for preconceived results.

Often, theory does not indicate whether a particular variable should be included or not. In this case there are some statistical indicators that can help.

- T-ratios – Explanatory variables with anemic t-ratios (|t-ratios| < 2) are candidates for exclusion from the model. Such variables will not pass a test of significance.
- Adjusted R^2 – If adjusted R^2 falls upon the addition of an explanatory variable, it is an indication that the variable does not belong. It can be shown that adjusted R^2 will fall when the added variable has a |t-ratio| < 1.
- Akaike Information Criterion and Schwarz Criterion – Like adjusted R^2, these statistics consider how fit is improved by adding an explanatory variable to a regression. Unlike adjusted R-squared, a fall in either of these statistics is an indication that the added variable belongs.

Akaike Information Criterion:

$$AIC = -2[(-n/2)(1 + \log(2\pi) + \log(\hat{\sigma}_2 / n))]/n + 2k/n$$

Schwarz Criterion:

$$SC = -2[(-n/2)(1 + \log(2\pi) + \log(\hat{\sigma}_2 / n))]/n + (k\log n)/n$$

- Altered coefficients – When a particular variable is removed from the regression and the coefficients on the remaining variables change markedly, it is an indication that the removed variable belongs.
- Ramsey's Reset Test – Ramsey (1969) has devised an F-test to determine if explanatory variables might be excluded from a regression:

  1. Ho: $\beta_2 = \beta_3 = 0$ Ha: β_2 and/or $\beta_3 \neq 0$
     (No variables excluded)   (Variables excluded)
  2. 5%
  3. If $F > F^c$, then reject Ho
  4. Get F and F^c
  5. Reject or Do Not Reject Ho

The F-statistic is calculated with the following formula:

$$F = \frac{SSR_U - SSR_R / 2}{(1 - SSR_U)/(n-k)}$$

An auxiliary regression must be run that includes the predicted values from the initial regression squared and cubed. Then the sum of the squared residuals from the initial regression (SSR_R) and the sum of the squared residuals from the auxiliary regression (SSR_U) are used to calculate an F-statistic that is compared to an F^c.

$$\text{SSR}_R: \ \Sigma e_i^2 \text{ from } Y_i = \hat{\beta}_0 + \hat{\beta}_1 X1_i + e_i$$

$$\text{SSR}_U: \ \Sigma e_i^2 \text{ from } Y_i = \hat{\beta}_0 + \hat{\beta}_1 X1_i + \hat{\beta}_2 \hat{Y}_i^2 + \hat{\beta}_3 \hat{Y}_i^3 + e_i$$

The critical F (F^c), is found in the F-table. The degrees of freedom in the numerator are equal to 2 (the two addition variables added to SSR_U) and the degrees of freedom in the denominator are equal to n–k.

If $F > F^c$ then we reject Ho which indicates that important explanatory variables may be omitted from the specification.

All of these rules are trumped by theory. When theory unequivocally indicates that a variable should be included, then these statistical indicators take a back seat.

Let's continue with our Andersen-Jordan example. They argued that monetary and fiscal policy were the only theoretically justified explanatory variables for their model. However, they were unsure about how to measure these variables. They tried a variety of measures for monetary policy (including changes in M1 and changes in the monetary base) and several fiscal policy variables. They understood that running a bank of regressions could cause skepticism about their results so they reported all their regression results and all the results pointed in the same direction: monetary policy affects nominal GDP but fiscal policy does not.

5.7 Underspecification

Underspecification is when an important explanatory variable is excluded from a regression. Let's omit monetary policy from the model and see what happens:

Correctly Specified Andersen-Jordan Equation

$$\text{NGDP}_t = 127.35 + 1.06 \, M2_{t-1} - 0.29 \, FP_{t-1} + e_t$$
$$\phantom{\text{NGDP}_t =} (3.75) \quad (5.55) \qquad (-0.71) \quad \leftarrow \text{t-ratios}$$

$$\text{SER} = 132.65 \quad \overline{\text{NGDP}} = 282.42 \quad R^2 = 0.47 \quad n = 42$$

$$\text{Adjusted } R^2 = 0.45 \quad \text{Akaike} = 12.68 \quad \text{Schwarz} = 12.81$$

Underspecified Specified Andersen-Jordan Equation

$$\text{NGDP}_t = 276.91 - 0.81 \, FP_{t-1} + e_t$$
$$\phantom{\text{NGDP}_t =} (10.15) \ (-1.56) \quad \leftarrow \text{t-ratios}$$

$$\text{SER} = 175.26 \quad \overline{\text{NGDP}} = 282.42 \quad r^2 = 0.06 \quad n = 42$$

$$\text{Adjusted } R^2 = 0.03 \quad \text{Akaike} = 13.22 \quad \text{Schwarz} = 13.30$$

Notice that adjusted R^2 has plummeted, indicating that the fit of the underspecified regression is much worse. The Akaike and the Schwarz statistics are higher, which also suggests a worse fit. Also notice how different the estimators are in both regressions. The constant term went from 127.35 to 276.91 and the coefficient on FP_{t-1} went from –0.29 to –0.81. Such dramatic differences imply that the omitted variable belongs in the regression.

Finally, the underspecified regression does not pass Ramsey's Reset test.

1. Ho: $\beta_2 = \beta_3 = 0$ Ha: β_2 and/or $\beta_3 \neq 0$
   (No variables excluded)   (Variables excluded)
2. 5%
3. If F > F^c, then reject Ho
4. 3.66 > 3.32; where F^c has d.f. NUM = 2 ; d.f. DEN = n – k = 42 – 4 = 38
                                (using NUM=2 and DEN=30 because of our F-table)
5. Reject Ho → Variables are excluded from this regression.

All indications are that the regression without the monetary policy variable is underspecified. The consequence of leaving a relevant explanatory variable out of a regression is severe; parameter estimates, and therefore all residual statistics, are biased. This means in repeated sampling, the average of the estimates will not equal the true value. $E[\hat{\beta}_1] \neq \beta_1$.

5.8 Overspecification

We can intentionally overspecify the original Andersen-Jordan model by adding a variable we know does not belong. $RAND_t$ is a series of random numbers generated by a computer.

Overspecified Andersen-Jordan Equation

$$NGDP_t = 152.46 + 1.05\ M2_{t-1} - 0.23\ FP_{t-1} + -8.42\ RAND_t + e_t$$
$$\quad (3.75)\quad (5.55)\qquad (-0.71)\qquad (-0.93)\quad \leftarrow \text{t-ratios}$$

$$SER = 132.87\quad \overline{NGDP} = 282.42\quad R^2 = 0.49\quad n = 42$$

$$\text{Adjusted } R^2 = 0.44\quad \text{Akaike} = 12.71\quad \text{Schwarz} = 12.87$$

Adjusted R^2 has fallen very slightly, while the Akaike and Schwarz statistics have both risen a tad. All three statistics thereby suggest that RAND does not belong in the regression. Notice that the estimators have hardly changed with the addition of RAND. The coefficient on FP_{t-1} went from 1.06 to 1.05. This also implies that RAND is extraneous.

Ramsey's Reset test cannot help to discern if a regression is overspecified, so we will not employ it here. It is fairly evident that RAND is an irrelevant explanatory variable given its anemic t-ratio and the indications noted above.

The consequence for including an irrelevant explanatory variable in a regression is inefficient (not best) estimators. An inefficient estimator will vary more in repeated sampling than the efficient estimator. Hypothesis tests should be conducted with caution under these circumstances since the t-ratios used in those tests will be derived from bloated standard errors. TYPE II errors will become more likely.

Terms

Adjusted R² ($\overline{R}^2$) – A statistic that tends to decrease when an irrelevant explanatory variable is added to a regression.

Akaike criterion – A statistic that tends to increase when an irrelevant explanatory variable is added to a regression.

Biased estimator – In repeated sampling, the average of the estimates will not equal the true value.

Inefficient estimator – An estimator that varies more in repeated sampling than the efficient estimator.

Multiple regression – A regression that includes more than one explanatory variable.

Overspecification – When a regression includes one or more irrelevant explanatory variables.

Ramsey's reset test – A statistical test to help determine if a regression is underspecified.

Schwarz criterion – A statistic that tends to increase when an irrelevant explanatory variable is added to a regression.

Underspecification – When an important explanatory variable is excluded from a regression.

Chapter 5   Problems

1. Use the data in SDATA.XLS and statistical software to run the following regression:

$$GPA_i = \hat{\beta}_0 + \hat{\beta}_1\ ST_i + e_i$$

where GPA = grade point average
and ST = study time per day

A) Interpret the value you obtained for $\hat{\beta}_0$.

B) Interpret the value you obtained for $\hat{\beta}_1$.

C) How much does $\hat{\beta}_1$ typically vary in repeated sampling?

D) Perform a test of significance on $\hat{\beta}_1$. Show the 5-step procedure.

E) What percent of the variation in GPA is explained by study time?

F) Perform a test to determine if $r^2 = 0$. Show the 5-step procedure.

G) According to these results, how many hours per day would your study time have to increase in order to raise your GPA by 0.1?

H) Plot the scattergram between GPA and ST with the estimated regression line drawn in.

I) What is the average distance of an observation from the regression line?

J) Will you cut back on your study time now that you have seen these results? Explain why.

2. Use the data in SDATA.XLS and statistical software to run the following regression:

$$GPA_i = \hat{\beta}_0 + \hat{\beta}_1 \, ST_i + \hat{\beta}_2 \, SAT_i + e_i$$

Where GPA = grade point average
ST = study time per day
SAT = SAT score

A) Interpret the value you obtained for $\hat{\beta}_0$.

B) Interpret the value you obtained for $\hat{\beta}_1$.

C) Perform a positive sign test on $\hat{\beta}_1$. Show the 5-step procedure.

D) Interpret the value you obtained for $\hat{\beta}_2$.

E) Perform a test to determine if $\hat{\beta}_0 < 1$. Show the 5-step procedure.

F) Interpret the value you obtained for R^2.

G) Which regression fits the data better, this one or the one in question 1? On what do you base your response?

H) The typical student in the survey studies about 3.0 hours per day and had an SAT score of 1125. What would you expect the average student's GPA to be given your research into this matter?

3. Use the data in CONSUMP.XLS and statistical software to run the following regression:

$$RCONPC_t = \hat{\beta}_0 + \hat{\beta}_1 \, REALYDPC_t + \hat{\beta}_2 \, REALR_t + e_t$$

where RCONPC = real consumer spending in the USA per capita
REALYDPC = real disposable income per capita
REALR = real interest rate on 1-year Treasury Bonds
CC = University of Michigan Index of Consumer Confidence

A) Do all the explanatory variables attain their expected signs?

B) Aside from CC, what explanatory variables might be missing from this regression?

C) Perform Ramsey's Reset test. Show the 5-step procedure. Are variables missing from the model according to this test?

4. Run the regression: $MBAPAY_i = \hat{\beta}_0 + \hat{\beta}_1 \, AVGMAT_i + \hat{\beta}_2 \, ACRATE_i + e_i$

where $MBAPAY_i$ = avg. starting salary of MBA students from school i
$AVGMAT_i$ = avg. GMAT score at school i
$ACRATE_i$ = acceptance rate at school i

A) Do all the explanatory variables attain their expected signs?
B) Aside from AVGPA, what explanatory variables might be missing from this regression?
C) Perform Ramsey's Reset test. Show the 5-step procedure. Are variables missing from the model according to this test?

5. Use the data in CONSUMP.XLS and statistical software to run the following regression:

$$RCONPC_t = \hat{\beta}_0 + \hat{\beta}_1 REALYDPC_t + \hat{\beta}_2 REALR_t + \hat{\beta}_3 CC_t + e_t$$

A) Does CC attain its expected sign? Explain.
B) Does a test of significance on CC justify its presence in the regression?
C) Does CC belong in the regression according to Adjusted R^2? Explain.
D) Does CC belong in the regression according to the Akaike Information Criterion? Explain.
E) Does CC belong in the regression according to the Schwarz Criterion? Explain.
F) Does this regression fit better than the regression from 1? Explain.
G) Perform Ramsey's Reset test. Show the 5-step procedure. Are variables missing from the model according to this test?
H) Do you think the estimators in $RCONPC_t = \hat{\beta}_0 + \hat{\beta}_1 REALYDPC_t + \hat{\beta}_2 REALR_t + e_t$ are biased? Inefficient? Neither? Explain.
I) Do you think the estimators in $RCONPC_t = \hat{\beta}_0 + \hat{\beta}_1 REALYDPC_t + \hat{\beta}_2 REALR_t + \hat{\beta}_3 CC_t + e_t$ are biased? Inefficient? Neither? Explain.

6. Use the data in MBAPAY.XLS and statistical software to run the following regression:

$$MBAPAY_i = \hat{\beta}_0 + \hat{\beta}_1 AVGMAT_i + \hat{\beta}_2 ACRATE_i + \hat{\beta}_3 AVGPA_i + e_i$$

where $MBAPAY_i$ = avg. starting salary of MBA students from school i
$AVGMAT_i$ = avg. GMAT score at school i
$ACRATE_i$ = acceptance rate at school i
$AVGPA_i$ = avg. GPA of incoming MBA students at school i

A) Does AVGPA attain its expected sign? Explain.
B) Does a test of significance on AVGPA justify its presence in the regression?
C) Does AVGPA belong in the regression according to adjusted R^2? Explain.
D) Does AVGPA belong in the regression according to the Akaike Information Criterion? Explain.
E) Does AVGPA belong in the regression according to the Schwarz criterion? Explain.
F) Does this regression fit better than the regression from 1? Explain.
G) Perform Ramsey's Reset test. Show the 5-step procedure. Are variables missing from the model according to this test?

H) Do you think the estimators in $\text{MBAPAY}_i = \hat{\beta}_0 + \hat{\beta}_1 \text{AVGMAT}_i + \hat{\beta}_2 \text{ACRATE}_i + e_i$ are biased? Inefficient? Neither? Explain.

I) Do you think the estimators in $\text{MBAPAY}_i = \hat{\beta}_0 + \hat{\beta}_1 \text{AVGMAT}_i + \hat{\beta}_2 \text{ACRATE}_i + \hat{\beta}_3 \text{AVGPA}_i + e_i$ are biased? Inefficient? Neither? Explain.

Test Yourself on Chapters 4 and 5

Dependent Variable: WHY
Method: Least Squares
Sample: 1978 2006
Included observations: 29

Variable	Coefficient	Std. Error	t-Statistic	Prob.
C	1.997710	51.03278	0.039146	0.9691
EX1	15.81597	3.734046	4.235611	0.0003
EX2	3.046501	2.188336	1.392154	0.1761
EX3	−0.000145	0.005735	−0.025229	0.9801

R-squared	0.765250	Mean dependent var	152.0576
Adjusted R-squared	0.737080	S.D. dependent var	51.28692
S.E. of regression	26.29775	Akaike info criterion	9.504286
Sum squared resid	17289.29	Schwarz criterion	9.692879
Log likelihood	−133.8121	F-statistic	27.16539
Durbin-Watson stat	0.723982	Prob(F-statistic)	0.000000

1. Use the Eviews output above and below to help with A through G.

   A) Interpret the coefficient on EX1.
   B) Interpret the coefficient on the constant term (C).
   C) Is EX2 significant at the 17 percent critical level? Explain.
   D) Perform a positive sign test on the coefficient attached to EX2. Show the 5-step procedure.
   E) Perform a test to determine if the coefficient on EX3 is greater than −1.11. Show the 5-step procedure.
   F) Perform a test to determine if R-squared is greater than zero. Show the 5-step procedure.
   G) Based on the information in the table above (and ignoring Ramsey's Reset test which we will perform in a moment) do you think the regression above is under or overspecified? Explain.
   H) Perform Ramsey's Reset Test on the regression above using the Eviews printout below. Show the 5-step procedure.

Ramsey RESET Test:

F-statistic	15.32735	Probability	0.000059
Log likelihood ratio	24.56517	Probability	0.000005

Test Equation:
Dependent Variable: WHY
Method: Least Squares
Sample: 1978 2006

Included observations: 29

Variable	Coefficient	Std. Error	t-Statistic	Prob.
C	1190.553	228.1171	5.219043	0.0000
EX1	–314.2471	60.00884	–5.236679	0.0000
EX2	–62.55620	12.06659	–5.184249	0.0000
EX3	–0.013078	0.006110	–2.140328	0.0432
FITTED^2	0.119787	0.021647	5.533578	0.0000
FITTED^3	–0.000222	4.06E–05	–5.474315	0.0000
R-squared	0.899370	Mean dependent var		152.0576
Adjusted R-squared	0.877494	S.D. dependent var		51.28692
S.E. of regression	17.95084	Akaike info criterion		8.795142
Sum squared resid	7411.349	Schwarz criterion		9.078031
Log likelihood	–121.5296	F-statistic		41.11217
Durbin-Watson stat	1.018779	Prob(F-statistic)		0.000000

I) What do the terms "FITTED^2" and "FITTED^3" refer to in the Eviews printout above?

2. Define the following terms:

A) unbiased estimator
B) best estimator
C) correlation coefficient (r)
D) Prob-value

3. Mark each statement TRUE or FALSE.

A) If a regression is overspecified, then it would be surprising to see the t-ratios become more robust once the extraneous variables were removed.
B) If a regression is underspecified, then it would be surprising to see the estimators change markedly once the missing variables were included.
C) If a regression is overspecified, then it would be surprising to see the estimators change markedly once the extraneous variables were removed.
D) A 95% confidence interval for a coefficient will be smaller than a 90% confidence interval.
E) The Andersen-Jordan equation indicates that monetary policy is more effective than fiscal policy.
F) Deriving the estimators for $Y_i = \hat{\beta}_0 + \hat{\beta}_1 X1_i + \hat{\beta}_2 X2_i + e_i$ will yield 3 normal equations.
G) The Akaike Criterion is monotonically decreasing with respect to the number of explanatory variables.
H) The higher the critical level of the hypothesis test, the less chance there is that the test will result in a TYPE II error.
I) A coefficient that is significant at the 1 percent critical level may not be significant at the 2 percent critical level.
J) A test of significance is more likely to result in a TYPE I error in an overspecified model.

Chapter 6

Alternate Functional Forms

6.1 Regression through the Origin

By suppressing the intercept term, the regression line is forced through the origin:

$$Y_i = \hat{\beta}_1 X_i + e_i$$

In this situation we still want to minimize $\Sigma e_i^{\,2}$ or min $\Sigma (Y_i - \hat{\beta}_1 X_i)^2$. Setting the derivative of this expression with respect to $\hat{\beta}_1$ equal to zero and solving gives:

$$\hat{\beta}_1 = \frac{\Sigma X_i Y_i}{\Sigma X_i^{\,2}}$$
(The details of this derivation are left to the reader as an exercise.)

There should be strong theoretical reasons for excluding the constant term. Just as when any important explanatory variable is excluded, the regression results will be biased if the intercept is inappropriately suppressed. In addition, R^2 and adjusted R^2 are invalid in regressions through the origin.

As an example of regression through the origin, consider Okun's law (Okun 1962). In the early 1960s Okun posited a linear relationship between unemployment and economic growth. Specifically, Okun estimated that the gap between potential and real GDP growth would widen 2 to 3 percentage points for each percentage point increase in the unemployment rate.

To test Okun's law in the postwar United States economy we regressed the gap between potential and real GDP growth on the change in the unemployment rate.

GDPGAP$_t$ = -0.08 – 1.87 CHGUN$_t$ + e$_t$
  (-0.05) (10.31) ← t-ratios

SER = 1.11 $|$GDPGAP$|$ = 1.55 R^2 = 0.70   n = 47

where GDPGAP is the real GDP growth minus potential GDP growth
  CHGUN is the change in the unemployment rate

The coefficient on CHGUN implies that a 1 percent increase in the unemployment rate will widen the GDPGAP by 1.87 percent; not quite the 2 to 3 percent Okun stipulated, but that was a different economy back then.

The constant term is not statistically different from zero in this regression and theoretically it should be equal to zero: if the change in the unemployment rate from one year to the next is zero, then the change in the GDPGAP should be zero as well. Therefore, we might test Okun's law with a regression through the origin.

$$GDPGAP_t = -1.87 \, CHGUN_t + e_t$$
$$(10.39) \qquad \leftarrow \text{t-ratio}$$

$$SER = 1.10 \quad |GDPGAP| = 1.55 \quad n = 47$$

The coefficient on CHGUN hardly changes when the constant term is omitted—just what we would expect when an extraneous variable is excluded. R^2 and adjusted R^2 are not reported since they are invalid in this case, as are Akaike and Schwarz. The SER indicates an inadequate fit.

6.2 Units of Measurement and Estimates

Regression estimates will be affected by changes in the units of measurement, but the substance of the regression results will be unaffected. Consider the case where personal consumption expenditures (PCON) are regressed on disposable personal income (DPI). Here are the raw data and the regression results:

YEAR	PCON	DPI
1959	317.6000	350.5000
1960	331.7000	365.4000
1961	342.1000	381.8000
1962	.	.
1963	.	.
1964	.	.
2006	9268.900	9529.100

$$PCON_t = -107.08 + 0.95 \, DPI_t + e_t$$
$$(-4.70) \quad (179.80) \quad \leftarrow \text{t-ratios}$$

$$SER = 101.07 \quad PCON = 3034.89$$

$$r^2 = 0.99 \quad n = 48$$

The interpretation here is that a 1-unit increase in DPI causes a .95-unit increase in PCON. In other words, the marginal propensity to consume is estimated to be 0.95. Our data are measured in billions of dollars. Wouldn't it be strange if our results changed simply because we measured PCON and DPI in millions of dollars? Here are the regression results when the data are in millions of dollars:

YEAR	PCON	DPI
1959	317600.0	350500.0
1960	331700.0	365400.0
1961	342100.0	381800.0
1962	.	.
1963	.	.
1964	.	.
1965	9268900.	9529100.

$$PCON_t = -107084.70 + 0.95 \, DPI_t + e_t$$
$$(-4.70) \quad (179.80) \quad \leftarrow \text{t-ratios}$$

$$SER = 101070.90 \quad PCON = 3034888.12$$

$$r^2 = 0.99 \quad n = 48$$

The new results still peg the marginal propensity to consume at 0.95. However, the constant term, the SER, and the mean of the dependent variable have been multiplied by 1,000.

We can get the coefficient on DPI to change decimal places as well. Watch what happens if we measure PCON in millions and DPI in billions of dollars.

YEAR	PCON	DPI
1959	317600.0	350.5000
1960	331700.0	365.4000
1961	342100.0	381.8000
1962	.	.
1963	.	.
1964	.	.
1965	9268900.	9529.100

$$PCON_t = -107084.70 + 951.12 \, DPI_t + e_t$$
$$\quad\quad\quad (-4.70) \quad (179.80) \quad \leftarrow \text{t-ratios}$$

$$SER = 101070.90 \quad PCON = 3034888.12$$

$$r^2 = 0.99 \quad n = 48$$

Even now our estimate of the marginal propensity to consume is unaffected because the coefficient on DPI is interpreted to mean if DPI increases by 1 unit (or 1 billion dollars), then PCON is expected to increase 951.12 units (or 951.12 million dollars.) In other words, PCON is expected to increase 95 cents when DPI increases by 1 dollar.

There is an important lesson to take away from this exercise: The magnitude of a coefficient says nothing about its significance. We can make coefficients larger or smaller simply by changing the units by which we measure the variables attached to them. However, the t-ratio is invariant to changes in the units of measurement.

6.3 The Double-Log Model

Ordinary-least squares fits straight lines between observations on a scattergram. However, it is possible to fit curvilinear lines by rescaling the data. Alternate functional forms rely on this rescaling.

Consider the demand for milk in the United States from 1959 to 2001.

The Demand for Milk

QMILK – milk consumption (gallons per person per year)

PMILK – price of milk (dollars per gallon)

Astute readers may notice that unlike most demand curves, this one has the price on the horizontal axis. Placing the independent variable, PMILK, on the X-axis is mathematically correct. Therefore, the demand curves drawn in economics textbooks and classrooms are incorrect in the mathematical sense. It has been suggested that the tradition of placing the price on the Y-axis is in homage to Alfred Marshall, who thusly drew demand curves in his 1890 text *Principles of Economics*.

It appears as if a bowed line, convex to the origin, would fit the data better than a straight line. This can be accomplished by rescaling – in this case taking the natural logarithms of the data.

The Demand for Milk (Natural Logarithms)

LNQMILK – the natural log of QMILK
LNPMILK – the natural log of PMILK

We can fit a straight line to the logged observations. When the axes of this diagram are put back into the original (non-logged) scale, the straight line bends to give the curved line in the original diagram.

It is quite simple to apply this technique. We have data on PMILK and QMILK. Take the natural logarithms of those data (LNPMILK, LNQMILK):

obs	PMILK	QMILK	LNPMILK	LNQMILK
1959	0.690000	31.29000	−0.371064	3.443299
1960	0.710000	30.69000	−0.342490	3.423937
1961	0.710000	29.72000	−0.342490	3.391820
1962	0.710000	29.35000	−0.342490	3.379293
1963	0.710000	29.20000	−0.342490	3.374169
.	.	.	.	.
.	.	.	.	.
.	.	.	.	.
2001	2.880000	7.410000	1.057790	2.002830

Now regress LNQMILK on LNPMILK:

$$\text{LNQMILK}_t = 3.09 - 0.99 \, \text{LNPMILK}_t + e_t$$

This is akin to fitting the straight line to the scattergram of LNQMILK and LNPMILK. Let's interpret these results carefully:

$$\hat{\beta}_0 = 3.09 \rightarrow \text{If PMILK} = 1, \text{ then LNQMILK} = 3.09 \text{ (QMILK} = 21.98)$$

$$\hat{\beta}_1 = -0.99 \rightarrow \text{If PMILK} \uparrow 1\%, \text{ then QMILK} \downarrow 0.99\%$$

The interpretation of $\hat{\beta}_0$ begins, "If PMILK = 1" because if PMILK = 1, then LNPMILK = 0. If we plug LNPMILK = 0 into the regression, we are left with LNQMILK = 3.09. Taking the anti-log of 3.09 gives QMILK = 21.98.

Because we have taken the natural logarithms of both variables, a 1 unit increase in LNPMILK can be interpreted as a 1 percent increase in PMILK. Thus, a 1 percent increase in PMILK causes 0.99 percent reduction in QMILK.

These results suggest the elasticity of the demand for milk is nearly unitary. If the price goes up 1 percent, demand falls by 0.99 percent. The interpretation of $\hat{\beta}_1$ as an elasticity is why this particular alternate functional form is sometimes called the "constant elasticity model." It also goes by the names "log-log model" or "double-log model."

The results and interpretations of the double-log model are compared with the linear model in the boxes below:

Linear:
$$\text{QMILK}_t = 35.17 - 11.27 \, \text{PMILK}_t + e_t \quad R^2 = .94$$

If PMILK = 0, then QMILK = 35.17

If PMILK $\uparrow$ 1 unit, then QMILK $\downarrow$ 11.27 units

Double-Log:
$$\text{LNQMILK}_t = 3.09 - 0.99 \, \text{LNPMILK}_t + e_t \quad R^2 = .96$$

If PMILK = 1, then LNQMILK = 3.09 (QMILK = 21.98)

If PMILK $\uparrow$ 1%, then QMILK $\downarrow$ 0.99%

The R^2's for both models indicate good fits. However, it is incorrect to say that the double-log model has a better fit than the linear model. The R^2's are not comparable since the dependent variables are not the same for both models. The adjusted R^2's are not comparable either.

6.4 The Log-Lin Model

Another alternate functional form is the semi-log, or log-lin, model. In this model the natural log of the dependent variable is taken, but not that of the independent variable. This model gives percentage changes in the dependent variable for absolute changes in the independent variable. The box below shows the results of applying the log-lin model to the milk data.

> Log-Lin:
>
> $LNQMILK_t = 3.84 - 0.70\ PMILK_t + e_t \qquad R^2 = .98$
>
> If PMILK = 0, then LNQMILK = 3.84 (QMILK = 46.53)
>
> If PMILK ↑ 1 unit, then QMILK ↓ 70%

The log-lin model has an interesting interpretation in regressions with a trend variable. A trend variable increases one unit each time period. The table below shows real GDP in the United States and a trend variable.

obs	RGDP	TREND
1948	1643.200	1.000000
1949	1634.600	2.000000
1950	1777.300	3.000000
1951	1915.000	4.000000
.	.	.
.	.	.
.	.	.
2006	11415.30	59.00000

Now run the log-lin model: $LNRGDP_t = 7.44 + 0.03\ TREND_t + e_t$

Interpret the coefficient on TREND: If TREND ↑ 1 unit, then RGDP ↑ 3%. Each year we expect real GDP to increase 3 percent. In other words, the average annual growth rate of real GDP from 1948 through 2006 was 3 percent. The log-lin model gives average annual growth rates when the x-variable is a trend.

6.5 The Lin-Log Model

The lin-log model is appropriate when the dependent variable changes an absolute amount for a given percentage change in the independent variable. Here it is applied to the milk data.

Lin-Log:
$QMILK_t = 23.18 - 16.52\ LNPMILK_t + e_t$ $R^2 = .99$

If PMILK = 1, then QMILK = 23.18

If PMILK $\uparrow$ 1%, then QMILK $\downarrow$ 0.1652 units

Again, a curvilinear line will be fit to the scattergram. The fit of this regression can be compared to that of the linear regression since both have QMILK as the dependent variable. We can compare R^2's since both regressions have the same number of explanatory variables. The lin-log model fits better with an R^2 of .99 compared to .94 in the linear model.

6.6 The Reciprocal Model

The reciprocal model uses the reciprocal of the independent variable. Often this model is used to estimate asymptotic relationships because of the unique interpretation of the intercept term.

Reciprocal:
$QMILK_t = 1.34 + 20.37\ (1/PMILK)_t + e_t$ $R^2 = .97$

As PMILK $\rightarrow \infty$, QMILK $\rightarrow$ 1.34

If PMILK $\uparrow$, then QMILK $\downarrow$

As PMILK approaches infinity, the reciprocal term approaches zero. Therefore, QMILK approaches 1.34.

There is no intuitive interpretation of the magnitude of the coefficient attached to the reciprocal (20.37). Since it is positive, an increase in PMILK will cause a decrease in QMILK. But the magnitude of that effect depends on the initial level of PMILK.

6.7 The Polynomial Model

The polynomial form is used to draw parabolas between the observations on a scattergram. A parabolic relationship does not make sense for a demand curve because it implies that there could be two quantities demanded at a given price. Nevertheless, the polynomial form was applied to the milk data as an example of how the results can be interpreted.

Polynomial:
$$QMILK_t = 44.07 - 24.54\ PMILK_t + 4.07\ PMILK^2_t + e_t$$

If PMILK = 0, then QMILK = 44.07

Since $\hat{\beta}_2 > 0$, then as PMILK $\uparrow$, QMILK $\downarrow$ up to a point and then QMILK $\uparrow$ (the relationship is U-shaped)

The magnitude of the coefficients on PMILK and $PMILK^2$ have no straightforward interpretation. However, when the coefficient on $PMILK^2$ is positive it suggests a U-shaped relationship. If the coefficient on $PMILK^2$ is negative then the parabola is an inverted U.

6.8 Mixing and Matching Alternate Forms

It is perfectly legitimate to mix and match alternate functional forms as in the multiple regression below. Each coefficient is interpreted individually, holding the others constant.

Mix and Match:
$$QMILK_t = 22.59 - 15.82\ LNPMILK_t + 3.58\ (1/PCOOKIE)_t + e_t$$

(where PCOOKIE is the price of cookies)

If PMILK = 1 and as PCOOKIE $\rightarrow \infty$, QMILK $\rightarrow$ 22.59

If PMILK $\uparrow$ 1%, then QMILK $\downarrow$ .1582 units, holding PCOOKIE constant

If PCOOKIE $\uparrow$, then QMILK $\downarrow$, holding PMILK constant

Hopefully there are good theoretical reasons for choosing such a peculiar alternate functional form.

6.9 Finding the Correct Functional Form

It is critical that regressions are run in the appropriate functional form. If the relationship between X and Y is curvilinear and the regression is run in the linear form, the results will be biased. Therefore, it is just as important to specify the correct functional form as it is to include all the important independent variables.

Theory is the best guide for determining the appropriate functional form. If a particular relationship is likely to be asymptotic, then the reciprocal form should be used. It is often instructive to see which functional form other researchers used on a given topic.

Unfortunately, theory and previous work is not always specific about the functional form of a statistical relationship. The second best solution is to let the data suggest the appropriate functional form. For instance, one functional form may fit much better than the others. Not all of the various functional forms can be directly compared for fit. Still, one can often discern whether a linear specification is appropriate or not.

Just looking at a scattergram of the relationship can be useful. We saw that the milk data suggested an alternate functional form.

Finally, Ramsey's Reset test is also a test for appropriate functional form. This is important to understand. Even if a regression includes all the relevant explanatory variables, it may not pass Ramsey's Reset test if it is in the wrong functional form.

Terms

Alternate functional form – A regression where at least one of the variables is transformed into different units such as natural logarithms or raised to some exponential power.

Regression through the origin – A regression where the constant term is suppressed.

Trend variable – An explanatory variable that takes on integer values that increase by one each period.

Chapter 6   Problems

1. Derive the formula for $\hat{\beta}_1$ in $Y_i = \hat{\beta}_1 X_i + e_i$ that minimizes Σe_i^2.

2. Use the data in OKUNUK.XLS and statistical software to run the following regression:

$$\text{GDPGAP}_t = \hat{\beta}_0 + \hat{\beta}_1\ \text{CHGUN}_t + e_t$$

where GDPGAP = real GDP growth minus potential GDP growth in the UK
CHGUN = change in the unemployment rate in the UK

   A) According to a test of significance, does $\hat{\beta}_0$ belong in the regression?
   B) According to economic reasoning, does $\hat{\beta}_0$ belong in the regression?
   C) Re-run the regression excluding $\hat{\beta}_0$. Does $\hat{\beta}_1$ change much from the prior regression?
   D) Which regression of the two fits best? On what do you base your response?

3. In the regression below, what would be the new values of $\hat{\beta}_0$, $\hat{\beta}_1$, their t-ratios, SER, r^2, and the mean of WEIGHT if WEIGHT was measured in ounces instead of pounds?

$$\text{WEIGHT}_i = 51.12 + 1.85\ \text{HEIGHT}_i + e_i$$
$$\phantom{\text{WEIGHT}_i = 51.12 + }(4.72)\quad (9.85)\quad \leftarrow \text{t-ratios}$$

$$\text{SER} = 20.38 \quad \overline{\text{WEIGHT}} = 156.78$$

$$r^2 = 0.49 \quad n = 4800$$

4. In the regression below, what would be the new values of $\hat{\beta}_0, \hat{\beta}_1$, their t-ratios, SER, r^2, and the mean of HEIGHT if AGE was measured in months instead of years and height was measured in inches instead of feet?

$$\text{HEIGHT}_i = 1.68 + 0.35\ \text{AGE}_i + e_i$$
$$\phantom{\text{HEIGHT}_i = 1.68 }(7.723)\quad (2.11)\ \leftarrow \text{t-ratios}$$

$$\text{SER} = 12.45 \quad \overline{\text{HEIGHT}} = 5.54$$

$$r^2 = 0.38 \quad n = 120$$

5. Use the data in EGG.XLS and statistical software to do the following problems:

Run the following regression: $\quad \text{QEGG}_t = \hat{\beta}_0 + \hat{\beta}_1\ \text{PEGG}_t + e_t$

where QEGG is per capita egg consumption each year 1973–1997
PEGG is the average price of a dozen eggs in the USA

i) A) Interpret the value you obtained for $\hat{\beta}_0$.

B) Interpret the value you obtained for $\hat{\beta}_1$.

C) If the price of eggs goes up \$1 per dozen, what is the expected change in egg consumption according to this regression?

ii) Run the regression in the double-log form.
A) Interpret the value you obtained for $\hat{\beta}_0$.

B) Interpret the value you obtained for $\hat{\beta}_1$.

C) If the price of eggs goes up 1 percent, what is the expected percentage change in egg consumption according to this regression?

iii) Run the regression in the semi-log form (where the natural log of PEGG is taken).

    A) Interpret the value you obtained for $\hat{\beta}_0$.

    B) Interpret the value you obtained for $\hat{\beta}_1$.

    C) If the price of eggs goes up 1 percent, what is the expected change in egg consumption according to this regression?

iv) Run the regression in the semi-log form (where the natural log of QEGG is taken).

    A) Interpret the value you obtained for $\hat{\beta}_0$.

    B) Interpret the value you obtained for $\hat{\beta}_1$.

    C) If the price of eggs goes up $1 per dozen, what is the expected percentage change in egg consumption according to this regression?

v) Run the regression in the reciprocal form.

    A) Interpret the value you obtained for $\hat{\beta}_0$.

    B) Interpret the value you obtained for $\hat{\beta}_1$.

    C) If the price of eggs goes up $1 per dozen, will egg consumption increase or decrease according to this regression.

vi) Run the regression in the polynomial form.

    A) Interpret the value you obtained for $\hat{\beta}_0$.

    B) Interpret the values you obtained for $\hat{\beta}_1$ and $\hat{\beta}_2$.

vii) A) Do you think the data in this study require an alternate functional form or is the linear form satisfactory? Explain.

    B) Which of the 6 regressions fits the data best?

6. Use the data in MATISSE.XLS and statistical software to do the following problems:

Does the size of a master's painting have an effect on its price? To shed light on this issue, run the following regression:

$$PRICE_i = \hat{\beta}_0 + \hat{\beta}_1 \ SIZE_i + e_i$$

    where PRICE is the price of paintings by Matisse sold at auction in dollars
             SIZE is the size of the paintings in square inches

i) A) Interpret the value you obtained for $\hat{\beta}_0$.

    B) Interpret the value you obtained for $\hat{\beta}_1$.

    C) If one Matisse canvas is 60 square inches larger than another, will it cost more? Exactly how much more (or less)?

    D) According to this regression, what would a 1500-square-inch Matisse sell for at auction?

ii) Run the regression in the double-log form.

   A) Interpret the value you obtained for $\hat{\beta}_0$.

   B) Interpret the value you obtained for $\hat{\beta}_1$.

   C) If one Matisse canvas is 5% larger than another, will it cost more? Exactly how much more (or less) in percentage terms?

   D) According to this regression, what would a 1500-square-inch Matisse sell for at auction?

iii) Run the regression in the semi-log form (where the natural log of price is taken).

   A) Interpret the value you obtained for $\hat{\beta}_0$.

   B) Interpret the value you obtained for $\hat{\beta}_1$.

   C) If one Matisse canvas is 60 square inches larger than another, will it cost more? Exactly how much more (or less) in percentage terms?

   D) According to this regression, what would a 1500-square-inch Matisse sell for at auction?

iv) Run the regression in the semi-log form (where the natural log of size is taken).

   A) Interpret the value you obtained for $\hat{\beta}_0$.

   B) Interpret the value you obtained for $\hat{\beta}_1$.

   C) If one Matisse canvas is 5% larger than another, will it cost more? Exactly how much more (or less)?

   D) According to this regression, what would a 1500-square-inch Matisse sell for at auction?

v) Run the regression in the reciprocal form.

   A) Interpret the value you obtained for $\hat{\beta}_0$.

   B) Interpret the value you obtained for $\hat{\beta}_1$.

   C) If one Matisse canvas is 60 square inches larger than another, will it cost more? Exactly how much more (or less)?

   D) According to this regression, what would a 1500-square-inch Matisse sell for at auction?

vi) Run the regression in the polynomial form.

   A) Interpret the value you obtained for $\hat{\beta}_0$.

   B) Interpret the values you obtained for $\hat{\beta}_1$ and $\hat{\beta}_2$.

   C) If one Matisse canvas is 60 square inches larger than another, will it cost more? Exactly how much more (or less)?

   D) According to this regression, what would a 1500-square-inch Matisse sell for at auction?

vii) A) Do you think the data in this study require an alternate functional form or is the linear form satisfactory? Explain.

   B) Which of the 6 regressions fits the data best?

7. Use the data in SDATA.XLS and statistical software to do the following problem:

Which functional form do you think is appropriate for the regression below:

$$GPA_i = \hat{\beta}_0 + \hat{\beta}_1 ST_i + e_i$$

Explain your response.

8. Use the data in EKC.XLS and statistical software to test the environmental Kuznets's theory. This theory posits an inverted–U shaped relationship between pollution and economic development. (See Dasgupta et al. 2002.)

   A) Run the following polynomial regression and discuss its implications for the Kuznets's curve:

$$CO2CAP_i = \hat{\beta}_0 + \hat{\beta}_1 \, GDPCAP_i + \hat{\beta}_2 \, GDPCAP_i^2 + e_i$$

   where   CO2CAP is per capita carbon dioxide emissions in 48 nations
   GDPCAP is per capita GDP in these nations

   B) Run the following regression and discuss its implications for the Kuznets's curve:

$$SO2CAP_i = \hat{\beta}_0 + \hat{\beta}_1 \, GDPCAP_i + \hat{\beta}_2 \, GDPCAP_i^2 + e_i$$

   where SO2CAP is per capita sulphur dioxide emissions in 48 nations

   C) Run the following regression and discuss its implications for the Kuznets's curve:

$$PART = \hat{\beta}_0 + \hat{\beta}_1 \, GDPCAP_i + \hat{\beta}_2 \, GDPCAP_i^2 + e_i$$

   where PART is suspended particulates in the largest city of the nation

9. Interpret every structural parameter in each of the following regressions considering:

WAGES = pay per hour of work
LNWAGES = natural log of WAGES
EXP = years of experience
EXPSQ = EXP squared

A) LNWAGES = 2.1 + 1.3 EXP + e

B) WAGES = 2.1 + 1.3 EXP − 2.3 EXPSQ + e

C) WAGES = 2.5 − 0.1 (1/EXP) + e

10. In the spaces below draw the following regression results:

A) LNWAGES = 2.1 + 1.3 EXP + e

B) WAGES = 2.1 + 1.3 EXP − 2.3 EXPSQ + e

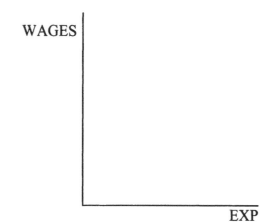

C) WAGES = 2.5 − 0.1 (1/EXP) + e

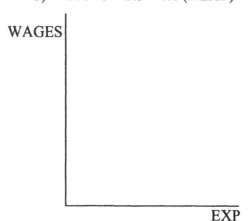

Chapter 7

Dichotomous Variables

7.1 Dichotomous Variables

Dichotomous variables take on values of zero or one only. Dichotomous variables are more commonly called "dummy" variables and sometimes are referred to as "limited" variables.

In the regression below, DRACE is a dummy variable.

$$EARNS_i = -0.78 + 0.76\ ED_i - 1.93\ DRACE_i + e_i$$

where EARNS = annual earnings (in 1963 in thousands of \$)
ED = years of education
DRACE = 1 if nonwhite; 0 otherwise

Here are the first few observations in the data set:

Obs	EARNS	ED	DRACE
1	1.920	2	0
2	12.403	9	0
3	5.926	17	1
4	7.000	9	0
5	6.900	12	0
6	6.500	13	0

The formulas for estimating the structural parameters and the residual statistics are unaffected by the presence of a dummy variable. However, the interpretations are somewhat different.

$\hat{\beta}_0 = -0.78 \rightarrow$ A white worker with 0 ED is expected to earn –0.78 units

$\hat{\beta}_1 = 0.76 \rightarrow$ If ED increases 1 unit, EARNS (nonwhites and whites) increases 0.76 units

$\hat{\beta}_2 = -1.93 \rightarrow$ A nonwhite earns 1.93 units less than a white with the same level of education

Graphing the interpretations indicates that the dummy variable allows for different intercepts for nonwhite and white workers. However, the slopes of the two regression lines are parallel.

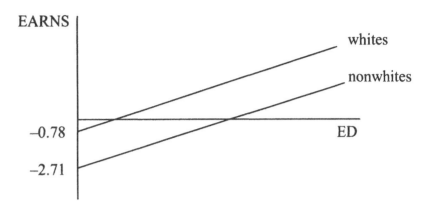

If the dummy variable was defined in the opposite manner (i.e. DRACE = 1 if white; 0 otherwise), then our regression results will be slightly altered. However, after interpretation, our diagram would remain unchanged. The new regression results would be:

$$EARNS_i = -2.71 + 0.76 \ ED_i + 1.93 \ DRACE_i + e_i$$

$\hat{\beta}_0 = -2.71 \rightarrow$ A nonwhite person with 0 ED is expected to earn -2.71 units

$\hat{\beta}_1 = 0.76 \rightarrow$ If ED increases 1 unit, EARNS (nonwhites and whites) increases 0.76 units

$\hat{\beta}_2 = 1.93 \rightarrow$ A white earns 1.93 units more than a nonwhite with the same level of education

Graphing the interpretations gives exactly the same diagram as previously.

7.2 Dummies for Seasonal Analysis

Dummy variables can be used to make more than two categories. In the example below, retail sales are divided into the four quarters of the year.

$$RSALES_t = 517462.20 + 63804.40 \ D2_t + 66323.00 \ D3_t + 115777.80 \ D4_t + e_t$$

where   RSALES is quarterly retail sales in the USA (millions of $)
D2 is 1 in the second quarter; 0 otherwise
D3 is 1 in the third quarter; 0 otherwise
D4 is 1 in the fourth quarter; 0 otherwise

$\hat{\beta}_0 \rightarrow$ in the 1st quarter RSALES average 51746.20

$\hat{\beta}_1 \rightarrow$ in the 2nd quarter RSALES are expected to be 63804.40 units higher than the 1st qtr

$\hat{\beta}_2 \rightarrow$ in the 3rd quarter RSALES are expected to be 66323.00 units higher than the 1st qtr

$\hat{\beta}_3 \rightarrow$ in the 4th quarter RSALES are expected to be 115777.80 units higher than the 1st qtr

The coefficients on the dummy variables tell us how much we can expect retail sales to differ from the first quarter due to seasonal factors. We can discern that retail sales are seasonally lowest in the first quarter, higher in the second quarter, still higher in the third, and highest in the fourth quarter.

Also notice that we need only three dummies to divide retail sales into four categories. That is because when D2 = D3 = D4 = 0, then by default we must be in the first quarter. Finally, we can obtain seasonally adjusted retail sales figures by adding the residuals from the regression above to the mean of retail sales. The graph below shows RSALES and the seasonally adjusted series.

Retail Sales and Seasonally Adjusted Retail Sales

7.3 Interactive Terms

Interactive terms interact with dummy variables to allow for different slopes for different categories. Going back to our earnings example, we have added an interactive term: DRACE*ED.

$$\text{EARNS}_i = -0.67 + 0.86\ \text{ED}_i - 1.82\ \text{DRACE}_i + 0.11\ \text{DRACE*ED}_i + e_i$$
$$\text{DRACE} = 1 \text{ if nonwhite; } 0 \text{ otherwise}$$
$$\text{DRACE*ED} = \text{DRACE} \times \text{ED}$$

$\hat{\beta}_0 = \quad -0.67 \rightarrow$ A white worker with 0 ED is expected to earn –0.67 units

$\hat{\beta}_1 = \quad 0.86 \rightarrow$ If ED $\uparrow$ 1 unit, EARNS for whites $\uparrow$ 0.86 units

$\hat{\beta}_2 = \quad -1.82 \rightarrow$ A nonwhite with zero ED earns 1.82 units less than a white with zero ED

$\hat{\beta}_3 = \quad 0.11 \rightarrow$ If ED $\uparrow$ 1 unit then EARNS for a nonwhite will increase 0.11 units over and above the 0.86 for a white

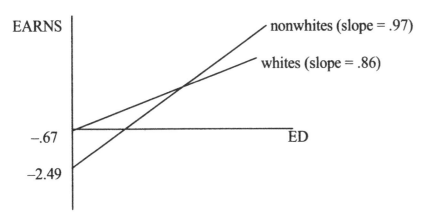

How would the regression results change if the dummy was flip-flopped? Again, the regression results would be altered, but so would the interpretations. The diagram above would be unchanged.

$$EARNS_i = -2.49 + 0.97\ ED_i + 1.82\ DRACE_i - 0.11\ DRACE*ED_i + e_i$$

DRACE = 1 if white; 0 otherwise
DRACE*ED = DRACE x ED

$\hat{\beta}_0 = -2.49 \rightarrow$ A nonwhite worker with 0 ED is expected to earn –2.49 units

$\hat{\beta}_1 = 0.97 \rightarrow$ If ED ↑ 1 unit, EARNS for a nonwhite ↑ 0.97 units

$\hat{\beta}_2 = 1.82 \rightarrow$ A white with zero ED earns 1.82 units more than a nonwhite with zero ED

$\hat{\beta}_3 = -0.11 \rightarrow$ If ED ↑ 1 unit then EARNS for a white will increase 0.11 units less than the 0.97 for a nonwhite

7.4 Linear Probability Models

Up to this point, we have considered using dummy variables only as independent variables. Dichotomous variables can be used as dependent variables as well. If ordinary least-squares is used to estimate a regression with a dummy dependent variable, then it is known as a linear probability model.

Let's consider a classic econometric study that uses a dichotomous dependent variable. Spector and Mazzeo (1980) investigated the factors affecting whether or not a student got a final letter grade of A in intermediate macroeconomics. Here are the results when ordinary least-squares is applied to their data:

$$AMACRO_i = -1.4980 + .4639\ GPA_i + .0111\ TUCE_i + .3786\ PSI_i + e_i$$
$$(2.86)(0.54)(2.72)$$

AMACRO = 1 if final grade in Macro Analysis is an A ; 0 otherwise
GPA = GPA of student at the beginning of Macro Analysis
TUCE = score on the TUCE exam prior to Macro Analysis (the TUCE is a 33-question multiple-choice exam that Tests Understanding of College Economics)
PSI = 1 if student received personalized instruction (tutoring); 0 otherwise

AMACRO is the dichotomous dependent variable. The regression also includes a dummy independent variable, PSI.

Interpretations:

If GPA, TUCE, and PSI = 0, then the probability of obtaining an A in Macro Analysis = −149.80%

If GPA increases one unit then the probability of obtaining an A in Macro Analysis increases 46.39%, holding TUCE constant, regardless of PSI.

If TUCE increases one unit then the probability of obtaining an A in Macro Analysis increases 1.11%, holding GPA constant, regardless of PSI.

A student who receives personalized instruction increases their odds of obtaining an A in Macro Analysis by 37.86%, holding GPA and TUCE constant.

These results are informative, but all linear probability models suffer from some drawbacks.

Problems with the linear probability model:

- The error terms are binomially—not normally—distributed, thereby invalidating hypothesis testing in small samples.
- R-squared is not a good measure of fit.
- Predicted probabilities can be out of bounds (i.e. >1 or < 0)

The fact that predicted probabilities can be out of bounds is especially disconcerting. Let's plug some numbers into our linear probability model. First, consider a student with a 3.5 GPA, a score of 28 on the TUCE exam, who received personalized instruction:

$$\hat{AMACRO}_i = -1.4980 + .4639 \, GPA_i + .0111 \, TUCE_i + .3786 \, PSI_i$$

$$.815 \quad = -1.4980 + .4639 \, (3.5) \ + .0111 \, (28) \quad + .3786 \, (1)$$

This student has an 81.5 percent chance of receiving an A in intermediate macroeconomics. However, a student with a GPA of 3.9, a 33 on the TUCE exam, who received personalized instruction has a 106 percent chance of obtaining an A:

$$\hat{AMACRO}_i = -1.4980 + .4639 \, GPA_i + .0111 \, TUCE_i + .3786 \, PSI_i$$

$$1.06 \quad = -1.4980 + .4639 \, (3.9) \ + .0111 \, (33) \quad + .3786 \, (1)$$

This is what is meant by a prediction that is out-of-bounds. Only the gods know for certain whether this student will receive an A in the course. And even they are only 100 percent sure.

Another out-of-bounds prediction occurs with this next student as well:

$$AM\hat{A}CRO_i = -1.4980 + .4639\ GPA_i + .0111\ TUCE_i + .3786\ PSI_i$$

$$-.26 \quad = -1.4980 + .4639\ (2.2) + .0111\ (20) + .3786\ (0)$$

According to the results above, a student with a GPA of 2.2, a TUCE score of 20, who did not receive personalized instruction will definitely not get an A. Indeed, it makes no sense to have a negative probability. The diagram below depicts what is happening.

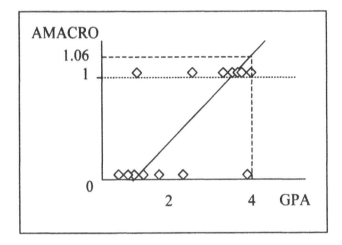

AMACRO can only be 1 or 0. Therefore, the observations on the scattergram will lie on these values. Here, AMACRO is plotted against GPA. High GPAs will be associated with AMACRO =1, while low GPA students are less likely to obtain an A. A linear probability model fits a straight line through the observations using the ordinary least-squares formulas. A student with a 3.9 GPA has 106 percent chance of obtaining an A when the ordinary least-squares line is used to make the prediction.

7.5 Logistic Models

Logistic models are based on the logistic equation. These models fit an S-shaped curve to scattergrams with dichotomous dependent variables. Logistic models give predictions that are less than one and greater than zero in all instances and thus avoid one of the drawbacks of linear probability models.

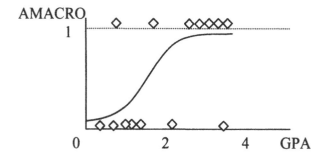

The logistic specification of Spector and Mazzeo's model for A's in macroanalysis is:

$$AMACRO_i = \frac{1}{1 + e^{-(\hat{\beta}_0 + \hat{\beta}_1 GPA_i + \hat{\beta}_2 TUCE_i + \hat{\beta}_3 PSI_i + e_i)}}$$

With a little algebra, this specification can be rewritten as:

$$\ln\left(\frac{AMACRO_i}{1 - AMACRO_i}\right) = \hat{\beta}_0 + \hat{\beta}_1 GPA_i + \hat{\beta}_2 TUCE_i + \hat{\beta}_3 PSI_i + e_i$$

There is an estimation problem with the logistic model. If $AMACRO_i = 0$ or 1, then $\ln\left(\frac{AMACRO_i}{1 - AMACRO_i}\right)$ is undefined. The maximum likelihood procedure overcomes this problem and is typically applied to the original logistic specification to obtain estimates of the structural parameters.

The maximum likelihood procedure is an algorithm that begins with initial values for the estimators and adjusts them based on the residuals (e_i's). The adjusted values of the estimators result in new e_i's and the algorithm decides how to adjust the estimates again given these new e_i's. This iterative process continues until sequential estimates of the estimators do not vary much.

Applying the maximum likelihood procedure to Spector and Mazzeo's data gives:

$$\ln\left(\frac{AMACRO_i}{1 - AMACRO_i}\right) = -13.0 + 2.8\ GPA_i + 0.1\ TUCE_i + 2.4\ PSI_i + e_i$$
$$(2.24) \qquad (0.72) \qquad (2.23) \qquad \text{Maddala } R^2 = .3821$$

Interpretations:

The estimators in logistic models do not have intuitive interpretations so we will only interpret two of them as examples.

If GPA, TUCE, and PSI = 0, then the natural log of the odds ratio = -13.0

If GPA increases 1 unit, then the natural log of the odds ratio increases 2.8 units, holding TUCE constant, regardless of PSI status.

Predicting with logistic models:

The predictions generated by the logistic model are between zero and one. Even the students with out-of-bounds predictions in the linear probability model are within bounds here.

It takes some effort to obtain these predictions. The students' GPA, TUCE, and PSI are plugged into:

$$\ln(\frac{AMACRO_i}{1 - AMACRO_i}) = -13.0 + 2.8 \text{ GPA}_i + 0.1 \text{ TUCE}_i + 2.4 \text{ PSI}_i + e_i$$

Then we can calculate $\ln(\frac{AMACRO_i}{1 - AMACRO_i})$ for each of our three students:

1.909	$= -13.0 + 2.8\,(3.5) + 0.1\,(28) + 2.4\,(1)$
3.620	$= -13.0 + 2.8\,(3.9) + 0.1\,(33) + 2.4\,(1)$
-4.904	$= -13.0 + 2.8\,(2.2) + 0.1\,(20) + 2.4\,(0)$

Finally, these can be converted into probabilities:

$$\ln(\frac{AMACRO_i}{1 - AMACRO_i}) = 1.909 \; ; \; \frac{AMACRO_i}{1 - AMACRO_i} = 6.746 \; ; \text{AMACRO} = .87$$

$$\ln(\frac{AMACRO_i}{1 - AMACRO_i}) = 3.620 \; ; \; \frac{AMACRO_i}{1 - AMACRO_i} = 37.34 \; ; \text{AMACRO} = .97$$

$$\ln(\frac{AMACRO_i}{1 - AMACRO_i}) = -4.904 \; ; \; \frac{AMACRO_i}{1 - AMACRO_i} = 0.007 \; ; \text{AMACRO} = .007$$

The student with an 81.5 percent chance of obtaining an A according to the linear probability model has an 87 percent chance according to the logistic model. The student with a 106 percent chance of obtaining an A according to the linear probability model has a 97 percent chance here. Finally, the student who had a negative 26 percent chance of obtaining an A has a 0.7 percent chance according to the logistic model.

Terms

Dummy variable (dichotomous variable) – Independent or dependent variables that take on the values of zero or one only.

Interactive term – A dummy variable combined with another independent variable.

Linear probability model – A regression with a dichotomous dependent variable that is estimated with ordinary least-squares.

Logistic model – An alternate function form that fits an S-shape to regressions with dichotomous dependent variables.

Maximum likelihood procedure – A technique for estimating the structural parameters of a non-linear econometric model, such as a logistic model.

Chapter 7   Problems

1. A) Interpret every structural parameter in the following regression:

$$PROFSAL_i = 17.969 + 1.3707\ EXP_i + 3.3336\ DUM_i + e_i$$

        where PROFSAL is the professor's salary
                   EXP is the professor's experience in years
                   DUM = 1 if the professor is male; 0 otherwise

   B) Draw a diagram reflecting the regression results with PROFSAL on the vertical axis and EXP on the horizontal axis.
   C) A male professor with 10 years experience is expected to make how much in salary?
   D) A female professor with 10 years experience is expected to make how much in salary?

   E) What would be the new values of the structural parameters if the dummy was flip-flopped?

   F) Using the flip-flopped results, how much would a male professor with 10 years experience make in salary?

2. Use the data in SDATA.XLS and statistical software to run the following regression:

$$GPA_i = \hat{\beta}_0 + \hat{\beta}_1\ ST_i + \hat{\beta}_2\ SAT_i + \hat{\beta}_3\ MALE_i + e_i$$

      where GPA = grade point average
             ST = study time per day
             SAT = SAT score
             MALE = 1 if the student is male; 0 otherwise

A) Interpret the coefficient on SAT.
B) Interpret the coefficient on the dummy variable.
C) Would a male or a female student with the same SAT scores and study time be expected to have a higher GPA? By exactly how much?
D) What would be the values of the four structural coefficients if the dummy variable had been defined as 1 = female ; 0 otherwise?

3. A) Interpret every structural parameter in the following regression:

$$PROFSAL_i = 16.1718 + 1.2016\ EXP_i + 3.2245\ DUM_i - 1.0001\ DUM*EXP_i + e_i$$

where PROFSAL is the professor's salary
EXP is the professor's experience in years
DUM = 1 if the professor is male; 0 otherwise

B) Draw a diagram reflecting the regression results with PROFSAL on the vertical axis and EXP on the horizontal axis.
C) What would be the new values of the structural parameters if the dummy was flip-flopped?

4. Use the data in SDATA.XLS and statistical software to run the following regression:

$$GPA_i = \hat{\beta}_0 + \hat{\beta}_1\ ST_i + \hat{\beta}_2\ MALE_i + \hat{\beta}_3\ INTER_i + e_i$$

where INTER is MALE x ST

A) Interpret all four structural parameters.
B) Who benefits more from an extra unit of ST, men or women? Exactly how much more.
C) What would be the new values for the structural parameters if the dummy for gender was defined: 1 = female ; 0 otherwise?
D) Graph your regression results, labeling all intercepts and slopes.

5. A) Interpret every structural parameter in the following regression:

$$GPA_i = 0.37 + 0.81\ HSGPA_i + 0.00001\ SAT_i - 0.38\ GREEK_i + e_i$$

where GPA is grade point average in college
HSGPS is high school GPA
SAT is SAT score
GREEK = 1 if student is a member of a sorority or fraternity;
0 otherwise

B) Draw a diagram reflecting the regression results with GPA on the vertical axis and SAT on the horizontal axis.

6. A) Interpret every structural parameter in the following regression:

$$PERSAV_t = 41.8081 + 0.0321\ INC_t - 19.7655\ DUM_t - 0.0021\ DUM*INC_t + e_t$$

where PERSAV is personal savings in the USA
INC is disposable personal income in the USA
DUM = 1 if 1982 or later;
0 otherwise

   B) Draw a diagram reflecting the regression results with PERSAV on the vertical axis and INC on the horizontal axis.

   C) What would be the new values of the structural parameters if the dummy was flip-flopped?

7. Use the data in WAGES.XLS and statistical software to run a regression where wages are explained by a constant term, education, experience, and a dummy variable for gender.

NAME	VARIABLE
WAGES	wages
LNWAGES	the natural logarithm of wages
ED	education in years
NONWH	1 if nonwhite ; 0 otherwise
FEM	1 if female ; 0 otherwise
MARRIED	1 if married ; 0 otherwise
EXPER	experience in years
EXPSQ	experience squared
UNION	1 if union member; 0 otherwise
PRO	1 if employed in a profession ; 0 otherwise

   A) Interpret the coefficient on education.
   B) Interpret the coefficient on the dummy variable.

8. Use the data in WAGES.XLS and statistical software to run a regression where wages are explained by a constant term, education, a dummy variable for gender, and an interactive term.

   A) Interpret all four structural parameters.
   B) Draw the regression results labeling the values of all intercepts and slopes.
   C) What would be the values of the structural parameters if the gender dummy was defined to be 1 if male; 0 otherwise?

9. Use the data in WAGES.XLS and statistical software to run a regression where the natural logarithm of wages is explained by a constant term, education, experience, and dummy variables for marital status, gender, race, union membership, and professional status.

   A) Interpret the coefficient on education.

B) Interpret the coefficient on marital status.

C) Interpret the coefficient on union membership.

D) Does this regression provide evidence of racial and gender discrimination? Explain.

10. Use the data in WAGES.XLS and statistical software to run a regression where MARRIED is explained by a constant term, WAGES, ED, and PRO.

A) Interpret all four structural parameters.

B) What is the probability that a college grad (ED = 16), in a profession with WAGES = 9.0 is married?

11. Use the data in EXTRAMARITAL.XLS and statistical software to estimate a linear probability model where EXTRA is explained by a constant term, AGE, HPPYM, RELIG, and YRSMAR.

EXTRA = 1 if person participated in an extramarital affair in the past year; 0 otherwise
AGE = the age of the person
HPPYM = person's perception of their marital happiness (1 = very unhappy; 5 = very happy)
RELIG = person's perception of their religiousness (1 = very unreligious; 5 = very religious)
YRSMAR = years married

A) Interpret all 5 structural parameters.

B) What is the probability that a 52-year-old person married for 27 years had an extramarital affair last year? Assume the person's RELIG = 2 and HAPPYM = 3.

12. Use the data in EXTRAMARITAL.XLS and statistical software to estimate a logistic model where EXTRA is explained by a constant term, AGE, HPPYM, RELIG, and YRSMAR. What is the probability that a 52-year-old person married for 27 years had an extramarital affair last year? Assume the person's RELIG = 2 and HAPPYM = 3.

Test Yourself on Chapters 6 and 7

1. Interpret every structural parameter in each of the following regressions considering:

$$WAGES = \text{pay per hour of work}$$
$$EXP = \text{years of experience}$$
$$EXPSQ = EXP \text{ squared}$$
$$ED = \text{years of education}$$
$$DGEN = 1 \text{ if male; 0 otherwise}$$
$$INTACT = DGEN \times EXP$$
$$LN \text{—} = \text{the natural log of a variable}$$

A) $LNWAGES_i = 2.1 + 1.3\ EXP_i + e_i$ Adjusted $R^2 = .77$

B) $LNWAGES_i = 2.1 + 1.3\ LNEXP_i + 2.3\ LNED_i + e_i$ Adjusted $R^2 = .79$

C) $WAGES_i = 2.1 + 1.3\ EXP_i + 3.5\ DGEN_i + 4.2\ INTACT_i + e_i$ Adjusted $R^2 = .80$

2. Which regression of the three above fits best? On what do you base your response?

3. What would be the values for the structural parameters for the regression above, 1 C), if DGEN was defined as 0 if male; 1 otherwise?

4. Draw diagrams that reflect the following regressions. Put WAGES on the Y axis and EXP on the X axis in each case.

A) $WAGES = 2.5 - .01\ (1/EXP) + U$
(Also, show where 2.5 is on the Y axis.)

B) $WAGES = 2.5 + 1.1\ EXP + 3.5\ DGEN - 3.0\ INTACT + U$
(Label all intercepts and slopes with their values.)

C) $WAGES = 2.5 + 1.1\ EXP - 0.22\ EXPSQ + U$

5. Given:

Dependent Variable: BINGE
Method: Least Squares
Sample(adjusted): 1 695
Included observations: 695 after adjusting endpoints

Variable	Coefficient	Std. Error	t-Statistic	Prob.
C	0.818558	0.125126	6.541884	0.0000
GPA	−0.125652	0.033407	−3.761217	0.0002
MALE	0.135596	0.036207	3.745041	0.0002

R-squared	0.056816	Mean dependent var	0.628777
Adjusted R-squared	0.052721	S.D. dependent var	0.483480
S.E. of regression	0.470563	Akaike info criterion	1.335963
Sum squared resid	153.0075	Schwarz criterion	1.362115
Log likelihood	−460.2471	F-statistic	13.87497
Durbin-Watson stat	2.015544	Prob(F-statistic)	0.000000

where   BINGE = 1 if student is a binge drinker; 0 otherwise
        GPA = grade point average
        MALE = 1 if male, 0 otherwise

A) Interpret the constant term.
B) Interpret the coefficient on GPA.

6. Given the following logistic regression results:

Dependent Variable: BINGE
Method: ML - Binary Logit (Quadratic hill climbing)

Sample(adjusted): 1 695
Included observations: 695 after adjusting endpoints
Convergence achieved after 4 iterations
Covariance matrix computed using second derivatives

Variable	Coefficient	Std. Error	z-Statistic	Prob.
C	2.174010	0.565780	3.842498	0.0001
GPA	-0.552753	0.159758	-3.459934	0.0005
MALE	0.581107	0.163816	3.547312	0.0004

What is the probability that a male with a GPA = 3.2 is a binge drinker? Show your calculations.

7. Label each statement below TRUE or FALSE.

A) In a regression through the origin, $\hat{\beta}_1 = \dfrac{\Sigma X_i Y_i}{\Sigma X_i^2}$.

B) Altering the units that the variables in a regression are measured in may alter the values of the structural parameters, but never their t-ratios.

C) If two models have the exact same dependent variable, then the one with the better fit is the better model.

D) R-squared is not a good measure of fit for a linear probability model.

E) The magnitude of a coefficient by itself says nothing about its significance.

F) A logistic model can yield a predicted value for the dependent variable that is equal to one, but never greater than one.

G) A linear probability model can yield a predicted value for the dependent variable that is equal to one, but never greater than one.

H) R-squared is invalid in regressions including dummy independent variables.

I) Regressions in the wrong functional form are biased.

J) Ramsey's Reset test can help to determine if a regression is in the correct functional form.

Chapter 8

Properties of Ordinary Least-Squares Estimators

The Ordinary Least-Squares Estimators are BLUE

Linear

Unbiased

Best

The Classical Linear Regression Model

Terms

Chapter 8 Problems

8.1 The Ordinary Least-Squares Estimators are BLUE

Although several choices are available when faced with calculating the structural parameters of $Y_i = \hat{\beta}_0 + \hat{\beta}_1 X_i + e_i$, the most popular technique is ordinary least-squares. That is because when we calculate $\hat{\beta}_0$ and $\hat{\beta}_1$ so that Σe_i^2 is minimized, our estimates have some very desirable statistical qualities. These qualities are captured in the acronym BLUE – best, linear, unbiased estimators.

8.2 Linear

The ordinary least-squares estimators are linear under certain conditions. Linear in this case means that the formulas for $\hat{\beta}_0$ and $\hat{\beta}_1$ are linear. That is, they do not contain any non-linearities such as exponents, reciprocals, or logarithms. This is certainly true of our formula for $\hat{\beta}_0 = \overline{Y} - \hat{\beta}_1 \overline{X}$. However, the formula for $\hat{\beta}_1 = \dfrac{\Sigma(X_i - \overline{X})Y_i}{\Sigma(X_i - \overline{X})^2}$ has a quotient and an exponent. We can get rid of these non-linearities by writing the formula as $\hat{\beta}_1 = \Sigma w_i Y_i$, where $w_i = \dfrac{\Sigma(X_i - \overline{X})}{\Sigma(X_i - \overline{X})^2}$. You may rightly claim that this does not get rid of the non-linearities. It only masks them in the term w_i.

However, we may consider the w_i's to be constants if the X_i's, which form the w_i's, are predetermined. This is rarely the case. Consider the following regression:

$GPA_i = \hat{\beta}_0 + \hat{\beta}_1 ST_i + e_i$ where GPA_i is grade point average of the ith student

                                              ST_i is average daily study time of the ith student

ST is our X-variable. It is predetermined if prior to collecting any data from students, we decided that ST should equal 0.5 hours, 1.0 hour, 1.5 hours, 2.0 hours, 2.5 hours, and 3.0 hours. Then we randomly selected a group of students who studied 0.5 hours and asked them their GPAs. Next we randomly select a group of students that studied 1.0 hour and asked them their GPAs. We continue in this manner through ST = 3.0 hours.

Typically data are not collected this way. Instead, we randomly select a student and ask them their ST and GPA. If a student reports ST = 0.75, we do not exclude that student from our study. In other words, our data on ST is stochastic, not predetermined. In this situation, our formula for $\hat{\beta}_1$ will not be linear.

A non-linear $\hat{\beta}_1$ is not an immediate problem and in no way makes $\hat{\beta}_1$ less desirable. However, some upcoming proofs will be more conveniently accomplished with a linear $\hat{\beta}_1$. In addition, it can be shown that $\hat{\beta}_1$ is linear even if the X_i's are not predetermined when the X_i's are not correlated with the error terms (u_i's) from the regression.

Concisely stated, $\hat{\beta}_0$ and $\hat{\beta}_1$ are linear if the X_i's are predetermined or if the X_i's are not correlated with the error terms from the regression. Linearity is not a highly desirable statistical attribute, but it will make some upcoming proofs easier.

8.3 Unbiased

Unbiased results are desirable in any scientific study. This is true of regression analysis as well. However, the term "unbiased" has a particular meaning in regard to statistical estimators. An estimator is unbiased if its expected value is equal to the true value of the parameter. More succinctly, $\hat{\beta}_1$ is unbiased if $E[\hat{\beta}_1] = \beta_1$.

It is highly unlikely that any particular sample regression will exactly yield the true values of β_1. However, if our estimate of β_1 is unbiased and we run the regression 10,000 times (using fresh data each time) and average together all 10,000 estimates of $\hat{\beta}_1$, the average will equal the true β_1.

How can we know this? We will do the proof in a moment. But the proof that the ordinary least-squares estimators are unbiased has been verified with Monte Carlo studies. A Monte Carlo study draws repeated samples from a known population and then analyzes the characteristics of the sample regressions.

In a sense we can play God by getting 5,000 observations on X and Y and assume that this is the entire population of observations. The structural parameters of a regression line through these 5,000 observations are the true β_0 and β_1. Now we can take a random sample of 40 observations from the 5,000 and run a sample regression. Indeed, we could program a computer to run 10,000 of these sample regressions drawing a fresh sample of 40 observations each time.

For an unbiased estimator, the average $\hat{\beta}_0$ and $\hat{\beta}_1$ from the 10,000 regressions with 40 observations each will be equal to the true β_0 and β_1 from the population regression with 5,000 observations.

With this intuition in hand, we can now prove that $\hat{\beta}_1$ is an unbiased estimate of β_1:

Assume $\hat{\beta}_1$ is a linear estimator of β_1.

$$\hat{\beta}_1 = \frac{\Sigma(X_i - \overline{X})Y_i}{\Sigma(X_i - \overline{X})^2} = \Sigma w_i Y_i ; \quad \text{where } w_i = \frac{(X_i - \overline{X})}{\Sigma(X_i - \overline{X})^2}$$

$$\hat{\beta}_1 = \Sigma w_i Y_i = \Sigma w_i (\beta_0 + \beta_1 X_i + u_i) = \beta_0 \Sigma w_i + \beta_1 \Sigma w_i X_i + \Sigma w_i u_i$$

$$\hat{\beta}_1 = \beta_1 + \Sigma w_i u_i \text{ since } \Sigma w_i = 0 \text{ and } \Sigma w_i X_i = 1$$

$$\text{Then } E[\hat{\beta}_1] = E[\beta_1 + \Sigma w_i u_i] = \beta_1 \text{ only if } E[\Sigma w_i u_i] = 0$$

It is fairly easy to show that $\Sigma w_i = 0$ and $\Sigma w_i X_i = 1$. These proofs are left to the reader as an exercise. For $\hat{\beta}_1$ to be unbiased we need $E[\Sigma w_i u_i] = 0$. This will hold if $E[u_i | X_i] = 0$. Thus we must assume that the expected value of the error terms is zero for each value of X_i in order to prove that $\hat{\beta}_1$ is an unbiased estimator of β_1.

It is straight forward to show that $\hat{\beta}_0 (= \overline{Y} - \hat{\beta}_1 \overline{X})$ is an unbiased estimator of β_0. Since $\overline{Y}$, $\overline{X}$, and $\hat{\beta}_1$ are unbiased estimators of the true $\overline{Y}$, $\overline{X}$, and β_1, then $\hat{\beta}_0$ will be an unbiased estimator of β_0. This is because $\hat{\beta}_0$ is a linear combination of these three unbiased estimators.

We are now in position to see that a regression in the incorrect functional form will yield biased estimates of the structural parameters. In such a regression, $E[u_i | X_i] \neq 0$, which is a direct violation of the assumption needed to prove unbiased parameter estimates. To see this, consider the example of the demand for milk from Chapter 6:

Here we have applied a straight line when an alternate functional form is appropriate. Notice $E[u_i | X_i] \neq 0$. When the value of X (PMILK) is low, u_i is likely to be positive, not 0. Similarly, when the value of X (PMILK) > 2.5, u_i is likely to be positive. When 1.0 < PMILK < 2.5, u_i is likely to be negative. Thus, $E[u_i]$ depends on X_i and is not always equal to zero.

If we are in the correct functional form but exclude an important explanatory variable from a regression, the structural parameters will be biased. Again, this is because $E[u_i | X_i] \neq 0$. Consider this example where you have left X_2, an important explanatory variable, out of a regression.

$$\text{TRUTH: } Y_i = \beta_0 + \beta_1 X_{1i} + \beta_2 X_{2i} + u_i$$
$$\text{YOU: } \quad Y_i = \hat{\beta}_0 + \hat{\beta}_1 X_{1i} + e_i$$

In this case, $e_i = \beta_2 X_{2i} + u_i$. Your error term, e_i, is composed of the u_i's plus the variable you omitted, X_2, times its coefficient, $\hat{\beta}_2$. It can be shown that

$$E[\hat{\beta}_1] = E[\beta_1 + \Sigma w_i u_i] = \beta_1 + \beta_2 (\alpha_1) \; ; \; \text{where } \alpha_1 \text{ is from } X_{2i} = \alpha_0 + \alpha_1 X_{1i} + u_I$$

Thus, we may conclude that the bias to $\hat{\beta}_0$ and $\hat{\beta}_1$ from omitting X_2 from the regression will be larger the more X_1 and X_2 are correlated. On the other hand, the structural parameters of the underfit regression will not be biased at all if $\alpha_1 = 0$; that is if X_1 and X_2 are completely uncorrelated. Nevertheless, all measures of goodness-of-fit are biased regardless of the value of α_1 since the e_i's are biased estimates of the u_i's. And the SE($\hat{\beta}_0$) and SE($\hat{\beta}_1$) are biased regardless of the zero correlation. Therefore, t-ratios are biased and hypothesis testing is invalid.

8.4 Best

We will now show that the ordinary least-squares estimators are best. It sounds as if our estimates are unbeatable, but the term "best" has a very particular meaning in this context. An estimator is said to be best if it varies the least out of all possible estimators in repeated sampling.

Consider once again our Monte Carlo experiment in which we have 5,000 observations on Y and X that are assumed to be the entire population of observations. If we run 10,000 regressions of Y on X with randomly drawn samples of 40 from this population, then we will have 10,000 separate estimates of β_0 and β_1. If the 10,000 estimates of β_1 average to the true β_1, then the ordinary least-squares estimator is unbiased. If the 10,000 estimates of β_1 have a smaller standard error than any other linear and unbiased estimator, then the ordinary least-squares estimator is best.

More concisely, the best estimator has minimum variance in its class. The best estimator is often referred to as an efficient estimator: it varies the least in repeated sampling. Monte Carlo experiments can be used to show one estimator is more efficient than another. But we can prove that the ordinary least-squares estimators are best. This is the proof of the famous Gauss-Markov theorem: The ordinary least-squares estimators are best in the class of all linear, unbiased estimators. Here is the proof that $\hat{\beta}_1$ is best:

Assume $\hat{\beta}_1$ is a linear and unbiased estimator of β_1.

$$\hat{\beta}_1 = \frac{\Sigma(X_i - \bar{X})Y_i}{\Sigma(X_i - \bar{X})^2} = \Sigma w_i Y_i ; \quad \text{where } w_i = \frac{(X_i - \bar{X})}{\Sigma(X_i - \bar{X})^2}$$

$$VAR(\hat{\beta}_1) = E\left[(\hat{\beta}_1 - \beta_1)^2\right] = E\left[(\beta_1 + \Sigma w_i u_i - \beta_1)^2\right] = \sigma^2 \Sigma w_i^2$$

Now consider another arbitrary estimator:

$$\tilde{\beta}_1 = \Sigma c_i Y_i; \text{ where } c_i = w_i + d_i$$

$$\tilde{\beta}_1 = \Sigma c_i (B_0 + B_1 X_i + u_i) = B_0 \Sigma c_i + B_1 \Sigma c_i X_i + \Sigma c_i u_i$$

$\tilde{\beta}_1$ is unbiased if and only if $\Sigma c_i = 0$ and $\Sigma c_i X_i = 1$, the c_i are fixed and $\Sigma u_i = 0$.

We can deduce that $\Sigma d_i = 0$ since $\Sigma c_i = \Sigma w_i + \Sigma d_i$ and $\Sigma c_i = 0$ and $\Sigma w_i = 0$.

Also, $\Sigma d_i X_i = 0$ since $\Sigma c_i X_i = \Sigma w_i X_i + \Sigma d_i X_i$ and $\Sigma c_i X_i = 1$ and $\Sigma w_i X_i = 1$.

$$VAR(\tilde{\beta}_1) = E\left[(\tilde{\beta}_1 - \beta_1)^2\right] = E\left[(\beta_1 + \Sigma c_i u_i - \beta_1)^2\right] = \sigma^2 \Sigma c_i^2$$

$\Sigma c_i^2 = \Sigma w_i^2 + \Sigma d_i^2 + 2\Sigma w_i d_i = \Sigma w_i^2 + \Sigma d_i^2$ since $\Sigma w_i d_i = 0$ (using $\Sigma d_i = 0$ and $\Sigma d_i X_i = 0$)

So that:

$$VAR(\tilde{\beta}_1) = \sigma^2 (\Sigma w_i^2 + \Sigma d_i^2) = \sigma^2 \Sigma w_i^2 + \sigma^2 \Sigma d_i^2 =$$

$$VAR(\hat{\beta}_1) + \sigma^2 \Sigma d_i^2$$

If $\Sigma d_i^2 \neq 0$, then $VAR(\tilde{\beta}_1) > VAR(\hat{\beta}_1)$; if $\Sigma d_i^2 = 0$, then $VAR(\tilde{\beta}_1) = VAR(\hat{\beta}_1)$
Q.E.D.

The most difficult step of this proof is in the third line:

$$VAR(\hat{\beta}_1) = E\left[(\hat{\beta}_1 - \beta_1)^2\right] = E\left[(\beta_1 + \Sigma w_i u_i - \beta_1)^2\right] = \sigma^2 \Sigma w_i^2. \text{ It is not easy to see that}$$

$E\left[(\beta_1 + \Sigma w_i u_i - \beta_1)^2\right] = \sigma^2 \Sigma w_i^2$. The positive β_1 cancels with the negative β_1 and we are left with:

$E[(\Sigma w_i u_i)^2] = \sigma^2 \Sigma w_i^2$ Expanding the left side:

$$E[(\Sigma w_i u_i)^2] = E[(w_1 u_1 + w_2 u_2 + \ldots + w_n u_n)(w_1 u_1 + w_2 u_2 + \ldots + w_n u_n)] =$$

$$E[w_1^2 u_1^2 + w_2^2 u_2^2 + \ldots + w_n^2 u_n^2 + 2w_1 u_1 w_2 u_2 + 2w_1 u_1 w_3 u_3 + \ldots + 2w_2 u_2 w_3 u_3 + 2w_2 u_2 w_4 u_4 + \ldots$$
$$+ 2w_{n-1} u_{n-1} w_n u_n]$$

However, if we assume that $E[u_i u_j] = 0$ for all $i \neq j$, then this last expression becomes:

$$E[w_1^2 u_1^2 + w_2^2 u_2^2 + \ldots + w_n^2 u_n^2]$$

Finally, assume $E[u_i^2] = E[u_j^2] = \sigma^2$ we have:

$$E[w_1^2 u_1^2 + w_2^2 u_2^2 + ... + w_n^2 u_n^2] = \sigma^2 E[w_1^2 + w_2^2 + ... + w_n^2] = \sigma^2 \Sigma w_i^2$$

Thus we are required to make two more assumptions in order to prove that $\hat{\beta}_1$ is best: 1) $E[u_i u_j] = 0$ for all $i \neq j$, which means the error terms are not related each other. Autocorrelation, or serial correlation, is when the error terms are related to one another. Therefore, we are assuming that the error terms are not serially correlated. 2) $E[u_i^2] = E[u_j^2] = \sigma^2$, which means that all the error terms have the same variance. When the error terms do not all have the same variance it is called heteroskedasticity. So we are assuming that the error terms are homoskedastic.

8.5 The Classical Linear Regression Model

Ordinary least-squares fits a straight line between observations on X and Y such that Σe_i^2 is minimized. We have just shown that this line will be best, linear, and unbiased if four assumptions are met.

The Assumptions of the Classical Linear Regression Model

1. The independent variable(s) is (are) predetermined or at least not correlated with the error term: $E[u_i X_i] = 0$
2. The expected value of the error terms is zero: $E[u_i \mid X_i] = 0$
3. The error terms are not related to one another: $E[u_i u_j] = 0$ for all $i \neq j$
4. The error terms all have the same variance: $E[u_i^2] = E[u_j^2] = \sigma^2$ for all $i \neq j$

Underspecified econometric models violate assumption 2. If assumption 2 does not hold, then we cannot get through the proof of unbiasedness. Indeed, underspecified regressions yield biased parameter estimates.

Similarly, regressions run using the incorrect functional form will yield biased results. This is because such regressions violate assumption 2.

If assumption 3 does not hold, then the error terms are said to be autocorrelated. We saw that assumption 3 was necessary to complete the Gauss-Markov proof. Hence, regressions that violate assumption 3 will yield inefficient (not best) estimators.

If assumption 4 is violated, then the error terms are said to be heteroskedastic. We saw that assumption 4 was necessary to complete the Gauss-Markov proof. Therefore, regressions that violate assumption 3 will yield inefficient (not best) estimators.

In Chapter 4 we did all sorts of hypothesis testing. In order to conduct hypothesis tests, it is necessary to make an additional assumption about the regression model: the error terms are normally distributed. If the error terms are normally distributed, then $\hat{\beta}_0$ and $\hat{\beta}_1$ will be normally distributed since they are linear functions of the error terms. In the section on bias above we saw that $\hat{\beta}_1$ is indeed a linear function of the u_i's : $\hat{\beta}_1 = \Sigma w_i Y_i = \Sigma w_i (\beta_0 + \beta_1 X_i + u_i)$. And $\hat{\beta}_0$ is a linear function of $\hat{\beta}_1$: $\hat{\beta}_0 = \overline{Y} - \hat{\beta}_1 \overline{X}$.

Once we know $\hat{\beta}_0$ and $\hat{\beta}_1$ are normally distributed we are able to carry out hypothesis tests based on the normal distribution. The t-table and F-table we use to look up critical values are only applicable if the error terms, and thus $\hat{\beta}_0$ and $\hat{\beta}_1$, are normally distributed.

There is a mathematical notation that succinctly sums up almost everything we have assumed about the error terms:

$$u_i \sim N(0, \sigma^2) \text{ for all i}$$

This states that the error terms are normally distributed with a mean of 0 and a variance of σ^2. Since $\hat{\beta}_0$ and $\hat{\beta}_1$ are linear functions of the u_i's, we know that:

$$\hat{\beta}_0 \sim N(\beta_0, \text{VAR}(\hat{\beta}_0))$$
$$\hat{\beta}_1 \sim N(\beta_1, \text{VAR}(\hat{\beta}_1))$$

Terms

Autocorrelation – When the error terms of a regression are related to one another: $E[u_i u_j] \neq 0$ for all $i \neq j$.

Best estimator – The estimator that varies the least out of all possible estimators in repeated sampling.

BLUE – An acronym for best, linear, unbiased estimator.

Gauss-Markov proof –The proof that $\hat{\beta}_0$ and $\hat{\beta}_1$ are best.

Heteroskedasticity – The error terms of a regression do not all have the same variance: $E[u_i] \neq E[u_j]$ for all $i \neq j$.

Linear estimator – An estimator whose formula is linear.

Monte Carlo study – An econometric study that draws repeated samples from a known population and then analyzes the characteristics of the sample regressions.

Unbiased estimator – An estimator whose expected value is equal to the true value of the parameter: $E[\hat{\beta}_1] = \beta_1$.

Chapter 8   Problems

1. Prove $\Sigma w_i = 0$ and $\Sigma w_i X_i = 1$.

2. Suppose $u_i \sim N(7, \sigma^2)$ for all i. Will $\hat{\beta}_1$ be biased? Explain.

3. Suppose $u_i \sim N(0, \sigma^2)$ for all i. Why can't we guarantee $\hat{\beta}_1$ will be efficient?

4. Given: Stalk Height$_i$ = 2.0 + 3.0 Rainfall$_i$ + 4.0 Fertilizer$_i$ + e$_i$

   A) Interpret the value of the intercept.
   B) Interpret the value of the coefficient on Rainfall.
   C) Suppose you were told that the true value of the coefficient on Rainfall is 3.1. Does this mean the estimate above is biased? Explain.
   D) Suppose you were told that the equation does not meet assumption 2 of the Classic Linear Regression Model (The error term has a zero population mean.) Does this mean that the coefficient on Rainfall is definitely not 3.0? Explain.
   E) When the data for this regression were gathered, Fertilizer was carefully applied to the various plots of corn so that each plot received exactly 2 lbs/acre of fertilizer more than the previous plot. Rainfall was measured using "dip canisters" in the standard meteorological way. Which of these explanatory variables is stochastic? Explain.
   F) Why can't we conclude that the estimates above are biased since one of the explanatory variables is stochastic?

5. From the article "Econometrics in Theory and Practice" by Steven Caudill, *Eastern Economic Journal*, vol. 16, no. 3 (Jul/Sept. 1990): 249–256.
   http://college.holycross.edu/eej/Volume16/V16N3P249_256.pdf

   A) What is the "Axiom of Specification"?
   B) Is the Axiom of Specification an assumption of the Classical Linear Regression Model? If not, then should it be? If so, then which assumption corresponds to it?
   C) What is the difference between "applied econometricians" and "econometric theorists"?
   D) What is "data mining"?

6. From the article "Let's Take the Con Out of Econometrics" by Edward E. Leamer, *American Economic Review*, vol. 73, no. 1 (March 1983): 31–43.
   http://www.mtholyoke.edu/~mirobins/leamer.pdf

   A) Distinguish between "experimental" and "nonexperimental" data. What is the drawback of using nonexperimental data?
   B) What is data mining? What is the drawback of data mining?
   C) What is sensitivity analysis?

Chapter 9

Multicollinearity

The Nature of Multicollinearity

Perfect Multicollinearity

Multicollinearity

Terms

Chapter 9 Problems

Test Yourself on Chapters 8 and 9

9.1 The Nature of Multicollinearity

In a multiple regression there are two or more explanatory variables. At times, some of these variables will be highly linearly related – a condition known as multicollinearity. When this occurs, ordinary least-squares has trouble discerning how much of the impact on the dependent variable can be attributed to each explanatory variable since changes in one explanatory variables are mirrored in the other.

Multicollinearity means that some or all of the explanatory variables move in lockstep or near lockstep. In this situation, regression analysis struggles to disentangle the effect each explanatory variable has on the Y-variable.

The material in this chapter is organized as follows:

- The difference between ordinary and perfect multicollinearity is explained
- The consequences of multicollinearity are spelled out
- Detection techniques are presented
- Remedies are considered

9.2 Perfect Multicollinearity

Perfect multicollinearity is when the explanatory variables in a regression are perfectly linearly related. Consider X_1 and X_2 below:

X_1	X_2
10.0	6.0
17.0	2.5
12.0	5.0
21.0	0.5

You might stare at these numbers for a long time before realizing that $X_2 = 11 - .5\,X_1$. In other words, X_2 is a perfect linear rewrite of X_1. The two variables are perfectly collinear. Notice that if the first observation on X_1 was 10.1 instead of 10.0, then the two variables would be highly linearly related, but no longer perfectly collinear.

When the explanatory variables in a regression are perfectly collinear, the structural parameters are undefined. From Chapter 5 we know that the formulas for $\hat{\beta}_1$ and $\hat{\beta}_2$ in $Y_i = \hat{\beta}_0 + \hat{\beta}_1 X_{1i} + \hat{\beta}_2 X_{2i} + e_i$ are:

$$\hat{\beta}_1 = \frac{(\Sigma y_i x_{1i})(\Sigma x_{2i}^2) - (\Sigma y_i x_{2i})(\Sigma x_{1i} x_{2i})}{(\Sigma x_{1i}^2)(\Sigma x_{2i}^2) - (\Sigma x_{1i} x_{2i})^2} ; \text{ where } y_i = Y_i - \overline{Y} ; x_{1i} = X_{1i} - \overline{X}_1 ; x_{2i} = X_{2i} - \overline{X}_2$$

and

$$\hat{\beta}_2 = \frac{(\Sigma y_i x_{2i})(\Sigma x_{2i}^2) - (\Sigma y_i x_{1i})(\Sigma x_{1i} x_{2i})}{(\Sigma x_{1i}^2)(\Sigma x_{2i}^2) - (\Sigma x_{1i} x_{2i})^2} ; \text{ where } y_i = Y_i - \overline{Y} ; x_{1i} = X_{1i} - \overline{X}_1 ; x_{2i} = X_{2i} - \overline{X}_2$$

It can be shown that the denominators of both of these equations are equal to zero when X_1 and X_2 are perfectly collinear. With the denominators equal to zero, both $\hat{\beta}_1$ and $\hat{\beta}_2$ are undefined. Therefore, $\hat{\beta}_0 = \overline{Y} - \hat{\beta}_1\overline{X}_{1i} - \hat{\beta}_2\overline{X}_{2i}$ is undefined as well.

You may wonder why a researcher would include perfectly collinear variables in a regression. Usually it happens by mistake. For instance, in a regression explaining GPA a researcher might include study time per day (ST/DAY) and study time per week (ST/WK) before realizing that ST/WK = 0 + 7 ST/DAY.

In another example, a regression explaining wages may include the number of unemployed people, the unemployment rate, and the number of people in the labor force.

$$\text{WAGES}_i = \hat{\beta}_0 + \hat{\beta}_1 \text{ \#UNEM}_i + \hat{\beta}_2 \text{ UNEMRATE}_i + \hat{\beta}_3 \text{ LFORCE}_i + e_i$$

In this case, the UNEMRATE = \#UNEM / LFORCE. A linear combination of two of the explanatory variables equals the third explanatory variable. This is perfect multicollinearity and the structural parameters are undefined.

There is only one thing to do in the face of perfect multicollinearity – drop one or more of the collinear variables.

9.3 Multicollinearity

Multicollinearity is when the explanatory variables in a regression are highly, but not perfectly, linearly related. In this case, the structural parameters and all the residual statistics can be calculated with the usual formulas.

Indeed, the ordinary least-squares estimators are BLUE in the presence of multicollinearity. There is no other linear estimator that will yield estimates that vary less in repeated sampling. However, the standard errors of the estimators will be larger than if there were no multicollinearity.

To understand this more clearly, consider the following regression:

$$Y_i = \hat{\beta}_0 + \hat{\beta}_1 X_{1i} + \hat{\beta}_2 X_{2i} + e_i$$

The standard error of $\hat{\beta}_1$ in the following regression can be written as:

$$SE(\hat{\beta}_1) = \sqrt{\frac{\Sigma e_i^2 / (n-k)}{\Sigma(X_{i1} - \overline{X}_1)^2(1 - r^2_{12})}} \ ;$$

where r^2_{12} is the square of the correlation coefficient between X_1 and X_2. Thus the more collinear X_1 and X_2, the larger the standard error of $\hat{\beta}_1$. In other words, the more severe the multicollinearity, the larger the standard errors of the estimators.

The main consequence of multicollinearity is bloated standard errors. This will lead to further problems. Since the t-ratios are calculated from the standard errors they will be smaller in absolute value than if there were no multicollinearity. This makes hypothesis testing precarious. Artificially anemic t-ratios can lead to more TYPE II errors.

In addition, the bloated standard errors can cause parameter estimates to be sensitive to model specification. Dropping an irrelevant variable, let alone a relevant one, can cause large swings in parameter estimates under multicollinearity. Model selection becomes tricky when multicollinearity is severe.

There are a variety of techniques available to detect multicollinearity. The simplest and most common technique is to check the correlation coefficient between the explanatory variables:

$$r = \frac{\Sigma(X_{1i} - \overline{X}_1)(X_{2i} - \overline{X}_2)}{(S.D.X_1)(S.D.X_2)}$$

Remember, r ranges between plus and minus unity. $|r| > 0.7$ means severe multicollinearity.

A more formal procedure for detecting multicollinearity requires the calculation of a set of variance inflation factors (VIFs). To find the VIFs, regress each explanatory variable on all the others in a bank of auxiliary regressions. Then, calculate VIF for each regression:

$$VIF(\hat{\beta}_i) = \frac{1}{1 - R_i^2}$$

If any VIF > 5, then multicollinearity is severe.

Once it has been detected, there are one or two things to consider when working with multicollinear explanatory variables. Often doing nothing is the best response. The consequences are not totally debilitating and can be taken into account. For instance, hypothesis testing should be conducted with a mind toward the fact that TYPE II errors are more likely to occur.

Dealing with multicollinearity is much like dealing with a common cold. There are some things you can do to alleviate the symptoms, but most of the time you simply have to put up with them. And like the common cold, the consequences of having multicollinearity usually are not life threatening.

Another thing to consider is dropping one of the collinear explanatory variables. This would be done only if it was determined that the variable could be expended without causing an underspecified model.

A better option would be to somehow combine the collinear variables. Sometimes it is possible to form ratios or differences of variables and thereby avoid dropping the information that belongs in the regression. With time-series data, taking first differences often remedies multicollinearity.

Finally, sometimes moving to an alternate functional form can alleviate the multicollinearity. Notice that it does not pay to change into an inappropriate functional form to relieve multicollinearity since the consequences of being in the wrong form are much worse than the consequences of multicollinearity.

Terms

Correlation coefficient – A statistic that estimates the degree of linear relationship between two variables.

Multicollinearity – When the explanatory variables in a regression are highly linearly related.

Perfect multicollinearity – When the explanatory variables in a regression are perfectly linearly related.

Variance inflation factor – A statistic used to detect multicollinearity.

Chapter 9   Problems

1. Use the data in CONSUMP.XLS and statistical software to run the regression:

$$RCONPC_t = \hat{\beta}_0 + \hat{\beta}_1 REALYDPC_t + \hat{\beta}_2 REALR_t + \hat{\beta}_3 CC_t + e_t$$

where: RCONPC = real consumer spending in the USA per capita
REALYDPC = real disposable income per capita
REALR = real interest rate on 1-year Treasury Bonds
CC = University of Michigan Index of Consumer Confidence

A) Which explanatory variables do not obtain their expected signs?

B) According to the correlation coefficients between the explanatory variables, would you classify the multicollinearity in this regression as severe, moderate, mild, or non-existent? Explain.

C) According to the correlation coefficients between the explanatory variables, which two variables are most collinear?

D) Calculate the three VIFs for this regression. Would you classify the multicollinearity in this regression as severe, moderate, mild, or non-existent? Explain.

E) Run the regression in first difference form. Which explanatory variables do not obtain their expected signs?

F) According to the correlation coefficients between the explanatory variables, would you classify the multicollinearity in this regression as severe, moderate, mild, or non-existent? Explain.

G) Calculate the three VIFs for this regression. Would you classify the multicollinearity in this regression as severe, moderate, mild, or non-existent? Explain.

H) Based on your look into this matter, what do you recommend doing about the multicollinearity in the original regression? Explain.

2. Use the data in ANMACRO.XLS and statistical software to run a regression where the demand for money (m2) is explained by a constant term, income (ngdp), interest rates (aaa), and prices (cpi).

VARIABLE	DESCRIPTION
m2	demand for m2
ngdp	nominal GDP
aaa	aaa corporate bond rate
cpi	consumer price index

A) Which explanatory variables do not obtain their expected signs?

B) According to the correlation coefficients between the explanatory variables, would you classify the multicollinearity in this regression as severe, moderate, mild, or non-existent? Explain.

C) According to the correlation coefficients between the explanatory variables, which two variables are most collinear?

D) Calculate the three VIFs for this regression. Would you classify the multicollinearity in this regression as severe, moderate, mild, or non-existent? Explain.

E) Run the regression in first difference form. Which explanatory variables do not obtain their expected signs?

F) According to the correlation coefficients between the explanatory variables, would you classify the multicollinearity in this regression as severe, moderate, mild, or non-existent? Explain.

G) Calculate the three VIFs for this regression. Would you classify the multicollinearity in this regression as severe, moderate, mild, or non-existent? Explain.

H) Based on your look into this matter, what do you recommend doing about the multicollinearity in the original regression? Explain.

Test Yourself on Chapters 8 and 9

1. Is a study that uses "experimental" data superior to a similar study that uses "nonexperimental" data? Explain.

2. Prove that $E[\hat{\beta}_1] = \beta_1$.

3. Assume $\hat{\beta}_1$ is linear and unbiased. Use that information to argue that $\hat{\beta}_0 (= \bar{Y} - \hat{\beta}_1 \bar{X})$ is unbiased as well.

4. Defend the process known as "data mining." Does this process not violate the theories of inference?

5. Discuss the pros and cons of the following remedies for multicollinearity:
   A) drop a variable
   B) try first differences
   C) try an alternate functional form such as the reciprocal form
   D) do nothing

6. Use the following equation to argue that the $SE(\hat{\beta}_1)$ is undefined under perfect

$$\text{multicollinearity:} \quad SE(\hat{\beta}_1) = \sqrt{\frac{\Sigma e_i^2 /(n-k)}{\Sigma(X_{i1} - \bar{X}_1)^2 (1 - r^2_{12})}} \quad ;$$

where r^2_{12} is the square of the
correlation coefficient between X1 and X2.

Mark each of the following statements TRUE or FALSE.

1. $\hat{\beta}_1$ is BLUE in the presence of serial correlation.

2. In order to show that $\hat{\beta}_1$ is best, it must be assumed that the e_i's are not correlated with each other.

3. In order to show that $\hat{\beta}_1$ is unbiased, it must be assumed that the true error terms are not correlated with each other.

4. One of the conditions necessary for hypothesis testing is that the u_i's are normally distributed.

5. One of the conditions necessary to prove that the OLS estimators are BLUE is that the u_i's are normally distributed.

6. A regression in the incorrect functional form violates assumption 4 of the Classical Linear Regression Model (CLRM).

7. In the presence of multicollinearity, the estimate of R-squared will be biased.

8. $VAR(\hat{\beta_1}) = E\left[(\hat{\beta_1} - \beta_1)^2\right] = E\left[(\beta_1 + \Sigma w_i u_i - \beta_1)^2\right] = \sigma^2 \Sigma w_i^2$

9. It is possible, although unlikely, that the structural parameters in an underspecified regression are unbiased.

10. With perfect multicollinearity, the OLS estimators are undefined.

11. Consider $Y_i = \hat{\beta_0} + \hat{\beta_1} X1_i + \hat{\beta_2} X2_i + \hat{\beta_3} X3_i + \hat{\beta_4} X4_i + e_i$. If X1 and X2 are highly collinear, then the standard errors of $\hat{\beta_1}$ and $\hat{\beta_2}$ will be bloated, but not those of $\hat{\beta_3}$ and $\hat{\beta_4}$.

12. $\Sigma w_i X_i = 0$; where $w_i = \dfrac{(X_i - \overline{X})}{X_i - \overline{X})^2}$

13. A predetermined explanatory variable is stochastic.

14. A VIF (variance inflation factor) less than 5 means multicollinearity is nonexistent.

15. $u_i \sim N(0, \sigma^2)$ indicates that the true error terms are normally distributed with an expected value of 0 and that each true error term has a variance equal to some constant, σ^2.

16. Assumptions 1 and 2 of the CLRM are necessary to prove that the OLS estimators are linear.

17. Assumptions 1 and 2 of the CLRM are necessary to prove that the OLS estimators are unbiased.

18. Assumptions 3 and 4 of the CLRM are necessary to prove that the OLS estimators are linear.

19. Assumptions 3 and 4 of the CLRM are necessary to prove that the OLS estimators are unbiased.

20. Assumptions 3 and 4 of the CLRM are necessary to prove that the OLS estimators are best.

Chapter 10

Heteroskedasticity

What is Heteroskedasticity?

Consequences of Heteroskedasticity

Detection

Remedies

Terms

Chapter 10 Problems

10.1 What is Heteroskedasticity?

Heteroskedasticity literally means different (hetero) spread (skedasticity). It occurs when the error terms from a regression do not all have the same variance. This is a direct violation of assumption 4 of the Classical Linear Regression Model which states that the error terms all have the same variance: $E[u_i^2] = E[u_j^2] = \sigma^2$.

Cross-sectional data are most likely to be heteroskedastic. The example below considers the relationship between the savings and income of 50 families.

Example: $SAVING_i = -2.28 + 0.43\ INCOME_i + e_i$

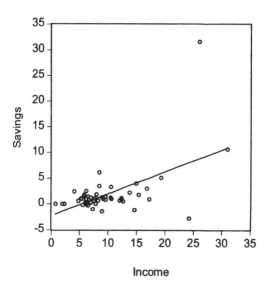

When family income is low, the regression errors tend to be small. As income increases, so does the magnitude of the residuals. Intuitively, this makes sense. When a family has low income, it is easy to predict their savings. However, there is more room for error when predicting the savings of a family with high income.

Heteroskedasticity is not the larger errors associated with higher levels of income. It is the wider frequency distributions of the error terms associated with higher levels of income. The difference is subtle, but important.

In practice, we detect heteroskedasticity by checking to see if the magnitude of the errors varies with one of the explanatory variables. The idea is that larger errors are evidence of wider frequency distributions. But let us consider the consequences of heteroskedasticity before turning to detection techniques.

10.2 Consequences of Heteroskedasticity

The structural parameters of a regression suffering from heteroskedasticity are not best. Since assumption 4 (the error terms all have the same variance: $E[u_i^2] = E[u_j^2] = \sigma^2$) of the Classical Linear Regression Model is violated, it is impossible to get through the Gauss-Markov proof. It is, however, possible to prove that the structural parameters are linear and unbiased.

The estimated SER, the estimated standard errors of the structural parameters, and therefore the t-ratios, the R^2, and F-statistics are all biased. So hypothesis testing of any sort is invalid in the presence of heteroskedasticity.

10.3 Detection

There are a variety of tests available to detect heteroskedasticity. Here we introduce three of them.

The graphical method involves plotting the squared residuals from the regression against the "culprit" variable. The culprit variable is the explanatory variable that is giving rise to the heteroskedasticity. In our example, there is no question that INCOME is the culprit variable – it is the only explanatory variable.

Here are the squared residuals from our example (EISSQ) graphed against income:

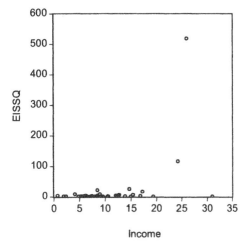

It is not obvious, but a case could be made that the squared residuals are getting larger as income increases. In general, any pattern to the squared residuals indicates heteroskedasticity. The chart on the left below shows no pattern, while the right is indicative of heteroskedasticity.

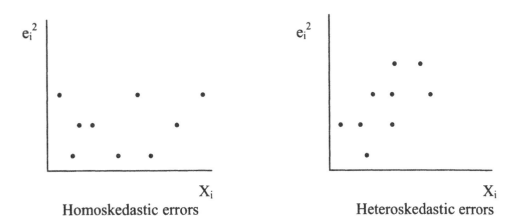

Homoskedastic errors   Heteroskedastic errors

The Park test (Park 1966) is a more formal way to look for patterns in the squared residuals. To test if $Y_i = \hat{\beta}_0 + \hat{\beta}_1 X_i + e_i$ suffers from heteroskedasticity, square the residuals and regress them on the explanatory variable giving rise to the heteroskedasticity. Use the double-log form if possible; if that is not possible, the semi-log form will do:

$$\ln(e_i^2) = \alpha_0 + \alpha_1 \ln(X_i) + \varepsilon_i$$

If α_1 is statistically significant, then heteroskedasticity is present.

To test if $SAVING_i = -2.28 + 0.43\ INCOME_i + e_i$ suffers from heteroskedasticity, square the residuals and regress them on the explanatory variable giving rise to heteroskedasticity:

$$\ln(e_i^2) = -1.49 + 0.70 \ln(INCOME_i) + \varepsilon_i$$
$$(1.29) \quad \leftarrow \quad \text{t-ratio} \quad n = 50$$

1) Ho: $\alpha_1 = 0$ (no hetero)   Ha: $\alpha_1 \neq 0$ (hetero exists)
2) 5%
3) If |t-ratio| > tc, reject Ho
4) $1.29 < 2.021$ (d.f = n – k)
5) Do Not Reject Ho: heteroskedasticity is not present in the original regression

The Park test contradicts what we suspected from the graphical analysis and finds no evidence of heteroskedasticity.

One of the most popular tests for heteroskedasticity is the White test (White 1980).

To test if $Y_i = \hat{\beta}_0 + \hat{\beta}_1 X1_i + \hat{\beta}_2 X2_i + e_i$ suffers from heteroskedasticity, run an auxiliary regression:

$$e_i^2 = \alpha_0 + \alpha_1 X1_i + \alpha_2 X1_i^2 + \alpha_3 X2_i + \alpha_4 X2_i^2 + \alpha_5(X1_i)(X2_i) + \varepsilon_i$$

If at least one of the coefficients α_0 through α_5 is significant, then heteroskedasticity is evident.

Let's add another explanatory variable to example so that we may put the White test to full use. SIZE is the number of people in the family.

$$SAVING_i = -2.62 + 0.42\ INCOME_i + 0.08\ SIZE_i + e_i$$

To test if this regression suffers from heteroskedasticity, run the auxiliary regression:

$$e_i^2 = \alpha_0 + \alpha_1 INCOME_i + \alpha_2 INCOME_i^2 + \alpha_3 SIZE_i + \alpha_4 SIZE_i^2 + \alpha_5(INCOME_i)(SIZE_i) + \varepsilon_i$$

$$n = 50 \ ; \ R^2 = .42$$

1) Ho: no hetero   Ha: hetero exists
2) 5%
3) If $nR^2 > \chi c$, then reject Ho
4) $50(.42) = 21.0$; $\chi c = 11.07$ (d.f. = k – 1 from the auxiliary regression = 5)
5) Reject Ho: heteroskedasticity is present in the original regression

The White test finds evidence of heteroskedasticity in the multiple regression of INCOME and SIZE on SAVINGS.

10.4 Remedies

As with multicollinearity and serial correlation, it is perfectly legitimate to do nothing in the face of heteroskedasticity. You will want to use the residual statistics with caution, or not at all, since they are biased. And hypothesis testing should be taken with a grain of salt. But the estimates of the structural parameters are unbiased and forecasts based on the regression are valid.

Sometimes running a regression in an alternate functional form can alleviate heteroskedasticity. It is left as an exercise for the reader to show that the heteroskedasticity in the example above is remedied by running the regression in the semi-log form. However, if you move to an incorrect functional form in order to remedy the heteroskedasticity, then you will be creating a more severe problem. Remember, regressions run in the wrong functional form yield biased results.

Another sly way to deal with heteroskedasticity is to form ratios as opposed to levels of the variables when possible. For instance, we might run a regression such as:

$$\frac{SAVING_i}{SIZE_i} = \hat{\beta}_0 + \hat{\beta}_1 \frac{INCOME_i}{SIZE_i} + e_i$$

Again, it is left to reader to show that in this particular case heteroskedasticity is reduced by forming these ratios. This regression explains savings per family member with income per family member.

Newey and West (1987) have developed superior estimates of the standard errors of the coefficients when the regression suffers from autocorrelation. The Newey-West standard errors are still biased, but less so than the usual estimates of the standard errors.

The Newey-West technique leaves the ordinary least-squares parameter estimates untouched. Remember that the ordinary least-squares parameter estimates are unbiased in the presence of autocorrelation. The standard errors of the parameter estimates, however, are biased. The Newey-West technique corrects for this bias. This technique has become so popular that many econometric software packages ask if you want to see "robust" standard errors for every regression, whether it suffers from heteroskedasticity or not.

Weighted least-squares is yet another possible way to cope with heteroskedasticity. It can be shown that weighted least-squares is the best, linear, unbiased, estimation technique in the presence of heteroskedasticity. The trick is finding the appropriate weights to correct for the non-constant variance of the error terms.

Suppose the error terms from $SAVING_i = \beta_0 + \beta_1 INCOME_i + u_i$ are heteroskedastic in that the variance of the error terms varies with INCOME. Multiply through the original regression by 1/INCOME.

$$\frac{SAVING_i}{INCOME_i} = \beta_0 \frac{1}{INCOME_i} + \beta_1 \frac{INCOME_i}{INCOME_i} + \frac{u_i}{INCOME_i}$$

Note that $INCOME_i/INCOME_i = 1$, so we can write:

$$\frac{SAVING_i}{INCOME_i} = \beta_0 \frac{1}{INCOME_i} + \beta_1 + \frac{u_i}{INCOME_i}$$

$\left(\dfrac{u_i}{INCOME_i}\right)$ are the new error terms. They will be homoskedastic if the variance of the u_i's is proportional to the square of INCOME.

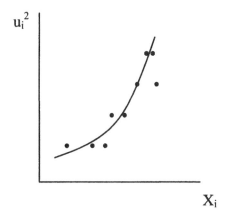

Error Terms Proportional to Income Squared

If we applying ordinary least-squares to the regression above, it is known as weighted least-squares. Notice that in practice this amounts to regressing $\dfrac{SAVING_i}{INCOME_i}$ on $\dfrac{1}{INCOME_i}$.

If the variance of the error terms is proportional to INCOME, rather than the square of INCOME, then multiplying through by $1/\sqrt{INCOME_i}$ will result in homoskedastic errors:

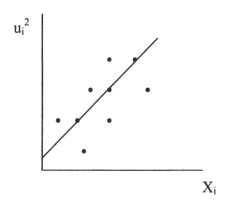

Error Terms Proportional to Income

$$\frac{SAVING_i}{\sqrt{INCOME_i}} = \beta_0 \left[\frac{1}{\sqrt{INCOME_i}} \right] + \beta_1 \left[\frac{INCOME_i}{\sqrt{INCOME_i}} \right] + \frac{u_i}{\sqrt{INCOME_i}}$$

Again, applying ordinary least-squares to the weighted data above is known as weighted least-squares. The error terms in the weighted least-squares regression $\left(\frac{u_i}{\sqrt{INCOME_i}} \right)$ are homoskedastic only if the variance of the u_i's is proportional to INCOME.

Most econometric software packages apply weighted least-squares on command. The researcher only needs to specify the weight. Typically this is the reciprocal of the explanatory variable giving rise to the heteroskedasticity or the reciprocal of the square root of the culprit variable.

Possible Remedies for Heteroskedasticity

- Do nothing
- Try alternate functional forms
- Take ratios if possible
- Apply the Newey-West technique
- Apply weighted least-squares

Terms

Culprit variable – The independent variable causing the heteroskedasticity.

Heteroskedasticity – The error terms of a regression do not all have the same variance: $E[u_j^2] = \sigma^2$.

Newey-West technique – Formulas for the standard errors of the estimators that are less biased in the presence of heteroskedasticity.

Weighted least-squares – A technique that remedies heteroskedasticity by dividing the data by some version of the culprit variable.

1. Given $Y_i = \hat{\beta}_0 + \hat{\beta}_1 X1_i + \hat{\beta}_2 X2_i + e_i$

   A) Write the auxiliary regression required for the Park test assuming X2 is the "culprit" variable.

   B) Suppose n = 23 and the t-ratio on X2 in the auxiliary regression is –2.222. Is heteroskedasticity present? Show the 5-step procedure for the Park test.

   C) Write the auxiliary regression required for the White test.

   D) Suppose n = 23 and the R-squared on the auxiliary regression is 0.55. Is heteroskedasticity present? Show the 5-step procedure for the White test.

   E) Write the weighted least-squares regression that would remedy the heteroskedasticity if it were proportional to X2.

2. A) Use the data in XFILE.XLS and statistical software to test the following regression for heteroskedasticity by applying White's test. Show the 5-step procedure.

   $$SAVING_i = \hat{\beta}_0 + \hat{\beta}_1 INCOME_i + \hat{\beta}_2 SIZE_i + e_i$$

   B) Run the original regression using weighted least-squares. Assume 1/INCOME is the correct weight. Then apply White's test for heteroskedasticity to the errors from this weighted regression. Show the 5-step procedure.

   C) Run the original regression using weighted least-squares. Assume $\sqrt{1/INCOME}$ is the correct weight. Then apply White's test for heteroskedasticity to the errors from this weighted regression. Show the 5-step procedure.

   D) Now apply White's test to the following regression. Show the 5-step procedure.

   $$SAVING_i = \hat{\beta}_0 + \hat{\beta}_1 \ln INCOME_i + \hat{\beta}_2 \ln SIZE_i + e_i$$

   E) Now apply White's test to the following regression. Show the 5-step procedure.

   $$\frac{SAVINGS_i}{SIZE_i} = \hat{\beta}_0 + \hat{\beta}_1 \frac{INCOME_i}{SIZE_i} + e_i$$

F) Now apply the Newey-West technique to the regression in 2.A). Based on the results do you think the standard errors of the structural parameters are biased upward or downward in the regression in 2.A)?

3. Use the data in ALCO5.XLS and statistical software to run a regression where "drink" is explained by a constant term, gpa, male, ofage, cig, pot, intra, and white.

VARIABLE	DESCRIPTION
drink	number of alcoholic drinks consumed per week
gpa	grade point average 0 – 4 scale
male	1 if the student is male; 0 otherwise
ofage	1 if the student is 21 or older; 0 otherwise
cig	1 if the student uses tobacco; 0 otherwise
pot	1 if the student uses marijuana: 0 otherwise
intra	1 if the student participates in intramural athletics; 0 otherwise
white	1 if the student is white; 0 otherwise

A) Which variables do not attain their expected signs?

B) Which variables are not significant at the 5% critical level?

C) Plot the squared residuals from the regression against gpa. Does the plot show evidence of heteroskedasticity? Explain.

D) Do a Park test for heteroskedasticity assuming gpa is the "culprit" variable. Show the 5-step procedure.

E) Perform White's test for heteroskedasticity. Show the 5-step procedure.

F) Run the original regression using weighted least-squares. Assume 1/gpa is the correct weight. Then apply White's test for heteroskedasticity to the errors from this weighted regression. Show the 5-step procedure.

G) Run the original regression using weighted least-squares. Assume $1/\sqrt{gpa}$ is the correct weight. Then apply White's test for heteroskedasticity to the errors from this weighted regression. Show the 5-step procedure.

H) Use the Newey-West technique to obtain heteroskedasticity-corrected standard errors with the original regression. Did heteroskedasticity appear to be biasing the standard errors of the structural parameters very much? Explain.

4. Linear probability models are prone to being heteroskedastic. Use the data in BINGE.XLS and statistical software to run a regression where BINGE is explained by a constant term, CIG, CLASS, INTRA, MALE, POT, and WHITE.

VARIABLE	DESCRIPTION
binge	1 if the student binged in the last two weeks; 0 otherwise
cig	1 if the student uses tobacco; 0 otherwise
class	1 if frshman; 2 if soph; 3 if jr; 4 if senior
intra	1 if the student participates in intramural athletics; 0 otherwise
male	1 if the student is male; 0 otherwise
pot	1 if the student uses marijuana: 0 otherwise
white	1 if the student is white; zero otherwise

A) Which variables do not attain their expected signs?

B) Which variables are not significant at the 5% critical level?

C) Perform White's test for heteroskedasticity. Show the 5-step procedure.

D) Apply the Newey-West technique to obtain heteroskedasticity-corrected standard errors with the original regression. Did heteroskedasticity appear to biasing the standard errors of the structural parameters very much? Explain.

Chapter 11

Serial Correlation

11.1 What is Serial Correlation?

Serial correlation, also known as autocorrelation, is when the error terms from a regression are related to one another.

A common way in which the error terms can be related is a first-order Markov scheme: $e_t = \rho\, e_{t-1} + \varepsilon_t$ where $-1 < \rho < +1$ and ε_t is white noise. (i.e., $\varepsilon_t \sim N(0, \sigma^2)$ for all t.

$$\text{positive autocorrelation is when } \rho > 0$$
$$\text{negative autocorrelation is when } \rho < 0$$

Autocorrelation is a time-series problem that occurs frequently with economic data. Second-order serial correlation is much less frequently encountered. As you might imagine, second-order serial correlation is when the current error term is related to the two prior error terms: $e_t = \rho_1 e_{t-1} + \rho\rho_2 e_{t-2} + \varepsilon_t$

11.2 Consequences of Serial Correlation

Serial correlation is a direct violation of assumption 3 of the Classical Linear Regression Model: The error terms are not related to one another: $E[u_i\, u_j] = 0$ for all $i \neq j$. Recall that assumption 3 was required to prove that the estimators are best, but not unbiased.

Therefore, in the presence of autocorrelation the structural parameters are not best. In addition, the residual statistics from the regression are biased:AE

$$\text{SER, S.E.(B's), T-ratios, F, } R^2$$
$$-\quad\quad -\quad\quad\quad + \quad + \ +$$

The signs under each statistic indicate the direction of the bias. Notice that each statistic is biased in a way that makes them appear better. For instance, the standard error of the regression (SER) indicates a good fit when it is low and it will be biased downward in the presence of autocorrelation.

The consequences of serial correlation are the same as those of heteroskedasticity with one small difference. In the presence of serial correlation, the direction of the bias in the residual statistics is known. With heteroskedasticity, the direction of the bias is unknown.

Since the standard errors and t-ratios are biased, hypothesis tests must be carried out with extreme caution in the presence of serial correlation. TYPE I errors will be more likely because the standard errors are biased downward.

11.3 Detection

Many techniques are available to detect serial correlation. We will consider two of them in this chapter and learn yet another in Chapter 12. Since serial correlation is when one error term is related to its predecessor, we might detect it by looking for patterns in the error terms. One way to see these patterns is to make a graph of the error terms from the regression over time.

Here are the residuals from a regression of consumer spending on disposable income from 1959 through 2005:

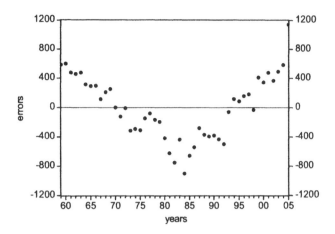

The pattern revealed here is indicative of positive serial correlation: $e_t = \rho \, e_{t-1} + \varepsilon_t$ and $\rho > 0$. Since ρ is positive any error term is likely to have the same sign as the one before it. This holds in the graph above. From 1959 through 1970, every error is positive. Once the error term becomes negative in 1971 there is a run of negative error terms until 1994 when they once again become positive. These long runs of positive and negative error terms are characteristic of positive serial correlation.

Another type of graph can indicate the phenomenon. Here the error terms from the same regression are plotted against their lagged values:

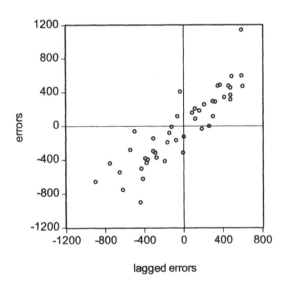

Almost all the observations lie in the first and third quadrants. This implies that when an error term is positive, the one before it is as well. And when an error term is negative, so is its predecessor. In other words, error terms tend to have the same sign as their predecessors. This implies a positive ρ in the first-order Markov scheme ($e_t = \rho\, e_{t-1} + \varepsilon_t$) and positive serial correlation.

The graphs below reflect negative serial correlation:

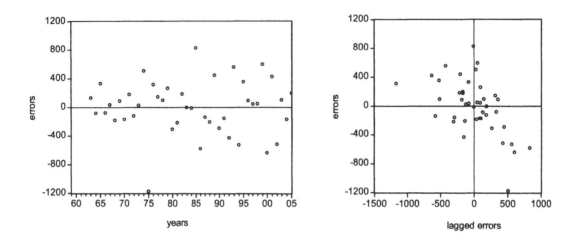

The graph on the left shows that the error terms zig-zag from positive to negative in sequence. If the current error term is positive, the subsequent error term is very likely to be negative. The graph on the right shows most of the observations in the second and fourth quadrants.

How do the graphs look when there is no serial correlation?

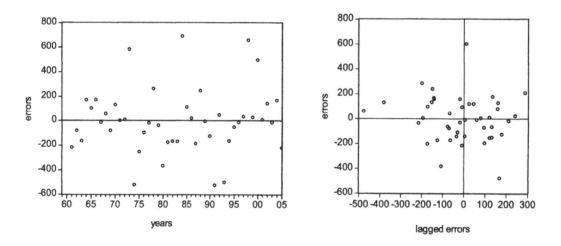

The graph on the left shows no pattern, but a random splay of errors over time. The observations on the graph on the right are almost evenly divided between all four quadrants.

One problem with the graphical method for detecting autocorrelation is that patterns can be difficult to discern. In practice, the graphs usually are not as clear cut as the ones shown here.

The most popular technique for detecting serial correlation is the Durbin-Watson test. (Durbin and Watson 1951) The test involves obtaining the residuals from the regression and calculating d, the test statistic:

$$d = \frac{\Sigma(e_t - e_{t-1})^2}{\Sigma e_t{}^2}$$

d ranges between 0 and 4 and will tend toward 2 if the error terms are not autocorrelated. If $d < 2$, suspect positive autocorrelation and apply the following 5-step procedure:

1) Ho: no positive auto   Ha: positive auto
2) 5%
3) If $0 < d < d_L$, then reject Ho
   If $d_L < d < d_U$, then inconclusive
4) calculate d and look up d_L and d_U in a table
5) reject or do not reject Ho

If $d > 2$, suspect negative autocorrelation and apply the following 5-step procedure:

1) Ho: no negative auto   Ha: negative auto
2) 5%
3) If $4 - d_L < d < 4$, then reject Ho
   If $4 - d_U < d < 4 - d_L$, then inconclusive
4) calculate d and look up d_L and d_U in a table
5) reject or do not reject Ho

Examples:

(1) $Y_t = 9734.2 - 3782.2\, X1_t + 2815.3\, X2_t + e_t$; n = 16

Since $d = 2.21$, suspect negative autocorrelation:

1) Ho: no negative auto   Ha: negative auto
2) 5%
3) If $4 - d_L < d < 4$, then reject Ho
   If $4 - d_U < d < 4 - d_L$, then inconclusive
4) d = 2.21 d_L = .98 d_U = 1.54   (n = 16; k = 3)
5) do not reject Ho → no negative auto

(2) $Y_t = 0.568 + 0.907\, X1_t + e_t$; n = 25

Since $d = .66$, suspect positive autocorrelation:

1) Ho: no positive auto   Ha: positive auto
2) 5%
3) If $0 < d < d_L$, then reject Ho
   If $d_L < d < d_U$, then inconclusive
4) d = .66 d_L = 1.29 d_U = 1.45   (n = 25; k = 2)
5) Reject Ho → positive auto is present

The Durbin–Watson test is invalid in certain situations:

- The test is not valid in regressions without a constant term.
- The test is not valid for small samples (n < 15).
- The test is not valid for autoregressive models.

Autoregressive models are regressions that include the lagged dependent variable as an explanatory variable: $Y_t = \hat{\beta}_0 + \hat{\beta}_1 X1_t + \hat{\beta}_2 Y_{t-1} + e_t$. The Durbin–Watson statistic is biased toward 2 in such models. Durbin's h–test (Durbin 1970) is available to test for serial correlation in these models, as are other tests.

Both the graphical procedure and the Durbin–Watson test outlined above only check for first-order serial correlation. That is, the serial correlation is expected to follow a first-order Markov scheme: $e_t = \rho\, e_{t-1} + \varepsilon_t$. Second-order serial correlation ($e_t = \rho_1\, e_{t-1} + \rho_2\, e_{t-2} + \varepsilon_t$) is rare, but not unheard of, with economic data.

11.4 Remedies

Consider
$$Y_t = \beta_0 + \beta_1 X_t + u_t.; \text{ where } u_t = \rho\, u_{t-1} + \varepsilon_t$$

lag and mult by ρ:
$$\rho\, Y_{t-1} = \rho\, \beta_0 + \beta_1\, \rho\, X_{t-1} + \rho\, u_{t-1}$$

subtract:
$$Y_t - \rho\, Y_{t-1} = \beta_0 - \rho\, \beta_0 + \beta_1\, X_t - \beta_1\, \rho X_{t-1} + u_t - \rho\, u_{t-1}$$

rearrange:
$$Y_t - \rho\, Y_{t-1} = \beta_0\,(1-\rho) + \beta_1\,(X_t - \rho\, X_{t-1}) + u_t - \rho\, u_{t-1}$$

This last equation is the generalized difference equation. The generalized differences of Y_t ($Y_t - \rho\, Y_{t-1}$) are regressed on the generalized differences of X_t ($X_t - \rho\, X_{t-1}$). When a regression is run using the generalized differences of the data, it is known as generalized least-squares (GLS). The error terms ($u_t - \rho\, u_{t-1}$) in the GLS regression are free from serial correlation. This can be seen by substituting $u_t = \rho\, u_{t-1} + \varepsilon_t$ into ($u_t - \rho\, u_{t-1}$). The result is ε_t which is white noise: a normally distributed stochastic variable that has a mean of zero, constant standard error, and is independently distributed (i.e., free from serial correlation).

The GLS estimators are efficient and the residual statistics are unbiased. GLS is the one and only remedy for autocorrelation. The problem, in practice, is that ρ is never known. It must be estimated. We consider four ways to estimate ρ:

(1) OLS Technique: Suppose the residuals of the following regression are autocorrelated: $Y_t = \hat{\beta}_0 + \hat{\beta}_1 X1_t + e_t$. Now estimate ρ by regressing the residuals on their lagged values: $e_t = \hat{\beta}_1 e_{t-1} + \varepsilon_t$. Notice there is no $\hat{\beta}_0$. $\hat{\beta}_1$ is the estimate of ρ. Run GLS with this estimate of ρ.

(2) Hildreth-Lu Scanning Procedure: Since ρ is expected to lie between plus and minus unity, a computer can easily check to see which value of ρ gives the best results in a GLS regression.

Assume $\rho = -1$; Run GLS; Assume $\rho = -.9$; Run GLS; Assume $\rho = -.8$; Run GLS; ...; Assume $\rho = +.9$; Run GLS; Assume $\rho = +1$; Run GLS. Of all these GLS regressions, use the one that has the best fit according to the R^2 or SER.

(3) Cochrane-Orcutt Iterative Procedure: This procedure estimates ρ with a formula and then runs the GLS regression. However, it does not stop there. The GLS regression will have its own residuals which can be plugged back into the formula for estimating ρ. Then GLS can be run again. Once again, the GLS residuals can be plugged into the formula for ρ and GLS can be reapplied. This process iterates until sequential estimates of ρ do not vary significantly.

(A) Estimate ρ with this formula → $\rho = \dfrac{\Sigma e_t e_{t-1}}{\Sigma e_{t-1}^2}$

(B) Run GLS and obtain the new e_t's

(C) Go back to (A)

(D) Stop when sequential estimates of ρ do not vary by much

(4) Maximum Likelihood Procedure: Most statistical software packages estimate the parameters of GLS regressions using a maximum likelihood procedure. Basically, this procedure assigns initial values to $\hat{\beta}_0$, $\hat{\beta}_1$, and ρ, then considers the residuals from this GLS model. The pattern of the residuals indicates adjustments to the initial values of $\hat{\beta}_0$, $\hat{\beta}_1$, and ρ. The residuals from the adjusted GLS model are considered and used to make further adjustments to $\hat{\beta}_0$, $\hat{\beta}_1$, and ρ. The process stops when sequential estimates of $\hat{\beta}_0$, $\hat{\beta}_1$, and ρ do not vary significantly.

11.5 Final Thoughts

Regressions that are underspecified or in the wrong functional form often test positive for serial correlation. When this occurs it is known as pseudoautocorrelation; graphs and/or the Durbin-Watson test pick up autocorrelation, but this is due to the regression missing an important explanatory variable or being in the wrong functional form. Both of these mistakes have worse consequences than autocorrelation. If autocorrelation is detected and remedial measures are ineffective, it is most likely pseudoautocorrelation.

One of the main consequences of serial correlation is the biased residual statistics. Especially troublesome are the biased standard errors of the coefficients of the regression because hypothesis testing is hazardous under these circumstances.

The Newey-West technique we employed to cope with heteroskedasticity is applicable in cases of autocorrelation as well. The technique corrects the biased standard errors of the structural parameters and leaves the estimates themselves alone. This allows for hypothesis testing in the presence of serial correlation.

Terms

Autoregressive model – A regression that uses the lagged dependent variable as an explanatory variable.

Cochrane-Orcutt iterative procedure – A procedure to estimate ρ for a generalized least-squares regression.

Durbin-Watson test – A test for serial correlation.

First-order Markov scheme ($e_t = \rho\, e_{t-1} + \varepsilon_t$) – A common way in which the error terms from a regression can be related.

Generalized least-squares (GLS) – A regression using the generalized differences of the data.

Hidreth-Lu scanning procedure – A procedure to estimate ρ for a generalized least-squares regression.

Maximum likelihood procedure – A technique for estimating the structural parameters of an econometric model, such as a GLS model.

Newey-West technique – Formulas for the standard errors of the structural parameters of a regression that correct for the bias caused by serial correlation or heteroskedasticity.

Pseudoautocorrelation – When a regression tests positive for autocorrelation but the symptoms are due to underspecification or using the wrong functional form.

Second-order serial correlation ($e_t = \rho_1 e_{t-1} + \rho_2 e_{t-2} + \varepsilon_t$) – When the current error term is related to the two prior error terms.

Serial correlation (autocorrelation) – When the error terms from a regression are related to one another.

White noise – A normally distributed stochastic variable that has a mean of zero, constant standard error, and is independently distributed (i.e., free from serial correlation).

Chapter 11   Problems

1. Complete the following table:

Sample Size	k	d stat	Autocorrelation present?
20	2	0.83	
32	3	1.24	
45	4	1.98	
100	5	3.72	
150	7	1.71	

2. Complete the following table:

Sample Size	k	d stat	Autocorrelation present?
15	2	1.60	
25	3	1.80	
45	4	2.48	
100	6	2.72	
150	10	2.11	

3. Use the data in CONSUMP.XLS and statistical software to run the following regression:

$$RCONPC_t = \hat{\beta}_0 + \hat{\beta}_1 REALYDPC_t + e_t$$

A) Plot the error terms over time. Do you suspect serial correlation? Explain.
B) Plot the error terms against their lagged values. Do you suspect serial correlation? Explain.
C) Perform a Durbin-Watson test. Show the 5-step procedure.

4. Use the data in ANMACRO.XLS and statistical software to run the following regression:

$$m2/cpi_t = \hat{\beta}_0 + \hat{\beta}_1 ngdp/cpi_t + e_t$$

A) Plot the error terms over time. Do you suspect serial correlation? Explain.
B) Plot the error terms against their lagged values. Do you suspect serial correlation? Explain.
C) Perform a Durbin-Watson test. Show the 5-step procedure.

5. Use the data in CONSUMP.XLS and statistical software to run the regression:

$$RCONPC_t = \hat{\beta}_0 + \hat{\beta}_1 REALYDPC_t + \hat{\beta}_2 REALR_t + \hat{\beta}_3 CC_t + e_t$$

where   RCONPC = real consumer spending in the USA per capita
        REALYDPC = real disposable income per capita
        REALR = real interest rate on 1-year Treasury Bonds
        CC = University of Michigan Index of Consumer Confidence

A) Plot the residuals from the regression over time. Does this plot suggest serial correlation is present? Positive or negative? Explain.
B) Plot the residuals from the regression against their lagged values. Does this plot suggest serial correlation is present? Positive or negative? Explain.

C) Does the regression suffer from serial correlation? Show the 5-step procedure of the Durbin-Watson test.

D) Estimate ρ by regressing the residuals on their lagged values (no constant term). What is the estimate of ρ?

E) Check for second-order serial correlation. Do you think it is present? Explain.

F) Estimate ρ and correct for first-order serial correlation using GLS with maximum likelihood estimation. What is this estimate of ρ?

G) Did GLS remedy the serial correlation? Show the 5-step procedure.

H) Compare the t-ratios from the original regression and the GLS regression. Are you surprised by which ones turn out to be larger? Explain.

I) Apply the Newey-West technique to the original regression. Are you surprised at the new standard errors of the estimators? Explain.

6. Use the data in ANMACRO.XLS and statistical software to run a regression where the demand for money (m2) is explained by a constant term, income (ngdp), interest rates (aaa), and prices (cpi).

A) Plot the residuals from the regression over time. Does this plot suggest serial correlation is present? Positive or negative? Explain.

B) Plot the residuals from the regression against their lagged values. Does this plot suggest serial correlation is present? Positive or negative? Explain.

C) Does the regression suffer from serial correlation? Show the 5-step procedure of the Durbin-Watson test.

D) Estimate ρ by regressing the residuals on their lagged values (no constant term). What is the estimate of ρ?

E) Check for second-order serial correlation. Do you think it is present? Explain.

F) Estimate ρ and correct for first-order serial correlation using GLS with maximum likelihood estimation. What is this estimate of ρ?

G) Did GLS remedy the serial correlation? Show the 5-step procedure.

H) Compare the t-ratios from the original regression and the GLS regression. Are you surprised by which ones turn out to be larger? Explain.

I) Apply the Newey-West technique to the original regression. Are you surprised at the new standard errors of the estimators? Explain.

Test Yourself on Chapters 10 and 11

1. Describe the following procedures:
   A) Park test
   B) Weighted least-squares
   C) Generalized least-squares
   D) Cochrane-Orcutt iterative procedure
   E) Hildreth-Lu scanning procedure
   F) Maximum likelihood procedure

2. Draw a diagram indicative of heteroskedasticity. Label the horizontal axis "culprit" and be sure to correctly label the vertical axis. Draw a diagram indicative of negative serial correlation. Be sure to label the axes of your diagram.

3. Describe the pros and cons of any 3 remedies for heteroskedasticity.

4. What is a first-order Markov scheme? What is second-order serial correlation? What is "white noise"?

5. Does the White test below indicate heteroskedasticity? Show the 5-step procedure.

White Heteroskedasticity Test:

F-statistic	0.491592	Probability	0.780723
Obs*R-squared	2.645362	Probability	0.754462

Test Equation:
Dependent Variable: RESID^2
Method: Least Squares
Sample: 1 50
Included observations: 50

Variable	Coefficient	Std. Error	t-Statistic	Prob.
C	−275.2148	329.0460	−0.836402	0.4074
ED	18.22919	33.65147	0.541706	0.5908
ED^2	−0.211078	0.952250	−0.221662	0.8256
ED*EXPER	−0.453429	0.645192	−0.702781	0.4859
EXPER	16.12281	15.23650	1.058170	0.2958
EXPER^2	−0.236866	0.208270	−1.137306	0.2616
R-squared	0.052907	Mean dependent var		19.62276
Adjusted R-squared	−0.054717	S.D. dependent var		66.54024
S.E. of regression	68.33644	Akaike info criterion		11.39893
Sum squared resid	205474.2	Schwarz criterion		11.62837
Log likelihood	−278.9733	F-statistic		0.491592
Durbin-Watson stat	2.086374	Prob(F-statistic)		0.780723

6. Does the regression featured in the Eviews printout below suffer from autocorrelation according to a Durbin-Watson test at the 5% critical level? Show the 5-step procedure.

Dependent Variable: WHY
Method: Least Squares
Sample: 1956 1980
Included observations: 25

Variable	Coefficient	Std. Error	t-Statistic	Prob.
C	−0.325482	8.371100	−0.038882	0.9693
EX1	0.913309	0.032584	28.02956	0.0000
EX2	−0.558162	2.745564	−0.203296	0.8408

R-squared	0.997461	Mean dependent var	640.6560
Adjusted R-squared	0.997230	S.D. dependent var	173.4284
S.E. of regression	9.127571	Akaike info criterion	7.372643
Sum squared resid	1832.876	Schwarz criterion	7.518908
Log likelihood	−89.15804	F-statistic	4321.229
Durbin-Watson stat	1.655326	Prob(F-statistic)	0.000000

----

1) Ho: no positive auto   Ha: positive auto   1) Ho: no negative auto   Ha: negative auto
2) 5%   2) 5%
3) If $0 < d < d_L$, then reject Ho   3) If $4 - d_L < d < 4$, then reject Ho
   If $d_L < d < d_U$, then inconclusive   If $4 - d_U < d < 4 - d_L$, then inconclusive
4) get the numbers   4) get the numbers
5) reject or do not reject Ho   5) reject or do not reject Ho

Mark each of the following statements TRUE or FALSE.

1. The "culprit variable" is the dependent variable in a heteroskedastic regression.
2. Application of Newey-West technique will alter the estimate of the SER.
3. The standard error of the regression (SER) is biased downward in a regression suffering from heteroskedasticity.
4. $E[u_i^2] = E[u_j^2] = \sigma^2$ for all $i \neq j$ is the definition of homoskedasticity.
5. In the presence of heteroskedasticity, tests of significance must be carried out with caution since the T-ratios of the structural parameters are biased.
6. The standard error of $\hat{\beta}_1$ is biased downward in the presence of serial correlation.
7. The R-squared from a GLS regression is not directly comparable to the R-squared from the same regression run using OLS.
8. The standard error of the regression (SER) is biased downward in a regression suffering from serial correlation.
9. After correcting for autocorrelation, one would expect the standard errors of the structural parameters to increase.
10. After correcting for heteroskedasticity, one would expect the standard errors of the structural parameters to increase.

Chapter 12

Time-Series Models

12.1 Distributed Lag Models

A distributed lag model occurs when one or more of the independent variables is lagged one or more periods:

$$Y_t = \beta_0 + \beta_1 X_t + \beta_2 X_{t-1} + \beta_3 X_{t-2} + \beta_4 Z_t + \beta_5 Z_{t-1} + u_t$$

There are several justifications for using lagged explanatory variables. For instance, changes in the explanatory variable may take time to impact the dependent variable. Or it may be that the trend in the explanatory variable over several periods is what affects the dependent variable.

The Permanent Income Hypothesis (PIH) offers an interesting application of a distributed lag model. The PIH asserts that spending depends not on actual income but expected future income. It has been observed that spending (CON) is more smooth over time than disposable personal income (DPI). The explanation for this is that windfalls do not change expected future income, so CON remains relatively more stable than DPI.

In econometrics terms, the PIH predicts that CON is better explained by expected DPI (EXDPI) as opposed to actual DPI:

$$CON_t = \hat{\beta}_0 + \hat{\beta}_1 EXDPI_t + e_t$$

The difficulty is that EXDPI is hard to measure especially for aggregate data. One of the first attempts to approximate EXDPI was to use the pattern of past and current incomes:

$$CON_t = \hat{\beta}_0 + \hat{\beta}_1 DPI_t + \hat{\beta}_2 DPI_{t-1} + \hat{\beta}_3 DPI_{t-2} + \hat{\beta}_4 DPI_{t-3} + e_t$$

Here a distributed lag model is used as a proxy for expected future income. If the lagged values of DPI are significant, then the PIH is supported.

Multicollinearity is typically a problem in distributed lag models. The correlation coefficient between DPI and DPI_{t-1} is typically close to unity. And distributed lag models can use up degrees of freedom.

The Koyck model (Koyck 1954) is an ingenious way to employ a distributed lag model while avoiding these drawbacks.

Suppose current consumption is a weighted average of DPI going back many periods. The weights decline geometrically:

$$CON_t = \beta_0 + \beta_1 (DPI_t + \lambda DPI_{t-1} + \lambda^2 DPI_{t-2} + \lambda^3 DPI_{t-3} + \ldots + \lambda^{n-1} DPI_{t-n+1}) + u_t$$

Lag this equation one period and multiply by λ:

$$\lambda CON_{t-1} = \lambda\beta_0 + \beta_1(\lambda DPI_{t-1} + \lambda^2 DPI_{t-2} + \lambda^3 DPI_{t-3} + ... + \lambda^n DPI_{t-n}) + \lambda u_{t-1}$$

Subtract the second equation from the first and you are left with:

$$CON_t - \lambda CON_{t-1} = \beta_0 - \lambda\beta_0 + \beta_1 DPI_t + u_t - \lambda u_{t-1}$$

which can be rewritten:

$$CON_t = (1 - \lambda)\beta_0 + \beta_1 DPI_t + \lambda CON_{t-1} + \varepsilon_t; \text{ where } \varepsilon_t = u_t - \lambda u_{t-1}$$

This is a Koyck distributed lag model. It amounts to regressing CON on contemporaneous DPI and CON_{t-1}. A distributed lag of n periods is estimated with the loss of just one observation. Multicollinearity is usually reduced in the Koyck model compared to the regular distributed lag model.

The coefficient on CON_{t-1} is an estimate of the weight (λ). The short run impact of DPI on CON is equal to β_1. The long run impact is equal to $\beta_1/(1-\lambda)$.

Any model that includes some form of the dependent variable as an explanatory variable can be called "autoregressive." The Koyck model is one example of an autoregressive model. The Durbin-Watson statistic is invalid in autoregressive models; use Durbin's h instead (Durbin 1970).

$$h = (1 - \frac{d}{2})\sqrt{\frac{n}{1 - n(\text{var}(\hat{\beta}))}}$$

1) Ho: no autocorrelation Ha: auto present
2) 5%
3) If $|h| > tc$, then reject Ho (d.f. = n–k)
4) Calculate h and get tc
5) Reject or do not reject Ho

Durbin's h is undefined if $n(\text{var}(\hat{\beta})) > 1$. In this case, the Lagrange Multiplier test may be used to test for serial correlation (Breusch 1978 and Godfrey 1978).

If $Y_t = \beta_0 + \beta_1 X_t + \beta_2 Y_{t-1} + u_t$ is suspected of suffering from serial correlation:

Run: $u_t = \alpha_0 + \alpha_1 X_t + \alpha_2 Y_{t-1} + \alpha_3 u_{t-1} + \gamma_t$

1) Ho: no serial correlation   Ha: serial correlation exists
2) 5%
3) If $nR^2 > \chi c$, then reject Ho (d.f. = k (from the auxiliary regression) – 1)

4) Calculate nR^2 and χc
5) Reject or do not reject Ho

Serial correlation has more serious consequences in autoregressive models and it is tricky to remedy. If an autoregressive model suffers from serial correlation then the structural parameters are biased as well as the residual statistics.

Remedies include respecifying the model. Maybe pseudoautocorrelation is the real problem. Instrumental variables and two-stage least squares are other possibilities, but we will not discuss these here.

12.2 Granger Tests

Often in time-series analysis, it pays to know if changes in one variable generally occur before changes in another variable. For instance, it would be hard to argue that inflation causes the FED to slow money growth when changes in the inflation rate do not consistently precede changes in the money supply.

Granger (1969) has developed a test to determine precedence in time-series data. In order to determine if changes in inflation rates precede changes in the money supply, run the following regression where M is the money supply and INFL is the inflation rate:

$$M_t = \hat{\beta}_0 + \hat{\beta}_1 M_{t-1} + \hat{\beta}_2 M_{t-2} + \hat{\beta}_3 INFL_{t-1} + \hat{\beta}_4 INFL_{t-2} + e_t$$

$\hat{\beta}_3$ and/or $\hat{\beta}_4$ will be statistically significant if changes in inflation do indeed precede changes in the money supply. The test for this is as follows:

1) Ho: $\hat{\beta}_3$ and $\hat{\beta}_4 = 0$; INFL does not precede M

   Ha: $\hat{\beta}_3$ and/or $\hat{\beta}_4 \neq 0$; INFL precedes M

$$F = \frac{(SSR_R - SSR)/R}{SSR/(n-k)}$$

2) 5%
3) If $F > F^C$, Reject Ho
4) 0.83 vs 3.32 (d.f. num. = R = 2; d.f. den. = n – k = 40 – 5 = 35)
5) Do Not Reject Ho → changes in INFL do not precede changes in M

Thus, we can conclude that changes in the inflation rate do not precede changes in the money supply. Regardless of how this test turned out, it is advisable to conduct the reverse Granger test as well by running the following regression:

$$INFL_t = \hat{\beta}_0 + \hat{\beta}_1 INFL_{t-1} + \hat{\beta}_2 INFL_{t-2} + \hat{\beta}_3 M_{t-1} + \hat{\beta}_4 M_{t-2} + e_t$$

And then perform the following 5-step procedure:

1) Ho: $\hat{\beta}_3$ and $\hat{\beta}_4 = 0$; M does not precede INFL

   Ha: $\hat{\beta}_3$ and/or $\hat{\beta}_4 \neq 0$; M precedes INFL

$$F = \frac{(SSR_R - SSR)/R}{SSR/(n-k)}$$

2) 5%

3) If $F > F^C$, Reject Ho
4) 2.58 vs 3.32 (d.f. num. = R = 2; d.f. den. = n – k = 40 – 5 = 35)
5) Do Not Reject Ho → changes in M do not precede changes in INFL

The results of this reverse test are a shocker since most economists think that inflation is most often the result of growth in the money supply. Perhaps we should only be lagging the dependent variables one period instead of two. The number of lags to use is left to the discretion of the researcher.

Even had we found that changes in the money supply precede changes in the inflation rate, we could not conclude that changes in the money supply CAUSE changes in inflation. Precedence does not necessarily imply causation. One observes many umbrellas being carried by pedestrians before a rainstorm, but surely those umbrellas do not cause the rain.

From the tests above we conclude that INFL does not "Granger-cause" M and M does not "Granger-cause" INFL.

Granger tests are useful to test for reverse-causality. Recall that the structural parameters in the following regression will be biased if Y has an impact on X1:

$$Y_t = \beta_0 + \beta_1 X1_t + u_t$$

In regression analysis, it is critical that changes in the explanatory variable (X1) cause changes in the dependent variable (Y). However, if Y impacts X1 we have a case of reverse causality. In such a case, it can be shown that the error terms (u_t) are correlated with X1. This violates assumption 1 of the Classical Linear Regression Model (the independent variable(s) is (are) predetermined or at least not correlated with the error term: $E[u_i X_i] = 0$) and the structural parameters will be biased.

12.3 Spurious Correlation and Nonstationarity

Spurious correlation is a strong relationship between variables that is the result of a statistical fluke, not an underlying causal relationship. This occurs often with economic data because economic variables have a tendency to grow over time. Thus, variables that are not causally related have high correlation coefficients anyway.

As an example, the correlation coefficient between the money supply (M2) and per capita milk consumption in the United States is –.95. Yet it is highly unlikely that increases in the money supply cause people to consume less milk. The correlation between the two is merely coincidental.

As you can imagine, spurious correlations are common with time-series data since so many variables exhibit long-term growth trends. Special care must be taken when working with trended data because regression results can be biased as a result of spurious correlations.
In the best circumstances, time-series regressions will use only stationary data—time-series whose basic properties do not change over time. Specifically, a time-series, X, is said to be stationary if:

1. the mean of X is constant over time
2. the variance of X is constant over time
3. the correlation between X_t and X_{t-k} (for all k) is constant

If one or more of these properties is not met, then X is nonstationary. The use of nonstationary time-series in regressions may result in spurious correlation and that means biased estimates of the structural parameters.

The graph below shows real GDP (rgdp) over the years since 1945. This time-series exhibits a pronounced upward trend and therefore cannot have a constant mean.

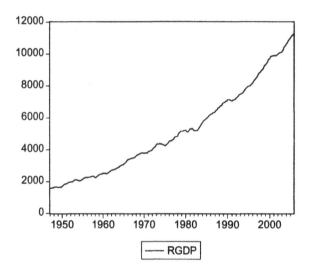

Whether or not the variance of rgdp is constant over time is difficult to tell from visual inspection. We could take the variance of the first half of the time-series and compare it to the variance of the second half.

There is no way to tell from visual inspection whether or not observations a given distance apart have a constant correlation. Checking the correlation between X_t and X_{t-k} requires a correlogram – a chart that shows the degree to which observations k spaces apart are correlated. Correlograms that do not approach zero quickly indicate nonstationary data.

It is quite tedious to obtain a correlogram by hand and we are glad to have computers do this for us. Given time-series data such as rgdp, take each pair of observations that are adjacent. This means taking the first and second observation, the second and third, the third and fourth, and so on. Now calculate the correlation coefficient (r) between all these pairs.

We are just getting started. Now take observations of rgdp that are a space apart. These are observations one and three, two and four, three, and five, and so on. Now calculate the correlation coefficient (r) between all these pairs. Repeat this for all pairs of observations up to 12 spaces apart (k = 12).

k	r
1	0.99
2	0.97
3	0.96
4	0.94
5	0.93
6	0.91
7	0.9
8	0.89
9	0.87
10	0.86
11	0.85
12	0.83

The table above indicates that adjacent observations in rgdp are highly correlated (r = 0.99). Even observations twelve years ago are highly correlated with this year's level of rgdp (r = 0.83). If we make a chart from the table above, we have a correlogram:

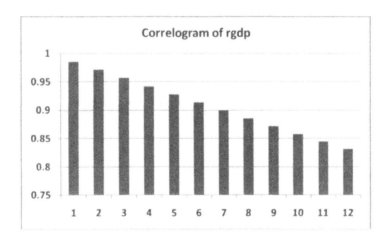

The vertical axis of the correlogram reports the correlation coefficients from the table, while the horizontal axis measures k. Correlograms that do not quickly decay toward r = 0, such as the one above, are typical of nonstationary time-series. Regressions that use nonstationary data will probably suffer from spurious correlation and yield biased results.

If a time-series is nonstationary, then it may be best to work with the first-differences of the data. First-differences are the change from one period to the next in the data series. The graphs below depict the first differences in rgdp (FD1RGDP):

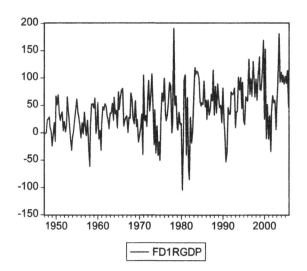

Visual inspection suggests a constant mean (perhaps), but it appears as if the latter half of the line has a larger variance than the first half. It is a tough call. The correlogram suggests significant correlations between observations at k = 1 through 4. In other words, the first differences in rgdp may be stationary since the correlations become insignificant after four lags.

k	r
1	0.42
2	0.38
3	0.21
4	0.20
5	0.11
6	0.13
7	0.07
8	0.02
9	0.14
10	0.11
11	0.10
12	-0.04

The second differences in rgdp (FD2RGDP) are the differences in the first-differences, or the change in the change, in rgdp.

The correlogram suggests that the second differences are stationary since they become insignificant after k = 1.

k	r
1	-0.47
2	0.12
3	-0.14
4	0.08
5	-0.11
6	0.07
7	-0.01
8	-0.15
9	0.14
10	-0.02
11	0.12
12	-0.18

It appears as if any regressions that use rgdp are using a nonstationary variable. This is a serious allegation because the results of any such regressions may be biased. It would be better to use the first-differences in rgdp since they appear to be stationary according to a check of the correlogram.

The premier test for stationarity is the Dickey-Fuller, or Unit Root, test (Dickey and Fuller 1979) To test if a time-series, X_t, is stationary:

a) run $(X_t - X_{t-1}) = \hat{\beta}_0 + \hat{\beta}_1 X_{t-1} + e_t$

b) perform a negative sign test on $\hat{\beta}_1$

1) Ho: $\hat{\beta}_1 = 0$ (X is nonstationary)   Ha: $\hat{\beta}_1 < 0$ (X is stationary)
2) 5%
3) If t-ratio $< -t^c*$, reject Ho
4) The t-ratio is the usual one, but t^c* is about 60% higher than tc from the usual t table. As n approaches infinity t^c* approaches 2.86 from higher levels.
5) state the results of the test

Using the data on rgdp as an example, we have:

a) $(rgdp_t - rgdp_{t-1}) = 25.92 + 0.03\ rgdp_{t-1} + e_t$
$$(5.72) \leftarrow t\text{–ratio}$$

b) negative sign test on $\hat{\beta}_1$:

1) Ho: $\hat{\beta}_1 = 0$ (X is nonstationary)   Ha: $\hat{\beta}_1 < 0$ (X is stationary)
2) 5%
3) If $5.72 < -2.91*$, reject Ho
4) Eviews gives the t^c for the Dickey-Fuller test
5) Do not reject Ho: rgdp is nonstationary

Now let's test if the first differences in rgdp are stationary:

a) $(d(rgdp_t) - d(rgdp)_{t-1}) = 90.68 - 0.51\ d(rgdp)_{t-1} + e_t$
$$(-4.31) \leftarrow t\text{–ratio}$$

b) negative sign test on $\hat{\beta}_1$:

1) Ho: $\hat{\beta}_1 = 0$ (X is nonstationary)   Ha: $\hat{\beta}_1 < 0$ (X is stationary)
2) 5%
3) If $-4.31 < -2.91*$, reject Ho
4) Eviews gives the t^c for the Dickey-Fuller test
5) Reject Ho: the first differences in rgdp are stationary

The augmented Dickey-Fuller test for a unit root (i.e., nonstationarity) adds a lagged dependent variable to the right-hand side:

$$(X_t - X_{t-1}) = \hat{\beta}_0 + \hat{\beta}_1 X_{t-1} + \hat{\beta}_2 (X_{t-1} - X_{t-2}) + e_t$$

It is left to the reader as an exercise to determine if the augmented Dickey-Fuller test gives the same results concerning the stationarity of rgdp and the first differences of rgdp.

If you discover that one or more of the time-series variables you are working with are nonstationary, then you might take first or second differences in order to avoid spurious correlation. However, it is unnecessary to difference nonstationary variables in a regression when they are cointegrated. Cointegrated variables are nonstationary to the same degree.
Suppose you are interested in this regression:

$$Y_t = \hat{\beta}_0 + \hat{\beta}_1 X_t + e_t$$

Suppose X and Y are both nonstationary so that the regression may suffer from spurious correlation. Further suppose that their first differences are stationary. To determine if X and Y are cointegrated, apply a Dickey-Fuller test to e_t:

a) Run the regression: $Y_t = \hat{\beta}_0 + \hat{\beta}_1 X_t + e_t$

b) Run the Dickey-Fuller regression: $(e_t - e_{t-1}) = \hat{\beta}_0 + \hat{\beta}_1 e_{t-1} + z_t$

c) perform a negative sign test on $\hat{\beta}_1$:

1) Ho: $\hat{\beta}_1 = 0$ (e_t is nonstationary)   Ha: $\hat{\beta}_1 < 0$ (e_t is stationary)
   (X and Y are not cointegrated)   (X and Y are cointegrated)
2) 5%
3) If t-ratio $< -tc^*$, reject Ho
4) the t-ratio is the usual one, but tc* is about 60% higher than tc from the usual t-table. As n approaches infinity, tc* approaches 2.86 from higher levels.
5) state the results of the test

Cointegrated variables can be used "as is" in regressions without concern for spurious correlation.

As an example, let's check a regression where the demand for money (m2) is explained by a constant term, income (ngdp), interest rates (aaa), and prices (cpi):

$$m2_t = \hat{\beta}_0 + \hat{\beta}_1 ngdp_t + \hat{\beta}_2 aaa_t + \hat{\beta}_3 cpi_t + e_t$$

Certainly m2, ngdp, and cpi are nonstationary since they exhibit obvious upward trends. Unit root tests indicate that all 4 variables are nonstationary in their levels. In addition, all four variables require second differencing in order to pass augmented Dickey-Fuller tests for stationarity. To check if the variables in this regression are cointegrated we apply an augmented Dickey-Fuller test to e_t by running the following regression:

$$(e_t - e_{t-1}) = \hat{\beta}_0 + \hat{\beta}_1 e_{t-1} + \hat{\beta}_2 (e_{t-1} - e_{t-2}) + z_t$$

And then applying a negative sign test to $\hat{\beta}_1$:

1) Ho: $\hat{\beta}_1 = 0$ (e_t is nonstationary)   Ha: $\hat{\beta}_1 < 0$ (e_t is stationary)
   (X and Y are not cointegrated)   (X and Y are cointegrated)
2) 5%
3) If $-2.84 < -2.94$, reject Ho
4) Eviews provides the t^c for this test.
5) Do not Reject Ho $\rightarrow$ the variables are not cointegrated.

It is close, but at the 5 percent critical level the variables in the regression are not cointegrated. It would be best to take second differences of all four time-series before running the regression in order to scrupulously avoid spurious correlation.

Terms

Autoregressive model – A regression that uses the lagged dependent variable as an independent variable.

Cointegrated variables – When the time-series in a regression are nonstationary to the same degree.

Correlogram – A chart that shows the degree to which observations k spaces apart are correlated.

Distributed lag model – A regression that lags one or more independent variables one or more times.

First-differences – The change from one period to the next in a time-series.

Koyck model – An autoregressive model used to mimic a distributed lag model with declining weights.

Second-differences – The change in the change of a time-series.

Spurious correlation –A strong relationship between variables that is the result of a statistical fluke, not an underlying causal relationship.

Stationary variable – A time-series with constant mean, variance and correlation between observations any given distance apart.

Chapter 12   Problems

1. Consider the following regression:

$$M_t = 2.00 - 0.10\,R_t + 0.70\,Y_t + 0.60\,M_{t-1} + e_t$$
$$(0.10) \qquad (0.35) \qquad (0.10) \qquad \leftarrow \text{standard errors}$$

$$R^2 = .9 \qquad\qquad DW = 1.80 \qquad\qquad n = 26$$

Where M is the demand for M1
    R is the interest rate on 10-year Treasuries
    Y is national income

A) Do the variables attain their expected signs?
B) Test for serial correlation in this regression. Show the 5-step procedure.
C) What is the short-run impact of a change in the interest rate on money demand?
D) What is the long-run impact?

2. Use the data in CONS.XLS and statistical software to run regressions of the following sort:

$$cons_t = \hat{\beta}_0 + \hat{\beta}_1 dpi_t + \hat{\beta}_2 dpi_{t-1} + \hat{\beta}_3 dpi_{t-2} + \hat{\beta}_4 dpi_{t-3} + ... + e_t$$

cons – the change in real consumer spending
dpi – the change in real disposable income

A) What lag length seems to be appropriate? Explain.
B) Is multicollinearity a problem in the regression with the appropriate lag length? Explain.
C) Run the Koyck version of this distributed lag model. What is the short-run impact of a change in disposable income on consumer spending?
D) What is the long-run impact?

3. Use the data in QLEISCOIN.XLS and statistical software to do the following problems.

COIN = percentage change in the composite index of coincident economic indicators
LEIS = percentage change in the composite index of leading economic indicators

A) Run a regression to determine if COIN is affected by LEIS and LEIS lagged 1 through 8 quarters. Do you think LEIS 8 quarters ago helps predict COIN this quarter? Explain.
B) How many lags of the LEIS should be used to explain COIN? Explain how you came to this conclusion.
C) Does the regression you settled on in B) above suffer from serial correlation according to the Durbin-Watson test? Show the 5-step procedure.
D) Does the regression you settled on in B) above suffer from serial correlation according to the Lagrange Multiplier test? Show the 5-step procedure.
E) Does the regression you settled on in B) above suffer from multicollinearity? On what do you base your response?

F) Employ a Koyck lag structure in the COIN/LEIS regression. Does this regression suffer from serial correlation according to the h test? Show the 5-step procedure.

G) Employ a Koyck lag structure in the COIN/LEIS regression. Does this regression suffer from serial correlation according to the Lagrange Multiplier test? Show the 5-step procedure.

H) Employ a Koyck lag structure in the COIN/LEIS regression. Does this regression suffer from multicollinearity? On what do you base your response?

I) According to the Koyck model, a 1 unit increase in LEIS implies COIN will be how much higher or lower in the short run?

J) In the long run the 1 unit increase in LEIS implies COIN will eventually change how much?

4. Use the data in MACRO.XLS and statistical software to determine if changes in real disposable personal income (RDPI) precede changes in real consumer spending (RCONS) or visa versa; use lag lengths of 8 for both variables.

A) Do you reject the null hypothesis that RDPI does not precede RCONS at the 5% critical level?

B) Would you reject the null hypothesis that RDPI does not precede RCONS at the 10% critical level? Explain.

C) Do you reject the null hypothesis that RCONS does not precede RDPI at the 5% critical level?

D) Would you reject the null hypothesis that RCONS does not precede RDPI at the 10% critical level? Explain.

5. Use the data in QLEISCOIN and statistical software to do Granger tests to determine if changes in the leading economic indicators (LEIS) precede changes in the coincident indicators (COIN).

A) Using lag lengths of 6, show the 5-step procedure for the Granger test to prove that changes in LEIS do not precede changes in COIN.

B) Using lag lengths of 6, show the 5-step procedure for the Granger test to prove that changes in COIN do not precede changes in LEIS.

C) Given your results in A) and B) above, can you unequivocally conclude that changes in LEIS precede changes in COIN?

D) Does your answer to C) above change when lag lengths of 10 are used?

E) Does your answer to C) above change when lag lengths of 12 are used?

6. Use the data in MACRO.XLS and statistical software to run Granger tests to determine if reverse causality is a problem in the following regression:

$$RGDP_t = \hat{\beta}_0 + \hat{\beta}_1 RINV_t + e_t$$

where RGDP is real GDP and RINV is real business spending on plant and equipment.

Is reverse causality a problem in the regression above? On what do you base your response?

7. Use the data in MACRO.XLS and statistical software to run Granger tests to determine if changes in M2 Granger-cause INFL or visa-versa.

   A) What are the appropriate lag lengths? Explain.
   B) What do you conclude? Explain.

8. Which of the following sets of variables are most likely to suffer from spurious correlation?

   A) The population of America and Dow Jones Industrial average
   B) GDP and the unemployment rate
   C) The inflation rate and government expenditures
   D) The change in the money supply and the federal funds rate

9. Using the data in MACRO.XLS and statistical software, which of the following variables appear to be nonstationary because of nonconstant means or nonconstant variances? Produce the graph for each variable and say if the problem is a nonconstant mean or variance, both, or neither.

   A) Real investment (rinv)
   B) The first difference in real investment
   C) The second difference in real investment
   D) The first difference in the money supply (m2)
   E) Interest rate on AAA corporate bonds (aaa)

10. Which variables from the list above appear to be nonstationary based on their autocorrelation functions? Produce the autocorrelation function for each variable and indicate if a variable is stationary, nonstationary, or questionable.

11. Which variables from the list above are nonstationary according to the Dickey-Fuller test? Show the 5-step procedure for each variable.

12. Use the data in RGDP.XLS to apply the augmented Dickey-Fuller test to real GDP (rgdp) and the first differences in rgdp. Show the 5-step procedure for each test.

13. Use the data in AJ.XLS to replicate the famous Andersen-Jordan study by regressing a constant term, lagged money supply (m2) and the lagged standardized federal deficit (fp) on nominal GDP (ngdp): $ngdp_t = \hat{\beta}_0 + \hat{\beta}_1 m2_{t-1} + \hat{\beta}_2 fp_{t-1} + e_t$

   A) Which explanatory variable has the more profound impact on nominal GDP? Explain your response.
   B) Which variables in the regression are nonstationary? Explain.
   C) Check for cointegration among the variables in the regression. Show the 5-step Dickey-Fuller procedure.

Test Yourself on Chapter 12

1. Given:

```
Dependent Variable: WHY
Method: Least Squares
Sample(adjusted): 1960 2001
Included observations: 42 after adjusting endpoints
```

Variable	Coefficient	Std. Error	t-Statistic	Prob.
C	−179.2567	163.7257	−1.094860	0.2803
EX	0.259430	0.091487	2.835696	0.0072
WHY(−1)	0.739760	0.198066	3.734916	0.0034

R-squared	0.997038	Mean dependent var	14665.26
Adjusted R-squared	0.996886	S.D. dependent var	4023.018
S.E. of regression	224.5044	Akaike info criterion	13.73442
Sum squared resid	1965686.	Schwarz criterion	13.85854
Log likelihood	−285.4227	F-statistic	6563.263
Durbin-Watson stat	0.866017	Prob(F-statistic)	0.000000

A) What is the short-run impact of EX on WHY?

B) What is the long-run impact of EX on WHY?

C) Does this regression suffer from serial correlation according to Durbin's h-test? Show the 5-step procedure.

D) Does this regression suffer from serial correlation according to the Lagrange multiplier test? Show the 5-step procedure.

$$h = (1 - \frac{d}{2})\sqrt{\frac{n}{1 - n(\text{var}(\hat{\beta}))}}$$

```
Breusch-Godfrey Serial Correlation LM Test:
```

F-statistic	20.57279	Probability	0.000056
Obs*R-squared	14.75185	Probability	0.000123

```
Test Equation:
Dependent Variable: RESID
Method: Least Squares
Date: 02/26/03   Time: 15:29
Presample missing value lagged residuals set to zero.
```

Variable	Coefficient	Std. Error	t-Statistic	Prob.
C	-93.87846	135.1921	-0.694408	0.4917
EX	0.104824	0.078148	1.341348	0.1878
WHY(-1)	-0.113005	0.083810	-1.348355	0.1855
RESID(-1)	0.622442	0.137231	4.535724	0.0001

E) Suppose the regression does suffer from serial correlation. What is the major consequence?

2. A) Using lags of two periods on both independent variables, write the Granger equation to test if the chicken came before the egg.

B) Given the Eviews printout that follows, did the chicken come before the egg? Explain how you know.

Pairwise Granger Causality Tests
Sample: 1951 1994
Lags: 2

Null Hypothesis:	Obs	F-Statistic	Probability
CHICK does not Granger Cause EGG	42	0.09849	0.04644
EGG does not Granger Cause CHICK		12.55461	0.17900

3. Are the first differences of M1 (FDM1) stationary? Using the Eviews printout below, show the 5-step procedure.

ADF Test Statistic	−0.615077	1% Critical Value*	−3.7667
		5% Critical Value	−3.0038
		10% Critical Value	−2.6417

Unit root test on FDM1.

4. A) List the three conditions for a variable to be stationary.
   B) What is spurious correlation?

5. A) What is "Granger causality"?
   B) What is the consequence of a dependent variable "Granger causing" an independent variable in the regression?

6. A) What is the permanent income hypothesis?
   B) Write the Koyck model that was used to test the permanent income hypothesis and explain why this regression is a test of the hypothesis.

7. A) Explain why two nonstationary time series are likely to be spuriously correlated.
   B) What is the consequence of using nonstationary variables in a regression?

8. A) Write the Granger regression to determine if changes in A precede changes in B. Assume lags of 2 periods.
   B) Why is it important to do the reverse Granger test before concluding that changes in A precede changes in B.

9. A) Draw the correlogram (autocorrelation function) of a stationary variable. (Be sure to label the axes of your drawing.)
   B) Draw the correlogram (autocorrelation function) of a nonstationary variable.

10. A) What is cointegration?
    B) Given $Y_t = Bo + B1 X_t + e_t$ describe how to determine if Y and X are cointegrated. Spell out the Dickey-Fuller regression involved.

References

Andersen, Leonall C. and Jerry L. Jordan. 1969. "Monetary and Fiscal Actions: A Test of Their Relative Importance in Economic Stabilization." *Federal Reserve Bank of St. Louis Review* 51(4): 12–16.

Breusch, T. S. 1978. "Testing for Autocorrelation in Dynamic Linear Models." *Australian Economic Papers*, 17: 334–355.

Caudill, Steven. 1990. "Econometrics in Theory and Practice." *Eastern Economic Journal* 16(3): 249–256.

Dasgupta, S.; B. Laplante; H. Wang; and D. Wheeler. 2002. "Confronting the Environmental Kuznets Curve." *The Journal of Economic Perspectives* 16(1): 147–168.

Dickey, D.A. and W.A. Fuller. 1979. "Distribution of the Estimators for Autoregressive Time Series with a Unit Root." *Journal of the American Statistical Association* 74: 427–431.

Durbin, J. 1970. "Testing for Serial Correlation in Least-Squares Regression When Some of the Regressors Are Lagged Dependent Variables." *Econometrica* 38: 410–421.

Durbin, J. and G.S. Watson. 1951. "Testing for Serial Correlation in Least-Squares Regression." *Biometrika* 38: 159–177.

Godfrey, L.G. 1978. "Testing against General Autoregressive and Moving Average Error Models When the Regressors include Lagged Dependent Variables." *Econometrica* 46: 1293–1302.

Granger, C.W.J. 1969. "Investigating Causal Relations by Econometric Models and Cross-Spectral Methods." *Econometrica* 37: 24–36.

Keynes, John Maynard. 1936. *The General Theory of Employment, Interest, and Money*. New York, NY: Macmillan.

Koyck, L.M. 1954. *Distributed Lags and Investment Analysis*. Amsterdam: North-Holland Publishing Company.

Leamer, Edward. 1983. "Let's Take the Con Out of Econometrics." *American Economic Review* 73(1): 31–43.

Levitt, Steven D. and Stephen J. Dubner. 2009. *Freakonomics: A Rogue Economist Explores the Hidden Side of Everything.* New York, NY: Harper Perennial.

Marshall, Alfred. 1890. *Principles of Economics.* London: Macmillan and Co., Ltd.

Newey, W.K. and K.D. West. 1987. "A Simple, Positive Semi-Definite, Heteroskedasticity and Autocorrelation Consistent Covariance Matrix." *Econometrica* 55(3): 703–708.

Okun, Arthur M. 1962. "Potential GNP: Its Measurement and Significance." *Proceedings of the Business and Economic Statistics Section of the American Statistical Association,* 89–104.

Park, R.E. 1966. "Estimation with Heteroscedastic Error Terms." *Econometrica* 34(4): 888.

Ramsey, J.B. 1969. "Tests of Specification Errors in Classical Linear Least Squares Regression Analysis." *Journal of the Royal Statistical Society, Series B* 31: 350–371.

Spector, Lee C. and Michael Mazzeo. 1980. "Probit Analysis and Economic Education." *Journal of Economic Education* 11(2): 37–44.

Theil, Henri. 1971. *Principles of Econometrics.* New York, NY: Wiley.

White, H. 1980. "A Heteroskedasticity Consistent Covariance Matrix Estimator and a Direct Test of Heteroskedasticity." *Econometrica* 48(4): 817–818.

Solutions to Odd End-of-Chapter Problems

1. The hours of study (per weekday) and GPA of three students are given below:

hours	GPA
2	2
4	3
2	3

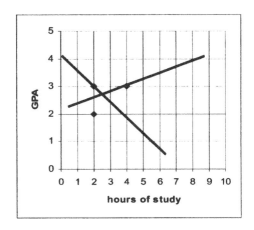

A) Draw two lines through these dots so that the sum of the vertical distances from the dots to the line equals zero. When the dot lies above the line the distance is positive. When the dot lies below the line the distance is negative. **Any line (except perfectly vertical) passing through hours = 2.67 and GPA = 2.67 works. Two such lines are pictured above.**

B) Now draw two lines through the dots so that the sum of the absolute value of the vertical distances between the dots and the line is minimized. **The minimum is one. Any line passing thru GPA = 3 and study hours = 4 and in between the two lines shown will yield this minimum.**

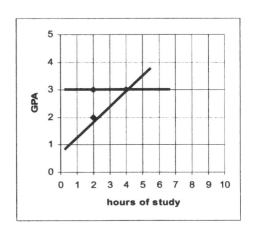

3. Suppose we estimate the following regression: CONS = –1218 + 0.97 DPI + u

A) What is the predicted value of CONS in 1960 given DPI = \$9,735 in 1960?

$$CONS = -1218 + 0.97 \ (9{,}735) = \$8{,}224.95$$

B) Actual CONS in 1960 equals \$8,837. Give several reasons why the forecast may be off from the actual.

   1) Important explanatory variables may be excluded from the analysis.
   2) The relationship bewteen CONS and DPI may have some randomness.
   3) The data may contain errors.
   4) Minor or immeasurable variables may be excluded from the analysis.

5. A) Specify an econometric model to test the theory that an increase in the money supply has no effect on real GDP.

$$RealGDP = \beta_0 + \beta_1 \ MS + u$$

B) What does this theory imply about the value of β_1?

$$\beta_1 = 0.$$

Chapter 2   Odd Problem Solutions

1. Which of the following is (are) NOT correct?

   A) $Y_i = \beta_0 + \beta_1 X_i + e_i$ D) $Y_i = \hat{\beta}_0 + \hat{\beta}_1 X_i + e_i$ G) $Y_i = \beta_0 + \beta_1 X_i$

   B) $\hat{Y}_i = \beta_0 + \beta_1 X_i + e_i$ E) $\hat{Y}_i = \hat{\beta}_0 + \hat{\beta}_1 X_i + e_i$ H) $\hat{Y}_i = \beta_0 + \beta_1 X_i + u_i$

   C) $Y_i = \beta_0 + \beta_1 X_i + u_i$ F) $Y_i = \hat{\beta}_0 + \hat{\beta}_1 X_i + u_i$ I) $E(Yi|Xi) = \hat{\beta}_0 + \hat{\beta}_1 X_i + e_i$

ABEFGHI

3. The savings and number of children of four families are given below:

sav	child
0.03	2
0.874	2
0.374	0
1.2	1

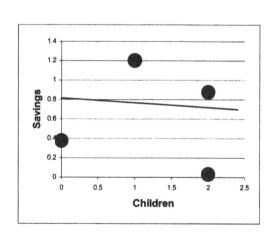

A) Calculate the values of $\hat{\beta}_0$ and $\hat{\beta}_1$ so that Σe_i^2 is minimized for

$sav_i = \hat{\beta}_0 + \hat{\beta}_1\ child_i + e_i$

B) Interpret the values you obtained.
C) Sketch your line in the graph.

SAVING	CHILD	Xi – X	(Xi – X) Yi	(Xi – X)2		
0.03	2	0.75	0.02	0.56	B1 =	–0.03
0.874	2	0.75	0.66	0.56		
0.374	0	–1.25	–0.47	1.56		
1.2	1	–0.25	–0.30	0.06	B0 =	0.66
0.62	1.25		–0.09	2.75		

Xi squared	$\hat{Y}_i$	$Y_i - \hat{Y}_1$	ei squared	(Yi – Y)2
4.00	0.60	–0.57	0.32	0.35
4.00	0.60	0.28	0.08	0.06
0.00	0.66	–0.29	0.08	0.06
1.00	0.63	0.57	0.33	0.34
9		0	0.81	0.81

C) Bo: If CHILD = 0, then SAV is expected to be 0.66 units
B1: If CHILD increases by 1 unit then SAV is expected to decrease by .03 units.

5. Calculate the values of the structural parameters for a regression of X on Y given:

Y	X
1.8	2
1.7	5
1.5	-2
0.6	5
25.4	6

Bo = 1.32
B1 = 1.53

7. Prove $\dfrac{\Sigma Y_i X_i - \bar{Y}\Sigma X_i}{\Sigma X_i^2 - \bar{X}\Sigma X_i} = \dfrac{\Sigma(X_i - \bar{X})(Y_i - \bar{Y})}{\Sigma(X_i - \bar{X})^2}$

Starting with the numerator of the second term, foil it out:

[Solution:]

$$\Sigma(X_i - \bar{X})(Y_i - \bar{Y}) = \Sigma(X_i Y_i - X_i \bar{Y} - \bar{X} Y_i + \bar{X}\bar{Y}) = \Sigma X_i Y_i - \bar{Y}\Sigma X_i - \bar{X}\Sigma Y_i + n\bar{X}\bar{Y}$$

The last two terms are equivalent and will cancel since one is negative and one is positive leaving:

$$\Sigma X_i Y_i - \overline{Y}\Sigma X_i$$

To prove that the two denominators are equal, foil out the denominator of the second term:

$$\Sigma(X_i - \overline{X})(X_i - \overline{X}) = \Sigma(X_i X_i - X_i\overline{X} - \overline{X}X_i + \overline{X}\overline{X}) = \Sigma X_i^2 - \overline{X}\Sigma X_i - \overline{X}\Sigma X_i + n\overline{X}\overline{X}$$

The last two terms are equivalent and will cancel since one is negative and one is positive leaving:

$$\Sigma X_i^2 - \overline{X}\Sigma X_i$$

9. Prove that $\Sigma e_i X_i = 0$ for the ordinary least-squares regression line.

Substitute in for the e_i and foil:

$$\Sigma e_i = \Sigma(Y_i - \hat{\beta}_0 - \hat{\beta}_1 X_i)X_i = \Sigma Y_i X_i - \hat{\beta}_0\Sigma X_i - \hat{\beta}_1\Sigma X_i^2$$

Sustitute in for $\hat{\beta}_0$ and distribute:

$$\Sigma Y_i X_i - (\overline{Y} - \hat{\beta}_1\overline{X})\Sigma X_i - \hat{\beta}_1\Sigma X_i^2 = \Sigma Y_i X_i - \overline{Y}\Sigma X_i - \hat{\beta}_1\overline{X}\Sigma X_i - \hat{\beta}_1\Sigma X_i^2$$

Combine the last two terms:

$$\Sigma Y_i X_i - \overline{Y}\Sigma X_i - \hat{\beta}_1(\Sigma X_i^2 - \overline{X}\Sigma X_i)$$

Divide through by $(\Sigma X_i^2 - \overline{X}\Sigma X_i)$:

$$\frac{\Sigma Y_i X_i - \overline{Y}\Sigma X_i - \hat{\beta}_1(\Sigma X_i^2 - \overline{X}\Sigma X_i)}{\Sigma X_i^2 - \overline{X}\Sigma X_i}$$

Notice that the first two terms in the numerator over the denominator $= \hat{\beta}_1$.

And the last term in the numerator over the denominator $= -\hat{\beta}_1$. So that this entire expression $= 0$.

Chapter 3   Odd Problem Solutions

1.A)   Calculate the values of the structural parameters for a regression of X on Y given:

Y	X
1.8	2
1.7	5
1.5	−2
0.6	5
25.4	6

$$\hat{\beta}_1 = 1.5$$

$$\hat{\beta}_0 = 1.3$$

B) Interpret the value you obtained for the intercept.
If X = 0, then Y is expected to equal 1.3

C) Interpret the value you obtained for the slope coefficient.
If X increases 1 unit, then Y is expected to increase by 1.5 units

D) Calculate r^2 for this regression. **$r^2 = .22$**

$$r^2 = 1 - \frac{\Sigma e_i^2}{\Sigma(Y_i - \bar{Y})^2} = 1 - \frac{362.0}{461.7} = .22$$

E) Interpret the value of r^2 for this regression.
22 percent of the variation in Y is explained by X.

F) Calculate the SER for this regression. **SER = 10.99**

$$SER = \sqrt{\frac{362.0}{3}} = 10.99$$

G) Interpret the value of the SER for this regression.
The typical distance of an observation from the regression line = 10.99

H) Calculate the standard error of the intercept term. **$SE(\hat{\beta}_0) = 7.3$**

$$SE(\hat{\beta}_0) = \sqrt{\frac{\hat{\sigma}^2 \Sigma X_i^2}{n\Sigma(X_i - \bar{X})^2}} = \sqrt{\frac{11353.3}{213.0}} = 7.3$$

I) Interpret the standard error of the intercept term.
In repeated sampling, $\hat{\beta}_0$ typically varies by 7.3

J) Calculate the standard error of the slope coefficient. **$SE(\hat{\beta}_1) = 1.7$**

$$SE(\hat{\beta}_1) = \sqrt{\frac{\hat{\sigma}^2}{\Sigma(X_i - \bar{X})^2}} = \sqrt{\frac{120.8}{42.6}} = 1.7$$

K) Interpret the standard error of the slope coefficient.
In repeated sampling, $\hat{\beta}_1$ typically varies by 1.7

3. Given the following: $GDP_i = \hat{\beta}_0 + \hat{\beta}_1 COR_i + e_i$

Nation	COR	GDP
Ukraine	7.4	2200
UK	1.4	21200
USA	2.5	31500
Vietnam	7.4	1770

where COR measures corruption in a nation on a scale of 0 (least) to 10 (most) and GDP measures output in dollars per capita:

A) Calculate the values of the structural parameters for the regression above.
$$\hat{\beta}_1 = -4194.5 \quad \hat{\beta}_0 = 33{,}776.7$$

$$\hat{\beta}_1 = -127124.25/30.31 = -4194.5 \qquad \hat{\beta}_0 = 14167.5 - (-4195.5 \times 4.68) = 33{,}776.7$$

B) Interpret the values of the structural parameters.
If COR = 0, then GDP is expected to equal 33,776.7
If COR increases 1 unit, then GDP is expected to decrease by 4194.5 units

C) Calculate r^2 for this regression. $r^2 = .82$

$$r^2 = 1 - \frac{\Sigma e_i^2}{\Sigma (Y_i - \bar{Y})^2} = 1 - \frac{113570352}{646790675} = .82$$

D) Interpret the value of r^2 for this regression.
82 percent of the variation in GDP is explained by COR

E) Calculate the SER for this regression. **SER = 7535.6**

$$SER = \sqrt{\frac{113570352}{2}} = 7535.6$$

F) Interpret the value of the SER for this regression.
The typical distance of an observation from the regression line is 7535.6

G) Does this regression have a good fit? Explain.
No because SER > ½ the mean of GDP
Or
Yes because $r^2 = .82$

H) Calculate the standard error of the intercept term. $SE(\hat{\beta}_0) = 7425.0$

$$SE(\hat{\beta}_0) = \sqrt{\frac{\hat{\sigma}^2 \Sigma X_i^2}{n\Sigma(X_i - \bar{X})^2}} = \sqrt{\frac{117.73 \times 56785267}{121.24}} = 7425.0$$

I) Interpret the standard error of the intercept term.

In repeated sampling, $\hat{\beta}_0$ typically varies by 7425.0

J) Would you be surprised if the intercept term equaled 26776.70 if you re-ran this regression with data on four different countries? Explain.

No because $\hat{\beta}_0$ typically varies by 7425.0 and 26776.70 is within range.

Chapter 4   Odd Problem Solutions

1. A professor has polled 25 students and asked them about their seat belt use (Do you wear your seat belt regularly?) and smoking (Do you smoke cigarettes?).

A) The correlation coefficient (r) between seat belt use and cigarette smoking is –.034. Are you surprised that the correlation is negative? Explain.

NO – people who smoke are more likely to go without a seatbelt because they are risk takers or don't value their lives as highly.

B) Do a test to determine if r is different than zero. Show the 5-step procedure.

1. Ho: r = 0   Ha: r ≠ 0
2. 5%
3. If | t-ratio | > t^c, then reject Ho
4. 0.163 < 2.069   (d.f. = n – 2 = 25 – 2 = 23)
5. Do Not Reject Ho → r is not statistically different than zero.

$$t - ratio = \frac{r\sqrt{n-2}}{\sqrt{(1-r^2)}} = \frac{-0.034\sqrt{25-2}}{\sqrt{1-.1156}} = \frac{-0.163}{.99} = -0.163$$

C) Do a test to determine if r is less than zero. Show the 5-step procedure.

1. Ho: r = 0   Ha: r < 0
2. 5%
3. If t-ratio < –t^c, then reject Ho
4. – 0.163 > –1.714   (d.f. = n – 2 = 25 – 2 = 23)
5. Do Not Reject Ho → r is not statistically less than zero.

D) Explain why seat belt use and smoking may be correlated despite the tests above.

There is some probability that we are making a TYPE II error.

3. Given the following regression results:

$$CORUPT_i = 5.47 - 0.05\ MIL_i + e_i$$
$$\quad\quad\quad (0.49)\ (0.05)\quad \leftarrow \text{standard errors}$$
$$\quad\quad\quad (0.00)\ (0.36)\quad \leftarrow \text{P-values}$$

$$SER = 2.35 \quad \overline{CORUPT} = 5.14 \quad r^2 = 0.02 \quad n = 48$$

$CORUPT_i$ is the corruption level of the country
(1 is low; 10 is high)
MIL_i is military presence in the country
(military personnel per 1000 citizens)

A) Do a test of significance on the coefficient on MIL. Show the 5-step procedure.

1. **Ho: $\beta_1 = 0$ Ha: $\beta_1 \neq 0$**
2. **5%**
3. **If $|\text{t-ratio}| > t^c$, then reject Ho**
4. **$1.00 < 2.021$ (using 40 d.f.) (d.f. $= n - k = 48 - 2 = 46$)**
5. **Do Not Reject Ho $\rightarrow$ β_1 is not statistically different than zero.**

B) Would the results of your test turn out differently if the critical level of the test was 40% instead of 5%? Explain.

Yes, we would reject Ho at the 40% critical level because the P-value is .36

C) Is the constant term significant at the 1% critical level? Answer this question without doing a test of significance. Just explain.

Yes – the constant term is significant at the 1% critical level because the P-value is 0.00

D) Form a 90% confidence interval around the coefficient on MIL.

90% CI for $\hat{\beta}_1 = -0.05$: $\hat{\beta}_1 +/- se(\hat{\beta}_1)(t^c)$

$-0.05 +/- 0.05\ (1.684) \quad \rightarrow \quad -0.13$ to 0.034

E) Determine if $r^2 = 0$ for this regression. (The F-statistic $= 0.95$.) Show the 5-step procedure.

1. **Ho: $r^2 = 0$ Ha: $r^2 > 0$**
2. **5%**
3. **If $F > Fc$, then reject Ho**

4. $0.95 < 4.08$ (d.f. = k − 1 in the numerator and n − k in the denominator) (1 & 46 using 1 & 40)
5. Do Not Reject Ho ; r^2 is not statistically greater than zero.

F) Would your results for E) be different if the critical level of test was 33%? Explain. (P-value for this test is 0.34.)

No, since the P-value > critical level of the test we still say do not reject Ho

G) Do a test to determine if the coefficient on MIL equals zero or if it is greater than zero. Show the 5-step procedure.

1) **Ho: $\beta_1 = 0$ Ha: $\beta_1 > 0$**
2) **5%**
3) **If t-ratio > t^c, then reject Ho**
4) **−1.00 < 1.684 (d.f. = n − k = 48 − 2 = 46) (using 40 d.f.)**
5) **Do Not Reject Ho → β_1 is not significantly positive**

H) Do a test to determine if the coefficient on MIL equals −0.1 or not. Show the 5-step procedure.

1. **Ho: $\beta_1 = -0.1$ Ha: $\beta_1 \neq -0.1$**
2. **5%**
3. **If $|$ t-ratio $|$ > t^c, then reject Ho**
4. **1 < 2.021 (d.f. = n − k = 48 − 2 = 46) (using 40 d.f.)**
5. **Do Not Reject Ho → β_1 is not statistically different than −0.1**

$$t - ratio = \frac{\hat{\beta}_0 - \beta_{Ho}}{SE(\hat{\beta}_0)} = \frac{-0.05 - (-0.1)}{0.05} = 1$$

Chapter 5   Odd Problem Solutions

1. Use the data in SDATA.XLS and statistical software to run the following regression:

$$GPA_i = \hat{\beta}_0 + \hat{\beta}_1 \, ST_i + e_i$$

where GPA = grade point average
and ST = study time per day

Dependent Variable: GPA
Method: Least Squares
Sample: 1 100
Included observations: 100

Variable	Coefficient	Std. Error	t-Statistic	Prob.
C	3.273582	0.057858	56.57915	0.0000
ST	0.026922	0.015906	1.692630	0.0937

R-squared	0.028404	Mean dependent var	3.347000
Adjusted R-squared	0.018490	S.D. dependent var	0.386503
S.E. of regression	0.382913	Akaike info criterion	0.937782
Sum squared resid	14.36903	Schwarz criterion	0.989885
Log likelihood	–44.88909	F-statistic	2.864998
Durbin-Watson stat	1.833710	Prob(F-statistic)	0.093703

A) Interpret the value you obtained for $\hat{\beta}_0$.

If ST = 0 , then GPA = 3.273582

B) Interpret the value you obtained for $\hat{\beta}_1$.

If ST increases 1 unit, then GPA is expected to increase 0.026922 units.

C) How much does $\hat{\beta}_1$ typically vary in repeated sampling? **0.015906**

D) Perform a test of significance on $\hat{\beta}_1$. Show the 5-step procedure.
1. **Ho: $\beta_1 = 0$ Ha: $\beta_1 \neq 0$**
2. **5%**
3. **If |t-ratio| tc, then reject Ho**
4. **1.692630 < 1.990 (d.f. = n–k = 100–2 = 98; using 80 d.f.)**
5. **Do Not Reject Ho → β_1 is not statistically different than zero.**

E) What percent of the variation in GPA is explained by study time? **2.8404%**

F) Perform a test to determine if $r^2 = 0$. Show the 5-step procedure.
1. **Ho: $r^2 = 0$ Ha: $r^2 > 0$**
2. **5%**
3. **If F > Fc, then reject Ho**
4. **2.864998 < 3.96 (d.f.: N = k – 1; D = n – k = 98; using 1 and 80 d.f.)**
5. **Do Not Reject Ho → R^2 is not statistically greater than zero.**

G) According to these results, how many hours per day would your study time have to increase in order to raise your GPA by 0.1?   **? x 0.026922 = 0.1 ; 3.7 hours (per day)**

H) Plot the scattergram between GPA and ST with the estimated regression line drawn in. **Be sure to put ST on the X-axis and GPA on the Y-axis.**

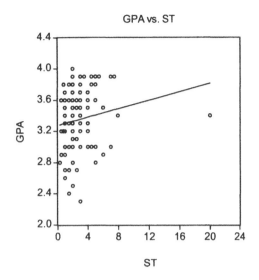

GPA vs. ST

I) What is the average distance of an observation from the regression line? **0.382913**

J) Will you cut back on your study time now that you have seen these results? Explain why.

Yes, these results indicate study time does not affect GPA.
Or
No, these results may be biased due to missing explanatory variables or the data may be corrupt because students exaggerated their study time or I am not typical.

3. Use the data in CONSUMP.XLS and statistical software to run the following regression:

$$RCONPC_t = \hat{\beta}_0 + \hat{\beta}_1 REALYDPC_t + \hat{\beta}_2 REALR_t + e_t$$

        where RCONPC = real consumer spending in the USA per capita
              REALYDPC = real disposable income per capita
              REALR = real interest rate on 1-year Treasury Bonds
              CC = University of Michigan Index of Consumer Confidence

A) Do all the explanatory variables attain their expected signs? **YES**

B) Aside from CC, what explanatory variables might be missing from this regression?
Wealth and age distribution of population, among other things.

C) Perform Ramsey's Reset test. Show the 5-step procedure. Are variables missing from the model according to this test?
1. **Ho: Ho: $\beta_3 = \beta_4 = 0$**   **Ha: β_3 and/or $\beta_4 \neq 0$**
   (No variables excluded)   **(Variables excluded)**
2. **5%**
3. **If F > F^c, then reject Ho**
4. **70.51342 > 3.23; where F^c has d.f. NUM = 2 ; d.f. DEN = n − k = 46−5 = 41**
                               (using NUM = 2 and DEN = 40 because of our F-table)

5. Reject Ho → Variables are excluded from this regression.

5. Use the data in CONSUMP.XLS and statistical software to run the following regression:

$$RCONPC_t = \hat{\beta}_0 + \hat{\beta}_1 REALYDPC_t + \hat{\beta}_2 REALR_t + \hat{\beta}_3 CC_t + e_t$$

where RCONPC = real consumer spending in the USA per capita
REALYDPC = real disposable income per capita
REALR = real interest rate on 1-year Treasury Bonds
CC = University of Michigan Index of Consumer Confidence

A) Does CC attain its expected sign? Explain. **Yes, we would expect consumers to spend more when they are more confident, because there is no need to save for future emergencies.**

B) Does a test of significance on CC justify its presence in the regression? **Yes**

C) Does CC belong in the regression according to Adjusted R^2? Explain. **Yes, it rises to 0.996646 from 0.993901.**

D) Does CC belong in the regression according to the Akaike information criterion? Explain. **Yes, it falls to 14.27868 from 14.85672.**

E) Does CC belong in the regression according to the Schwarz criterion? Explain. **Yes, it falls to 14.43769 from 14.97598.**

F) Does this regression fit better than the regression from 1? Explain. **Yes, based on adjusted r-squared, Akaike, and Schwarz.**

G) Perform Ramsey's Reset test. Show the 5-step procedure. Are variables missing from the model according to this test?
   1. **Ho: Ho: $\beta_4 = \beta_5 = 0$**   **Ha: β_4 and/or $\beta_5 \neq 0$**
      (No variables excluded)   **(Variables excluded)**
   2. **5%**
   3. **If F > F^c, then reject Ho**
   4. **37.97626 > 3.23; where F^c has d.f. NUM = 2 ; d.f. DEN = n – k = 46 – 6 = 40**
   5. **Reject Ho → Variables are excluded from this regression.**

H) Do you think the estimators in $RCONPC_t = \hat{\beta}_0 + \hat{\beta}_1 REALYDPC_t + \hat{\beta}_2 REALR_t + e_t$ are biased? Inefficient? Neither? Explain. **Biased, because at least one important explanatory variable is missing – CC.**

I) Do you think the estimators in $RCONPC_t = \hat{\beta}_0 + \hat{\beta}_1 REALYDPC_t + \hat{\beta}_2 REALR_t +$

$\hat{\beta}_3 CC_t + e_t$ are biased? Inefficient? Neither? Explain. **Biased, because Ramsey's suggests at least one variable is missing and theory points to wealth as being important for consumer spending.**

Chapter 6   Odd Problem Solutions

1. We have $Y_i = \hat{\beta}_1 X_i + e_i$

   We want to min $\sum e_i^2$; or min $\sum(Y_i - \hat{\beta}_1 X_i)^2$

   To find the equation for $\hat{\beta}_0$ that minimize this expression, take the derivative with respect to $\hat{\beta}_0$ and set it equal to zero:

$$\frac{d\Sigma(Y_i - \hat{\beta}_1 X_i)^2}{d\hat{\beta}_1} = 2\Sigma(Y_i - \hat{\beta}_1 X_i)(-X_i) = 0$$

   Dividing both sides of this equation by –2 leaves $\Sigma(Y_i - \hat{\beta}_1 X_i)(X_i) = 0$

   Now distribute the summation sign: $\Sigma Y_i X_i - \hat{\beta}_1 \Sigma X_i^2 = 0$;

   Moving the second term to the other side gives: $\Sigma Y_i X_i = \hat{\beta}_1 \Sigma X_i^2$

   The result is known as a "normal equation".

   Rearranging terms and dividing through by ΣX_i^2 gives:

$$\hat{\beta}_1 = \frac{\Sigma X_i Y_i}{\Sigma X_i^2}$$

3. In the regression below, what would be the new values of $\hat{\beta}_0$, $\hat{\beta}_1$, their t-ratios, SER, r^2, and the mean of WEIGHT if WEIGHT was measured in ounces instead of pounds?

WEIGHT$_i$ = 51.12 + 1.85 HEIGHT$_i$ + e$_i$
(4.72)   (9.85)   ← t-ratios
————
SER = 20.38 $\overline{\text{WEIGHT}}$ = 156.78
r^2 = 0.49   n = 4800

WEIGHT$_i$ = 817.92 + 29.6 HEIGHT$_i$ + e$_i$
(4.72)   (9.85)   ← t-ratios
————
SER = **326.08** $\overline{\text{WEIGHT}}$ = **2508.48**
r^2 = **0.49**   n = **4800**

5. Use the data in EGG.XLS and statistical software to do the following problems:
   Run the following regression: $QEGG_t = \hat{\beta}_0 + \hat{\beta}_1 PEGG_t + e_t$

   where QEGG is per capita egg consumption each year 1973–1997
   PEGG is the average price of a dozen eggs in the USA

i)   A) Interpret the value you obtained for $\hat{\beta}_0$.
     If PEGG = 0, then QEGG = 341.1228
     B) Interpret the value you obtained for $\hat{\beta}_1$.
     If PEGG ↑ 1 unit, then QEGG ↓ 83.70535 units
     C) If the price of eggs goes up $1 per dozen, what is the expected change in egg consumption according to this regression? **↓ 83.70535 units**

ii) Run the regression in the double-log form.
     A) Interpret the value you obtained for $\hat{\beta}_0$.
     If PEGG = 1, then LNQEGG = 5.544318 (or QEGG = 255.78)
     B) Interpret the value you obtained for $\hat{\beta}_1$.
     If PEGG ↑ 1 %, then QEGG ↓ 0.361304 %
     C) If the price of eggs goes up 1 percent, what is the expected percentage change in egg consumption according to this regression? **↓ 0.361304 %**

iii) Run the regression in the semi-log form (where the natural log of PEGG is taken).
     A) Interpret the value you obtained for $\hat{\beta}_0$.
     If PEGG = 1, then QEGG = 256.3509
     B) Interpret the value you obtained for $\hat{\beta}_1$.
     If PEGG ↑ 1 %, then QEGG ↓ 0.9196824 units
     C) If the price of eggs goes up 1 percent, what is the expected change in egg consumption according to this regression? **↓ 0.9196824 units**

iv) Run the regression in the semi-log form (where the natural log of QEGG is taken).
     A) Interpret the value you obtained for $\hat{\beta}_0$.
     If PEGG = 0, then LNQEGG = 5.877692 (or QEGG = 356.98)

B) Interpret the value you obtained for $\hat{\beta}_1$.

If PEGG ↑ 1 unit, then QEGG ↓ 32.9175 %

C) If the price of eggs goes up $1 per dozen, what is the expected percentage change in egg consumption according to this regression? **↓ 32.9175 %**

v) Run the regression in the reciprocal form.

A) Interpret the value you obtained for $\hat{\beta}_0$.

As PEGG → ∞, QEGG → 157.0288

B) Interpret the value you obtained for $\hat{\beta}_1$.

If PEGG ↑, QEGG ↓

C) If the price of eggs goes up $1 per dozen, will egg consumption increase or decrease according to this regression? **decrease**

vi) Run the regression in the polynomial form.

A) Interpret the value you obtained for $\hat{\beta}_0$.

If PEGG = 0, then QEGG = 567.0630

B) Interpret the values you obtained for $\hat{\beta}_1$ and $\hat{\beta}_2$.

As PEGG ↑, QEGG ↓ to a point and then QEGG ↑ with further increases in PEGG.

vii) A) Do you think the data in this study require an alternate functional form or is the linear form satisfactory? Explain. **Theory is not helpful in this case. Ramsey's Reset test says nonlinear since it flunks the linear form and passes the nonlinear forms. The scattergram suggests a curvilinear shape. Therefore, an alternate form is recommended.**

B) Which of the 6 regressions fits the data best? **One cannot say since all 6 cannot be compared. However, of those having QEGG as the dependent variable, the polynomial fits best with an adjusted r-squared of 0.813771. Of those having LNQEGG as the dependent variable, the double-log fits best with an r-squared = 0.766749.**

7. Use the data in SDATA.XLS and statistical software to do the following problem:

Which functional form do you think is appropriate for the regression below:

$$GPA_i = \hat{\beta}_0 + \hat{\beta}_1 ST_i + e_i$$

Explain your response.

A scattergram does not suggest the need for an alternate functional form. Ramsey's Reset test is no help since all the functional forms pass the test. However, lin-log and reciprocal regressions fit the data slightly better than a linear regression. Perhaps the reciprocal specification is best since it fits better than the linear and theory suggests an asymptotic relationship (the more you study the closer your GPA comes to 4.0).

9. Interpret every structural parameter in each of the following regressions considering:

WAGES = pay per hour of work
LNWAGES = natural log of WAGES
EXP = years of experience
EXPSQ = EXP squared

A) LNWAGES = 2.1 + 1.3 EXP + e
   If EXP = 0, then LNWAGES = 2.1 (or WAGES = 8.17)
   If EXP ↑ 1 unit, then WAGES ↑ 130%
B) WAGES = 2.1 + 1.3 EXP − 2.3 EXPSQ + e
   If EXP = 0, then WAGES = 2.1
   As EXP ↑, so do WAGES, up to a point, then WAGES decline with further EXP
C) WAGES = 2.5 − 0.1 (1/EXP) + e
   As EXP → ∞, WAGES → 2.5
   As EXP ↑, WAGES ↑

Chapter 7   Odd Problem Solutions

1. A) Interpret every structural parameter in the following regression:

$$PROFSAL_i = 17.969 + 1.3707\ EXP_i + 3.3336\ DUM_i + e_i$$

Where PROFSAL is the professor's salary
EXP is the professor's experience in years
DUM = 1 if the professor is male; 0 otherwise

A female with no experience is expected to have PROFSAL = 17.969
If EXP increases 1 unit, then PROFSAL is expected to increase 1.3707 units for males and females
A male is expected to earn 3.3336 more than a female, holding EXP constant

B) Draw a diagram reflecting the regression results with PROFSAL on the vertical axis and EXP on the horizontal axis.

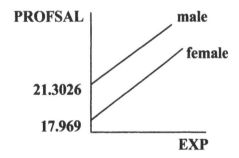

C) A male professor with 10 years experience is expected to make how much in salary?
   PROFSAL= 17.969 + 1.3707(10) +3.3336(1) = 35.0096

D) A female professor with 10 years experience is expected to make how much in salary?
PROFSAL= 17.969 +1.3707(10) + 3.3336(0) = 31.676
What would be the new values of the structural parameters if the dummy was flip-flopped?
$$PROFSAL_i = 21.3026 + 1.3707\ EXP_i - 3.3336\ DUM_i + e_i$$
Using the flip-flopped results, how much would a male professor with 10 years experience make in salary? **35.0096**

3. A) Interpret every structural parameter in the following regression:

$$PROFSAL_i = 16.1718 + 1.2016\ EXP_i + 3.2245\ DUM_i - 1.0001\ DUM*EXP_i + e_i$$

where PROFSAL is the professor's salary
EXP is the professor's experience in years
DUM = 1 if the professor is male; 0 otherwise

A female with no EXP is expected to make 16.1718
For every unit increase in EXP, PROFSAL is expected to increase by 1.2016 for females
A male with 0 EXP will earn 3.2245 more than a female with 0 EXP
If EXP increases 1 unit, then PROFSAL for a male will increase 1.0001 less than the
1.2016 for a female

B) Draw a diagram reflecting the regression results with PROFSAL on the vertical axis and EXP on the horizontal axis.

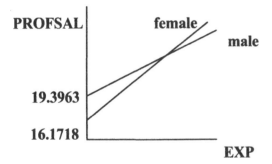

C) What would be the new values of the structural parameters if the dummy was flip-flopped?

$$PROFSAL_i = 19.3963 + 0.2015\ EXP_i - 3.2245\ DUM_i + 1.0001\ DUM*EXP_i + e_i$$

5. A) Interpret every structural parameter in the following regression:

$$GPA_i = 0.37 + 0.81\ HSGPA_i + 0.00001\ SAT_i - 0.38\ GREEK_i + e_i$$

where GPA is grade point average in college
HSGPS is high school GPA
SAT is SAT score
GREEK = 1 if student is a member of a sorority or fraternity;
0 otherwise

If HSGPA and SAT = 0 and the student is not greek, then GPA = 0.37
If HSGPA increases 1 unit, then GPA increases 0.81 units, holding SAT constant
If SAT increases 1 unit, then GPA increases 0.00001 units, holding HSGPA constant
A greek student is expected to have a GPA 0.38 lower than a non-greek with the same HSGPA and SAT.

B) Draw a diagram reflecting the regression results with GPA on the vertical axis and SAT on the horizontal axis.

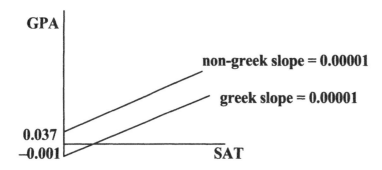

7. Use the data in WAGES.XLS and statistical software run to run a regression where wages are explained by a constant term, education, experience, and a dummy variable for gender.

NAME	VARIABLE
WAGES	wages
LNWAGES	the natural logarithm of wages
ED	education in years
NONWH	1 if nonwhite ; 0 otherwise
FEM	1 if female ; 0 otherwise
MARRIED	1 if married ; 0 otherwise
EXPER	experience in years
EXPSQ	experience squared
UNION	1 if union member; 0 otherwise
PRO	1 if employed in a profession; 0 otherwise

A) Interpret the coefficient on education.
   If ED increases 1 unit, then WAGES increases 0.940489 units, holding EXPER constant.

B) Interpret the coefficient on the dummy variable.
   A female's wages are 2.337621 less than a male's with the same ED and EXPER.

Dependent Variable: WAGES
Method: Least Squares
Date: 12/05/07   Time: 13:49
Sample: 1 534
Included observations: 534

Variable	Coefficient	Std. Error	t-Statistic	Prob.
C	−4.166703	1.186608	−3.511439	0.0005
ED	0.940489	0.078859	11.92616	0.0000
EXPER	0.113297	0.016707	6.781255	0.0000
FEM	−2.337621	0.388042	−6.024141	0.0000
R-squared	0.253171	Mean dependent var		9.023947
Adjusted R-squared	0.248944	S.D. dependent var		5.138874
S.E. of regression	4.453528	Akaike info criterion		5.832733
Sum squared resid	10511.97	Schwarz criterion		5.864796
Log likelihood	−1553.340	F-statistic		59.88904
Durbin-Watson stat	1.857160	Prob(F-statistic)		0.000000

9. Use the data in WAGES.XLS and statistical software to run a regression where the natural logarithm of wages is explained by a constant term, education, experience, and dummy variables for marital status, gender, race, union membership, and professional status.

A) Interpret the coefficient on education.
If ED increases 1 unit, then WAGES increase 8.4356%, holding experience constant.

B) Interpret the coefficient on marital status.
A married person is expected to have WAGES 7.1460% higher than an unmarried person, holding ED and EXPER constant.

C) Interpret the coefficient on union membership.
A union member is expected to have WAGES 20.2786% higher than a nonunion person, holding ED and EXPER constant.

D) Does this regression provide evidence of racial and gender discrimination? Explain.
Definitely, gender discrimination – the coeff. on FEM is negative and significant. For racial discrimination the evidence is not so strong – the coeff. on nonwhite is negative, but only significant at the 10.47% level.

11. Use the data in EXTRAMARITAL.XLS and statistical software to estimate a linear probability model where EXTRA is explained by a constant term, AGE, HPPYM, RELIG, and YRSMAR.

EXTRA = 1 if person participated in an extramarital affair in the past year; 0 otherwise
AGE = the age of the person
HPPYM = person's perception of their marital happiness (1 = very unhappy; 5 = very happy)
RELIG = person's perception of their religiousness (1 = very unreligious; 5 = very religious)
YRSMAR = years married

A) Interpret all 5 structural parameters.
A person with AGE = HPPYM = RELIG = YRSMAR = 0 has an 81.8833 % chance of an affair in the past year.
As AGE ↑ 1 unit, the chance of having had an affair in the past year ↓ 0.5948%, holding the other variables (HPPYM, RELIG, YRSMAR) constant.
As HPPYM ↑ 1 unit, the chance of having had an affair in the past year ↓ 8.7451%, holding the other variables (AGE, RELIG, YRSMAR) constant.

As RELIG ↑ 1 unit, the chance of having had an affair in the past year ↓ 5.4697%, holding the other variables (AGE, HPPYM, YRSMAR) constant.
As YRSMAR ↑ 1 unit, the chance of having had an affair in the past year ↑ 1.6910%, holding the other variables (AGE, HPPYM, RELIG) constant.

B) What is the probability that a 52-year-old person married for 27 years had an extramarital affair last year? Assume the person's RELIG = 2 and HAPPYM = 3.

EXTRA = 0.81883 – 0.005948 (52) – 0.087451 (3) – 0.054697 (2) + 0.016910 (27) = 0.594

59.4%

Chapter 8   Odd Problem Solutions

1. Prove $\Sigma w_i = 0$ and $\Sigma w_i X_i = 1$.

[Solution:]

$$\Sigma w_i = \frac{\Sigma(X_i - \overline{X})}{\Sigma(X_i - \overline{X})^2} = \frac{\Sigma Xi - n\overline{X}}{\Sigma(X_i - \overline{X})^2} = \frac{0}{\Sigma(X_i - \overline{X})^2}$$

$$\Sigma w_i X_i = \frac{\Sigma(X_i - \overline{X})X_i}{\Sigma(X_i - \overline{X})^2} = \frac{\Sigma X_i^2 - \overline{X}\Sigma X_i}{\Sigma X_i^2 - \overline{X}\Sigma X_i} = 1$$

3. Suppose $u_i \sim N(0, \sigma^2)$ for all i. Why can't we guarantee $\hat{\beta}_1$ will be efficient? **Because maybe E[$u_i u_j$] ≠ 0 for all i ≠ j**

5. From the article "Econometrics in Theory and Practice" by Steven Caudill, *Eastern Economic Journal*, vol. 16, no. 3 (July/Sept. 1990): 249–256. http://college.holycross.edu/eej/Volume16/V16N3P249_256.pdf

A) What is the "Axiom of Specification"?

The Axiom of Specification is a set of criteria beyond the assumptions of the classic linear regression model that a regression must meet if the estimators are to be BLUE.

B) Is the Axiom of Specification an assumption of Classical Linear Regression Model? If not, then should it be? If so, then which one corresponds to it?
The Axiom of Specification is an implicit assumption of the CLRM. Most econometricians would put it under assumption 2: E[u_i] = 0, since this assumption will be violated if the set of dependent variables is not unique, complete, small in number, observable, or unknown parameters are not constant.

C) What is the difference between "applied econometricians" and "econometric theorists"?
Applied econometricians are interested in testing theories and not so interested in Classical assumptions. They are more likely to data mine. Econometric theorists are concerned with adhering to the Classical assumptions and not so concerned with testing any particular economic theory. They are more likely to do proofs.

D) What is "data mining"?
Allowing the data to determine the best model, not theory.

Chapter 9   Odd Problem Solutions

1. Use the data in CONSUMP.XLS and statistical software to run the regression:

$$RCONPC_t = \hat{\beta}_0 + \hat{\beta}_1 REALYDPC_t + \hat{\beta}_2 REALR_t + \hat{\beta}_3 CC_t + e_t$$

where RCONPC = real consumer spending in the USA per capita
REALYDPC = real disposable income per capita
REALR = real interest rate on 1-year Treasury Bonds
CC = University of Michigan Index of Consumer Confidence

A) Which explanatory variables do not obtain their expected signs?
They all obtain their expected signs.

B) According to the correlation coefficients between the explanatory variables, would you classify the multicollinearity in this regression as severe, moderate, mild, or non-existent? Explain. **Mild to non-existent with r's of 0.016, 0.135, and 0.276.**

C) According to the correlation coefficients between the explanatory variables, which two variables are most collinear? **REALR and CC**

D) Calculate the three VIFs for this regression. Would you classify the multicollinearity in this regression as severe, moderate, mild, or non-existent? Explain.
VIF = 1.02; 1.08; 1.10 >>>> nonexistent to mild

E) Run the regression in first difference form. Which explanatory variables do not obtain their expected signs? **They all obtain their expected signs.**

F) According to the correlation coefficients between the explanatory variables, would you classify the multicollinearity in this regression as severe, moderate, mild, or non-existent? Explain. **Mild with r's of 0.26, 0.28, and 0.34.**

G) Calculate the three VIFs for this regression. Would you classify the multicollinearity in this regression as severe, moderate, mild, or non-existent? Explain.
Nonexistent to mild with VIFs of 1.124, 1.176, and 1.176.

H) Based on your look into this matter, what do you recommend doing about the multicollinearity in the original regression? Explain.
There was no or very little multicollinearity in the original regression.

Chapter 10   Odd Problem Solutions

1. Given $Y_i = \hat{\beta}_0 + \hat{\beta}_1 X1_i + \hat{\beta}_2 X2_i + e_i$

A) Write the auxiliary regression required for the Park test assuming X2 is the "culprit" variable. $\ln(e_i^2) = \alpha_0 + \alpha_1 \ln(X2_i) + \varepsilon_i$

B) Suppose n = 23 and the t-ratio on X2 in the auxiliary regression is –2.222. Is heteroskedasticity present? Show the 5-step procedure for the Park test.
1) Ho: $\alpha_2 = 0$ (no hetero)   Ha: $\alpha_2 \neq 0$ (hetero exists)
2) 5%
3) If |t-ratio| > tc, reject Ho
4) 2.222 > 2.080 (d.f.= n – k)
5) Reject Ho: heteroskedasticity is present in the original regression

C) Write the auxiliary regression required for the White test.
$e_i^2 = \alpha_0 + \alpha_1 X1_i + \alpha_2 X1_i^2 + \alpha_3 X2_i + \alpha_4 X2_i^2 + \alpha_5(X1_i)(X2_i) + \varepsilon_i$

D) Suppose n = 23 and the R-squared on the auxiliary regression is 0.55. Is heteroskedasticity present? Show the 5-step procedure for the White test.

1) Ho: no hetero   Ha: hetero exists
2) 5%
3) If $nR^2 > \chi c$, then reject Ho
4) 23(.55) = 12.65 ; χc = 11.07 (d.f. = k – 1 from the auxiliary regression = 5)
5) Reject Ho: heteroskedasticity is present in the original regression

E) Write the weighted least-squares regression that would remedy the heteroskedasticity if it were proportional to X2.

[Solution:]

$$\frac{Y_i}{\sqrt{X2_i}} = \beta_0 \left[\frac{1}{\sqrt{X2_i}} \right] + \beta_1 \left[\frac{X1_i}{\sqrt{X2_i}} \right] + \beta_2 \left[\frac{X2_i}{\sqrt{X2_i}} \right] + \frac{u_i}{\sqrt{X2_i}}$$

3. Use the data in ALCO5.XLS and statistical software to run a regression where "drink" is explained by a constant term, gpa, male, ofage, cig, pot, intra, and white.

VARIABLE	DESCRIPTION
drink	number of alcoholic drinks consumed per week
gpa	grade point average 0 – 4 scale
male	1 if the student is male; 0 otherwise
ofage	1 if the student is 21 or older; 0 otherwise
cig	1 if the student uses tobacco; 0 otherwise
pot	1 if the student uses marijuana: 0 otherwise
intra	1 if the student participates in intramural athletics; 0 otherwise
white	1 if the student is white; 0 otherwise

A) Which variables do not attain their expected signs? **Perhaps INTRA; otherwise the signs are correct.**

B) Which variables are not significant at the 5% critical level? **WHITE**

C) Plot the squared residuals from the regression against gpa. Does the plot show evidence of heteroskedasticity? Explain. **Yes, higher gpa yields wider variance on the squared errors.**

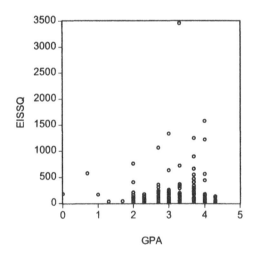

D) Do a Park test for heteroskedasticity assuming gpa is the "culprit" variable. Show the 5-step procedure.
   1) **Ho: $\alpha_2 = 0$ (no hetero)   Ha: $\alpha_2 \neq 0$ (hetero exists)**
   2) **5%**
   3) **If |t-ratio| > tc, reject Ho**
   4) **6.376729 > 1.984 (d.f. = n – k=694 – 2 = 692)**
   5) **Reject Ho: heteroskedasticity is present in the original regression**

E) Perform White's test for heteroskedasticity. Show the 5-step procedure.
   1) **Ho: no hetero   Ha: hetero exists**
   2) **5%**
   3) **If $nR^2 > \chi c$, then reject Ho**
   4) **89.95281 > χc = 43.77 (d.f. = k – 1 from the auxiliary regression = 31 – 1 = 30)**

5) Reject Ho: heteroskedasticity is present in the original regression

F) Run the original regression using weighted least-squares. Assume 1/gpa is the correct weight. Then apply White's test for heteroskedasticity to the errors from this weighted regression. Show the 5-step procedure.

> **1) Ho: no hetero   Ha: hetero exists**
> **2) 5%**
> **3) If $nR^2 > \chi c$, then reject Ho**
> **4) 209.4133 > χc = 43.77 (d.f. = k – 1 from the auxiliary regression = 31 – 1 = 30)**
> **5) Reject Ho: heteroskedasticity is present in the WLS regression**

G) Run the original regression using weighted least-squares. Assume $1/\sqrt{gpa}$ is the correct weight. Then apply White's test for heteroskedasticity to the errors from this weighted regression. Show the 5-step procedure.

> **1) Ho: no hetero   Ha: hetero exists**
> **2) 5%**
> **3) If $nR^2 > \chi c$, then reject Ho**
> **4) 125.3590 > χc = 43.77 (d.f. = k–1 from the auxiliary regression = 31 – 1 = 30)**
> **5) Reject Ho: heteroskedasticity is present in the WLS regression**

H) Use the Newey-West technique to obtain heteroskedasticity-corrected standard errors with the original regression. Did heteroskedasticity appear to be biasing the standard errors of the structural parameters very much? Explain. **The heteroskedasticity appears to be biasing the SEs of the structural parameters a moderate to minor amount. They are all slightly higher in the Newey-West regression except for the SE on WHITE which is slightly lower.**

Dependent Variable: DRINK
Method: Least Squares
Date: 02/22/08   Time: 14:39
Sample: 1 699
Included observations: 695
Excluded observations: 4
Newey-West HAC Standard Errors & Covariance (lag truncation=6)

Variable	Coefficient	Std. Error	t-Statistic	Prob.
C	8.951717	2.463179	3.634213	0.0003
GPA	–2.705399	0.705993	–3.832049	0.0001
MALE	4.538337	0.674783	6.725629	0.0000
OFAGE	1.799706	0.638602	2.818198	0.0050
CIG	3.045336	0.833358	3.654294	0.0003
POT	4.579583	0.780064	5.870777	0.0000
INTRA	2.990046	1.619902	1.845819	0.0653
WHITE	1.839064	0.897039	2.050149	0.0407

R-squared	0.278284	Mean dependent var	7.589928
Adjusted R-squared	0.270930	S.D. dependent var	9.241721
S.E. of regression	7.891096	Akaike info criterion	6.980791
Sum squared resid	42779.07	Schwarz criterion	7.033095
Log likelihood	–2417.825	F-statistic	37.84261
Durbin-Watson stat	2.009937	Prob(F-statistic)	0.000000

Chapter 11   Odd Problem Solutions

1. Complete the following table:

Sample Size	k	d stat	Autocorrelation present?
20	2	0.83	Yes
32	3	1.24	Yes
45	4	1.98	No
100	5	3.72	Yes
150	7	1.71	Inconclusive

3. Use the data in CONSUMP.XLS and statistical software to run the following regression:

$$RCONPC_t = \hat{\beta}_0 + \hat{\beta}_1 REALYDPC_t + e_t$$

A) Plot the error terms over time. Do you suspect serial correlation? Explain.

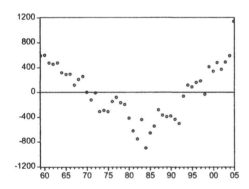

Obvious pattern of positive serial correlation with runs of + and then − errors.

B) Plot the error terms against their lagged values. Do you suspect serial correlation? Explain.

Obvious + auto with observations splayed mainly in I and III quadrants.

C) Perform a Durbin-Watson test. Show the 5-step procedure.

   1) **Ho: no positive auto   Ha: positive auto**

   2) **5%**

   3) **If $0 < d < d_L$, then reject Ho**
      If $d_L < d < d_U$, then inconclusive

   4) **$d = 0.201834$; $d_L = 1.48$; $d_U = 1.57$ (using $k = 2$ and $n = 45$)**

   5) **reject Ho: positive auto is present**

5. Use the data in CONSUMP.XLS and statistical software to run the regression:

$$RCONPC_t = \hat{\beta}_0 + \hat{\beta}_1 REALYDPC_t + \hat{\beta}_2 REALR_t + \hat{\beta}_3 CC_t + e_t$$

     where: RCONPC = real consumer spending in the USA per capita
              REALYDPC = real disposable income per capita
              REALR = real interest rate on 1-year Treasury Bonds
              CC = University of Michigan Index of Consumer Confidence

A) Plot the residuals from the regression over time. Does this plot suggest serial correlation is present? Positive or negative? Explain.

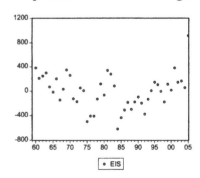

Positive autocorrealtion is suggested since there are long runs of positive and negative errors.

B) Plot the residuals from the regression against their lagged values. Does this plot suggest serial correlation is present? Positive or negative? Explain.

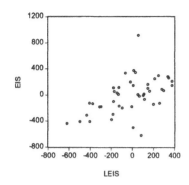

An upward splay of observations indicates positive serial correlation.

C) Does the regression suffer from serial correlation? Show the 5-step procedure of the Durbin-Watson test.

1) **Ho: no positive auto   Ha: positive auto**
2) **5%**
3) **If $0 < d < d_L$, then reject Ho**
   If $d_L < d < d_U$, then inconclusive
4) **$d = 0.846499$; $d_L = 1.38$; $d_U = 1.67$ (n = 46; k = 4)**
5) **Reject Ho: positive serial correlation is present**

D) Estimate ρ by regressing the residuals on their lagged values (no constant term). What is the estimate of ρ? **0.574174**

E) Check for second order serial correlation. Do you think it is present? Explain.
   No because the second lag of the errors is not significant in
   $eis_t = \rho_1 eis_{t-1} + \rho_2 eis_{t-2} + \varepsilon_t$

F) Estimate ρ and correct for first order serial correlation using GLS with maximum likelihood estimation. What is this estimate of ρ? **0.863657**

G) Did GLS remedy the serial correlation? Show the 5-step procedure.

1) **Ho: no negative auto   Ha: negative auto**
2) **5%**
3) **If $4 - d_L < d < 4$, then reject Ho**
   If $4 - d_U < d < 4 - d_L$, then inconclusive
4) **d= 2.144248; $d_L = 1.34$; $d_U = 1.72$ (n = 45; k = 5)**
5) **do not reject ho; GLS remedied the negative autocorrelation**

H) Compare the t-ratios from the original regression and the GLS regression. Are you surprised by which ones turn out to be larger? Explain. **The absolute values of the t-stats are lower after correcting for serial correlation and that is to be expected since they were biased to look better than they actually were in the original regression.**

I) Apply the Newey-West technique to the original regression. Are you surprised at the new standard errors of the estimators? Explain. **The SEs rise after applying the Newey-West technique as expected since they were biased downward in the original regression.**

1. Consider the following regression:

$$M_t = 2.00 - 0.10\ R_t + 0.70\ Y_t + 0.60\ M_{t-1} + e_t$$
$$\quad\quad\quad (0.10)\quad (0.35)\quad (0.10)\quad\quad \leftarrow \text{standard errors}$$

$$R^2 = .9 \quad\quad\quad DW = 1.80 \quad\quad\quad n = 26$$

Where M is the demand for M1
R is the interest rate on 10-year Treasuries
Y is national income

A) Do the variables attain their expected signs? **Yes**
B) Test for serial correlation in this regression. Show the 5-step procedure.

Durbin's h- test
  1) **Ho: no autocorrelation Ha: auto present**
  2) **5%**
  3) **If $|h| > t^c$, then reject Ho (d.f. = n – k)**
  4) **$h = (.1)(5.93) = 0.59$; $t^c = 2.074$**
  5) **Do not reject Ho; no auto present**

C) What is the short-run impact of a change in the interest rate on money demand?
   –0.10
D) What is the long-run impact? **Is equal to $\beta_1/(1-\lambda) = -0.10/(1-.60) = -0.25$**

3. Use the data in QLEISCOIN and statistical software to do the following problems.

COIN = percentage change in the composite index of coincident economic indicators
LEIS = percentage change in the composite index of leading economic indicators

A) Run a regression to determine if COIN is affected by LEIS and LEIS lagged 1 through 8 quarters. Do you think LEIS 8 quarters ago helps predict COIN this quarter? Explain. **No, the sign on LEIS (–8) is negative and it is insignificant.**
B) How many lags of the LEIS should be used to explain COIN? Explain how you came to this conclusion. **Lag length 7 works well (all correct signs and only lags 6 and 5 are insign.); 6 works well (all correct signs and only lag 5 is insign.); 5 is not an improvement over 6 (all correct signs with lag 2 insign.); 4 and 3 are same as 5; finally, 2 has all correct signs and statistical sign. So, 7, 6, and 5 are good responses.**
C) Does the regression you settled on in B) above suffer from serial correlation according to the Durbin-Watson test? Show the 5-step procedure.

Working with a lag of 6:

1) Ho: no positive auto   Ha: positive auto
2) 5%
3) If $0 < d < d_L$, then reject Ho
   If $d_L < d < d_U$, then inconclusive
4) $d = 1.239550$; $d_L = 1.6$; $d_U = 1.83$ (n=173; k = 8)
5) Reject Ho; positive serial correlation is present

D) Does the regression you settled on in B) above suffer from serial correlation according to the Lagrange Multiplier test? Show the 5-step procedure.

Lagrange Multiplier test (lag of 6)

1) Ho: no serial correlation   Ha: serial correlation exists
2) 5%
3) If $nR^2 > \chi c$, then reject Ho (d.f. = k (from the auxiliary regression) – 1=8)
4) $30.19793 > 15.51$, reject Ho (chi-squared = 16.92 for lag of 7)
5) Reject Ho; auto present

E) Does the regression you settled on in B) above suffer from multicollinearity? On what do you base your response? **Not very much, mild to moderate — the VIF = 1.37**

F) Employ a Koyck lag structure in the COIN/LEIS regression. Does this regression suffer from serial correlation according to the h test? Show the 5-step procedure.

1) Ho: no autocorrelation Ha: auto present

$$h = (1 - \frac{d}{2})\sqrt{\frac{n}{1 - n(\text{var}(\hat{\beta}))}} \qquad h = (1 - \frac{2.13}{2})\sqrt{\frac{178}{1 - 178(0.05^2)}} = -1.16$$

2) 5%
3) If $|h| > t^c$, then reject Ho (d.f. = n – k)
4) $h = (.06)(17.94) = 1.07$; $t^c = 1.984$ (d.f. = 178 – 3; using d.f. = 100)
5) Do not reject Ho; no auto present

G) Employ a Koyck lag structure in the COIN/LEIS regression. Does this regression suffer from serial correlation according to the Lagrange Multiplier test? Show the 5-step procedure.

1) Ho: no serial correlation   Ha: serial correlation exists
2) 5%
3) If $nR^2 > \chi c$, then reject Ho (d.f. = k (from the auxiliary regression) – 1)
4) $5.808074 < 7.81$,
5) Do Not Reject Ho; auto is not present

H) Employ a Koyck lag structure in the COIN/LEIS regression. Does this regression suffer from multicollinearity? On what do you base your response? **Not very much—the VIF = 1.01**

I) According to the Koyck model, a 1 unit increase in LEIS implies COIN will be how much higher or lower in the short run? **0.327359 higher**

J) In the long-run the 1 unit increase in LEIS implies COIN will eventually change how much? $\beta_1/(1 - \lambda) = 0.33/(1 - 0.603959) = 0.83$

5. Use the data in QLEISCOIN and statistical software to do Granger tests to determine if changes in the leading economic indicators (LEIS) precede changes in the coincident indicators (COIN).

A) Using lag lengths of 6, show the 5-step procedure for the Granger test to prove that changes in LEIS do not precede changes in COIN.

Pairwise Granger Causality Tests
Sample: 1959:1 2003:4
Lags: 6

Null Hypothesis:	Obs	F-Statistic	Probability
COIN does not Granger Cause LEIS	173	8.00292	1.5E–07
LEIS does not Granger Cause COIN		15.6394	4.4E–14

1) **Ho: LEIS does not Granger Cause COIN**
   Ha: LEIS does Granger Cause COIN
2) **5%**
3) **If F > F^C , Reject Ho**
4) **15.6394 > 2.18 (d.f. num. = R = 6; d.f. den. = n – k = 173 – 13 = 160; using 120)**
5) **Reject Ho → changes in LEIS precede changes in COIN**

B) Using lag lengths of 6, show the 5-step procedure for the Granger test to prove that changes in COIN do not precede changes in LEIS.

1) **Ho: COIN does not Granger Cause LEIS**
   Ha: COIN does Granger Cause LEIS
2) **5%**
3) **If F > F^C , Reject Ho**
4) **8.00292 > 2.18 (d.f. num. = R = 6; d.f. den. = n – k = 173 – 13 = 160; using 120)**
5) **Reject Ho → changes in COIN precede changes in LEIS**

Dependent Variable: LEIS
Method: Least Squares
Date: 04/16/10   Time: 08:47
Sample(adjusted): 1960:4 2003:4
Included observations: 173 after adjusting endpoints

Variable	Coefficient	Std. Error	t-Statistic	Prob.
C	0.523021	0.131798	3.968344	0.0001
COIN(–1)	–0.990878	0.175292	–5.652734	0.0000
COIN(–2)	–0.051971	0.200176	–0.259625	0.7955
COIN(–3)	–0.119829	0.189817	–0.631286	0.5288
COIN(–4)	0.098743	0.178740	0.552438	0.5814

COIN(–5)	–0.052785	0.165461	–0.319020	0.7501
COIN(–6)	0.179148	0.144364	1.240950	0.2164
LEIS(–1)	0.653975	0.092049	7.104657	0.0000
LEIS(–2)	0.176288	0.109281	1.613163	0.1087
LEIS(–3)	0.277366	0.109328	2.537014	0.0121
LEIS(–4)	–0.019450	0.105757	–0.183911	0.8543
LEIS(–5)	0.125042	0.102509	1.219815	0.2243
LEIS(–6)	0.024625	0.085896	0.286678	0.7747

R-squared	0.438093	Mean dependent var	0.394833
Adjusted R-squared	0.395950	S.D. dependent var	1.183041
S.E. of regression	0.919467	Akaike info criterion	2.742126
Sum squared resid	135.2672	Schwarz criterion	2.979079
Log likelihood	–224.1939	F-statistic	10.39538
Durbin-Watson stat	1.975072	Prob(F-statistic)	0.000000

Dependent Variable: LEIS
Method: Least Squares
Date: 04/16/10   Time: 08:49
Sample(adjusted): 1960:4 2003:4
Included observations: 173 after adjusting endpoints

Variable	Coefficient	Std. Error	t-Statistic	Prob.
C	0.250640	0.089861	2.789191	0.0059
LEIS(–1)	0.508384	0.077577	6.553257	0.0000
LEIS(–2)	–0.068384	0.087131	–0.784839	0.4337
LEIS(–3)	0.140603	0.085915	1.636523	0.1036
LEIS(–4)	–0.196359	0.085897	–2.285992	0.0235
LEIS(–5)	–0.011192	0.086981	–0.128668	0.8978
LEIS(–6)	–0.013386	0.077324	–0.173115	0.8628

squared	0.269459	Mean dependent var	0.394833
.ljusted R-squared	0.243054	S.D. dependent var	1.183041
S.E. of regression	1.029277	Akaike info criterion	2.935211
Sum squared resid	175.8621	Schwarz criterion	3.062800
Log likelihood	–246.8957	F-statistic	10.20483
Durbin-Watson stat	1.993804	Prob(F-statistic)	0.000000

$$F = \frac{(SSR_R - SSR)/R}{SSR/(n-k)} = \frac{(175.8621 - 135.2672)/6}{135.2672/(173-13)} = \frac{6.7658}{.84542} = 8.0029059$$

C) Given your results in A) and B) above, can you unequivocally conclude that changes in LEIS precede changes in COIN? **No**

D) Does your answer to C) above change when lag lengths of 10 are used? **No**

Pairwise Granger Causality Tests
Sample: 1959:1 2003:4
Lags: 10

Null Hypothesis:	Obs	F-Statistic	Probability
COIN does not Granger Cause LEIS	169	4.36968	2.3E–05
LEIS does not Granger Cause COIN		10.9508	8.0E–14

E) Does your answer to C) above change when lag lengths of 12 are used? **No**

Pairwise Granger Causality Tests
Sample: 1959:1 2003:4
Lags: 12

Null Hypothesis:	Obs	F-Statistic	Probability
COIN does not Granger Cause LEIS	167	4.01460	2.4E–05
LEIS does not Granger Cause COIN		9.44066	2.8E–13

7. Use the data in MACRO.XLS and statistical software to run Granger tests to determine if changes in M2 Granger-cause INFL or visa-versa.

   A) What are the appropriate lag lengths? Explain. **Lower lags (2 – 4) are closer to showing some significance but no hypothesis is rejected for any lags up to at least 12.**
   B) What do you conclude? Explain. **Since no hypothesis is rejected at almost all lag lengths, it appears as if changes in M2 do not Granger-cause INFL and visa-versa.**

9. Using the data in MACRO.XLS and statistical software, which of the following variables appear to be nonstationary because of nonconstant means or nonconstant variances? Produce the graph for each variable and say if the problem is a nonconstant mean or variance, both, or neither.

A) Real investment (rinv)
Nonstationary- Nonconstant mean; variance

B) The first difference in real investment
Stationary or not due to nonconstant variance

C) The second difference in real investment
Stationary or not due to nonconstant variance

D) The first difference in the money supply (m2)

Nonstationary- nonconstant variance & mean

E) Interest rate on AAA corporate bonds (aaa)

Nonstationary- nonconstant mean

11. Which variables from the list above are nonstationary according to the Dickey-Fuller test? Show the 5-step procedure for each variable.

A) Real investment (rinv)

ADF Test Statistic	2.548323	1% Critical Value*	−3.4597
		5% Critical Value	−2.8739
		10% Critical Value	−2.5733

1) Ho: B1 = 0 (X is nonstationary)   Ha: B1 < 0 (X is stationary)
2) 5%
3) If t-ratio < −tc*, reject Ho
4) 2.548323 < −2.8739
5) Do not reject Ho – rinv is nonstationary

B) The first difference in real investment

ADF Test Statistic	−12.72571	1% Critical Value*	−3.4598
		5% Critical Value	−2.8740
		10% Critical Value	−2.5733

1) Ho: B1 = 0 (X is nonstationary)   Ha: B1 < 0 (X is stationary)
2) 5%
3) If t-ratio < –tc*, reject Ho
4) –12.72571 < –2.8740
5) Reject Ho – fd1rinv is stationary

C) The second difference in real investment

ADF Test Statistic	–26.49940	1% Critical Value*	–3.4599
		5% Critical Value	–2.8740
		10% Critical Value	–2.5734

1) Ho: B1 = 0 (X is nonstationary)   Ha: B1 < 0 (X is stationary)
2) 5%
3) If t-ratio < –tc*, reject Ho
4) –26.49940 < –2.8740
5) Reject Ho – fd2rinv is stationary

D) The first difference in the money supply (m2)

ADF Test Statistic	–4.709242	1% Critical Value*	–3.4667
		5% Critical Value	–2.8771
		10% Critical Value	–2.5750

1) Ho: B1 = 0 (X is nonstationary)   Ha: B1 < 0 (X is stationary)
2) 5%
3) If t-ratio < –tc*, reject Ho
4) –4.709242 < –2.8771
5) Reject Ho – fd1m2 is stationary

E) Interest rate on AAA corporate bonds (aaa)

ADF Test Statistic	–1.432218	1% Critical Value*	–3.4597
		5% Critical Value	–2.8739
		10% Critical Value	–2.5733

1) Ho: B1 = 0 (X is nonstationary)   Ha: B1 < 0 (X is stationary)
2) 5%
3) If t-ratio < –tc*, reject Ho
4) –1.432218 > –2.8739
5) Do not reject Ho – AAA is nonstationary

13. Use the data in AJ.XLS to replicate the famous Andersen-Jordan study by regressing a constant term, lagged money supply (m2) and the lagged standardized federal deficit (fp) on nominal GDP (ngdp): $ngdp_t = \hat{\beta}_0 + \hat{\beta}_1 m2_{t-1} + \hat{\beta}_2 fp_{t-1} + e_t$

A) Which explanatory variable has the more profound impact on nominal GDP? Explain your response. **Only m2 is statistically significant.**

B) Which variables in the regression are nonstationary? Explain. **Line graphs are inconclusive. Correlograms suggest that the first differences in M2 and NGDP are nonstationary. Dickey-Fuller tests indicate that first the differences of M2, and NGDP are nonstationary.**

C) Check for cointegration among the variables in the regression. Show the 5-step Dickey-Fuller procedure.

1) **Ho: $\hat{\beta}_1 = 0$ (e_t is nonstationary)   Ha: $\hat{\beta}_1 < 0$ (e_t is stationary)**
   (X and Y are not cointegrated)   (X and Y are cointegrated)
2) **5%**
3) **If t-ratio $< -tc^*$, reject Ho**
4) **$-3.11 < -2.9350$**
5) **Reject Ho $\rightarrow$ The regression is cointegrated.**

Solutions to Test Yourself Problems

1. Given

Y_i	X_i
11.2	5.4
−27.1	6.7
33.4	7.1
0.02	−8.8

A) Calculate the values for the structural parameters of $Y_i = \hat{\beta}_0 + \hat{\beta}_1 X_i + e_i$.

(Show your work, making the details of your calculations apparent.)

$\hat{\beta}_1 = 0.4 \quad \hat{\beta}_0 = 3.33$

B) Interpret the values you obtained for $\hat{\beta}_0$ and $\hat{\beta}_1$ above.

If X = 0, then Y is expected to equal 3.33

If X increases 1 unit, then Y is expected to increase 0.4 units

C) According to the SER, is the fit of the regression adequate? Explain.

No, the SER (= 30.58) is greater than ½ Y-bar (= 4.38)

D) What percent of the variation in Y is explained by X in this regression?

r2 = .015 – 1.5 percent of the variation in Y is explained by X.

E) Suppose we ran this regression again with a new set of observations on Y and X. Would you be surprised if $\hat{\beta}_1$ turned out to be –2.0? Explain why or why not.

SE($\hat{\beta}_1$) = 2.31. No, because -2.0 is very close to the expected variation in $\hat{\beta}_1$ in repeated sampling.

2. Answer the following questions:

A) Distinguish between the population regression function and the sample regression function.

The population regression function is the line that minimizes the Σe_i^2 for the entire population of error-free observations on X and Y. The sample regression function minimizes the Σe_i^2 for a sample from the entire population of observations of X and Y that may contain errors.

B) Distinguish between cross-sectional and time-series data.

Cross-sectional data are observations on X and Y at a given point in time. Time-series data are observations on X and Y over time.

C) What is a normal equation?

A normal equation will be encountered when deriving formulae for structural parameters in regression equations. Once the derivatives, or partial derivatives, of the function to be minimized are taken and set equal to zero, the normal equation(s) can be found by beginning to solve for the unknown(s). Normal equations have no negative terms.

D) Explain why a perfectly vertical regression line is impossible.

Any observations on a scattergram that do not lie directly on a vertical line will have an infinite vertical distance to the line. Since regression lines minimize the sum of the squared vertical distances to the line, a vertical line cannot provide that minimum.

3. Which of the following is (are) NOT correct? **A, E, F, H, I**

A) $Y_i = \beta_0 + \beta_1 X_i$ D) $Y_i = \hat{\beta}_0 + \hat{\beta}_1 X_i + e_i$ G) $E(Y_i|X_i) = \beta_0 + \beta_1 X_i$

B) $= \beta_0 + \beta_1 X_i$ E) $\hat{Y}_i = \hat{\beta}_0 + \hat{\beta}_1 X_i + e_i$ H) $\hat{Y}_i = \beta_0 + \beta_1 X_i + u_i$

C) $Y_i = \beta_0 + \beta_1 X_i + u_i$ F) $Y_i = \hat{\beta}_0 + \hat{\beta}_1 X_i + u_i$ I) $E(Y_i|X_i) = \hat{\beta}_0 + \hat{\beta}_1 X_i + e_i$

4. Answer True or False:

A) **F** Sabermetrics is the application of statistical analysis to war.

B) **T** Unless all the observations lie on a straight line, it is impossible to fit a line such that $\Sigma|e_i| = 0$.

C) **T** When a line is fit to observations on a scattergram so that Σe_i^2 is minimized, then $\Sigma e_i = 0$.

D) **F** When a line is fit to observations on a scattergram so that Σe_i^2 is minimized, then sometimes more than one line meets this criteria.

E) **F** $\Sigma(X_i - \bar{X})(Y_i - \bar{Y}) = \bar{X}\Sigma Y_i - \bar{Y}\Sigma X_i$

F) **T** $\Sigma(X_i - \bar{X}) = 0$

G) **T** A large SER and low r^2 can be the result of the Y- variable being very random.

H) **T** If $r^2 = 0$, then β_1 must $= 0$.

I) **F** If $r^2 = 1$, then β_1 must $= 1$.

J) **T** If SER $= 0$, then r^2 must $= 1$.

Solutions to Test Yourself on Chapters 4 and 5

Dependent Variable: WHY
Method: Least Squares
Sample: 1978 2006
Included observations: 29

Variable	Coefficient	Std. Error	t-Statistic	Prob.
C	1.997710	51.03278	0.039146	0.9691
EX1	15.81597	3.734046	4.235611	0.0003
EX2	3.046501	2.188336	1.392154	0.1761
EX3	−0.000145	0.005735	−0.025229	0.9801
R-squared	0.765250	Mean dependent var		152.0576

Adjusted R-squared	0.737080	S.D. dependent var	51.28692
S.E. of regression	26.29775	Akaike info criterion	9.504286
Sum squared resid	17289.29	Schwarz criterion	9.692879
Log likelihood	-133.8121	F-statistic	27.16539
Durbin-Watson stat	0.723982	Prob(F-statistic)	0.000000

1. Use the Eviews output above and below to help with A) through G)

A) Interpret the coefficient on EX1. **If EX1 increases 1 unit, then WHY is expected to increase 15.81597 units, holding EX2 and EX3 constant.**

B) Interpret the coefficient on the constant term. **If X1 = X2 = X3 = 0, then WHY is expected to equal 1.997710.**

C) Is EX2 significant at the 17 percent critical level? Explain. **No, its prob value is greater than .17**

D) Perform a positive sign test on the coefficient attached to EX2. Show the 5-step procedure.

1) **Ho: $\beta_2 = 0$ Ha: $\beta_2 > 0$**
2) **5%**
3) **If t-ratio > t^c, then reject Ho**
4) **1.392154 < 1.708 (d.f. = n– k = 29 – 4 =25)**
5) **Do Not Reject Ho → β_0 is not significantly positive**

E) Perform a test to determine if the coefficient on EX3 is greater than –1.11. Show the 5-step procedure.

1) **Ho: $\beta_3 = -1.11$ Ha: $\beta_3 > -1.11$**
2) **5%**
3) **If t-ratio > t^c, then reject Ho**
4) **193.6 > 1.708 (d.f. = n – k = 29 – 4 = 25)**
5) **Reject Ho → β_0 is significantly greater than –1.11**

$$t\text{-}ratio = \frac{\hat{\beta}_0 - \beta_{Ho}}{SE(\hat{\beta}_0)} = \frac{-0.000145 + 1.11}{0.005735} = 193.6$$

F) Perform a test to determine if R-squared is greater than zero. Show the 5-step procedure.
1. **Ho: $r^2 = 0$ Ha: $r^2 > 0$**
2. **5%**
3. **If F > Fc, then reject Ho**

---

4. 27.16539 > 2.99 (d.f. = k – 1 = 3 in the numerator and n – k = 25 in the denominator)
5. Reject Ho → r^2 is statistically greater than zero.

G) Based on the information in the table above (and ignoring Ramsey's Reset test which we will perform in a moment) do you think the regression above is under or overspecified? Explain. **Overspecified because EX2 and EX3 are insignificant.**

H) Perform Ramsey's Reset Test on the regression above using the Eviews printout below. Show the 5-step procedure.

Ramsey RESET Test:

F-statistic	15.32735	Probability	0.000059
Log likelihood ratio	24.56517	Probability	0.000005

Test Equation:
Dependent Variable: WHY
Method: Least Squares
Sample: 1978 2006
Included observations: 29

Variable	Coefficient	Std. Error	t-Statistic	Prob.
C	1190.553	228.1171	5.219043	0.0000
EX1	–314.2471	60.00884	–5.236679	0.0000
EX2	–62.55620	12.06659	–5.184249	0.0000
EX3	–0.013078	0.006110	–2.140328	0.0432
FITTED^2	0.119787	0.021647	5.533578	0.0000
FITTED^3	–0.000222	4.06E–05	–5.474315	0.0000

R-squared	0.899370	Mean dependent var	152.0576
Adjusted R-squared	0.877494	S.D. dependent var	51.28692
S.E. of regression	17.95084	Akaike info criterion	8.795142
Sum squared resid	7411.349	Schwarz criterion	9.078031
Log likelihood	–121.5296	F-statistic	41.11217
Durbin-Watson stat	1.018779	Prob(F-statistic)	0.000000

1. **Ho:** $\hat{\beta}_4 = \hat{\beta}_5 = 0$ **Ha:** $\hat{\beta}_4$ **and/or** $\hat{\beta}_5 \neq 0$

      (No variables excluded)   **(Variables excluded)**

2. **5%**
3. **If F > F^c, then reject Ho**
4. **15.32735 > 3.42; where F^c has d.f. NUM = 2 ; d.f. DEN = n – k = 23**
5. **Reject Ho → variables are excluded**

I) What do the terms "FITTED^2" and "FITTED^3", refer to in the Eviews printout? **These terms represent possible missing variables. They are the predicted WHY values from the original regression squared and cubed.**

2. Define the following terms

A) unbiased estimator - **an estimator that averages out to the true value in repeated sampling.** $E(\hat{\beta}_0) = \hat{\beta}_0$

B) best estimator – **an estimator that varies less than any other possible estimator in repeated sampling. Var** $(\hat{\beta}_0) <$ **Var** $(\tilde{\beta}_0)$ **where** $\tilde{\beta}_0$ **is any other possible estimator of** β_0.

C) correlation coefficient (r) – **measures the degree of linear correlation between two variables.**

D) Prob-value – **the lowest level of significance that can be used in a hypothesis test while still rejecting Ho.**

3. Mark each statement TRUE or FALSE.

A) **F** If a regression is overspecified, then it would be surprising to see the t-ratios become more robust once the extraneous variables were removed.

B) **F** If a regression is underspecified, then it would be surprising to see the estimators change markedly once the missing variables were included.

C) **T** If a regression is overspecified, then it would be surprising to see the estimators change markedly once the extraneous variables were removed.

D) **F** A 95% confidence interval for a coefficient will be smaller than a 90% confidence interval.

E) **T** The Andersen-Jordan equation indicates that monetary policy is more effective than fiscal policy.

F) **T** Deriving the estimators for $Y_i = \hat{\beta}_0 + \hat{\beta}_1 X1_i + \hat{\beta}_2 X2_i + e_i$ will yield 3 normal equations.

G) **F** The Akaike Criterion is monotonically decreasing with respect to the number of explanatory variables.

H) **T** The higher the critical level of the hypothesis test, the less chance there is that the test will result in a TYPE II error.

I) **F** A coefficient that is significant at the 1 percent critical level may not be significant at the 2 percent critical level.

J) **F** A test of significance is more likely to result in a TYPE I error in an overspecified model.

1. Interpret every structural parameter in each of the following regressions considering:

> WAGES = pay per hour of work
> EXP = years of experience
> EXPSQ = EXP squared
> ED = years of education
> DGEN = 1 if male, 0 otherwise
> INTACT = DGEN X EXP
> LN --- = the natural log of a variable

A) $LNWAGES_i = 2.1 + 1.3 \ EXP_i + e_i$ Adjusted $R^2 = .77$
   If EXP = 0, LNWAGES = 2.1 (WAGES = 8.2)
   If EXP ↑ 1 unit, then WAGES ↑ 130%

B) $LNWAGES_i = 2.1 + 1.3 \ LNEXP_i + 2.3 \ LNED_i + e_i$ Adjusted $R^2 = .79$
   If EXP and ED = 1, then LNWAGES = 2.1 (WAGES = 8.2)
   If EXP ↑ 1%, then WAGES ↑ 1.3%, holding ED constant
   If ED ↑ 1%, then WAGES ↑ 2.3%, holding EXP constant

C) $WAGES = 2.1 + 1.3 \ EXP_i + 3.5 \ DGEN_i + 4.2 \ INTACT_i + e_i$ Adjusted $R^2 = .80$
   For a female with 0 EXP, WAGES = 2.1
   For a female, if EXP ↑ 1 unit, then WAGES ↑ 1.3 units
   For a male with 0 EXP, WAGES are 3.5 units higher than a female with 0 EXP
   For a male, if EXP ↑ 1 unit, then WAGES ↑ 4.2 units more than the 1.3 units they
   would increase for a female

2. Which regression of the three above fits best? On what do you base your response? **You cannot say since the regressions have different dependent variables.**

3. What would be the values for the structural parameters for the regression above, 1 C), if DGEN was defined as 0 if male ; 1 otherwise?
   WAGES = 5.6 + 5.5 EXP − 3.5 DGEN − 4.2 INTACT + e

4. Draw diagrams that reflect the following regressions. Put WAGES on the Y axis and EXP on the X axis in each case.

   A) WAGES = 2.5 − .01 (1/EXP) + e
      (Also, show where 2.5 is on the Y axis.)

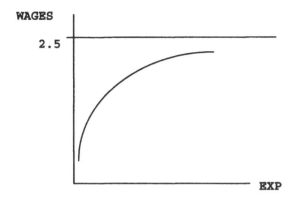

B) WAGES = 2.5 + 1.1 EXP + 3.5 DGEN – 3.0 INTACT + e
(Label all intercepts and slopes with their values.)

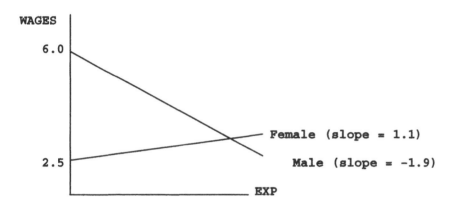

C) WAGES = 2.5 + 1.1 EXP – 0.22 EXPSQ + e

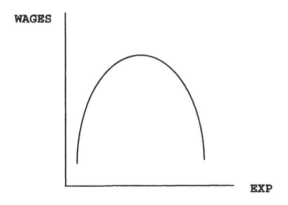

5. Given:

Dependent Variable: BINGE
Method: Least Squares
Sample(adjusted): 1 695
Included observations: 695 after adjusting endpoints

Variable	Coefficient	Std. Error	t-Statistic	Prob.
C	0.818558	0.125126	6.541884	0.0000
GPA	−0.125652	0.033407	−3.761217	0.0002
MALE	0.135596	0.036207	3.745041	0.0002

R-squared	0.056816	Mean dependent var		0.628777
Adjusted R-squared	0.052721	S.D. dependent var		0.483480
S.E. of regression	0.470563	Akaike info criterion		1.335963
Sum squared resid	153.0075	Schwarz criterion		1.362115
Log likelihood	−460.2471	F-statistic		13.87497
Durbin-Watson stat	2.015544	Prob(F-statistic)		0.000000

where   BINGE = 1 if student is a binge drinker, 0 otherwise
             GPA = grade point average
             MALE = 1 if male, 0 otherwise

A) Interpret the constant term.
The probability of a female with 0 GPA binging is 81.8558%

B) Interpret the coefficient on GPA.
If GPA ↑ 1 unit, then the probability of binging ↓ 12.5652% (for males and females)

6. Given the following logistic regression results:

Dependent Variable: BINGE
Method: ML - Binary Logit (Quadratic hill climbing)
Sample(adjusted): 1 695
Included observations: 695 after adjusting endpoints
Convergence achieved after 4 iterations
Covariance matrix computed using second derivatives

Variable	Coefficient	Std. Error	z-Statistic	Prob.
C	2.174010	0.565780	3.842498	0.0001
GPA	−0.552753	0.159758	−3.459934	0.0005
MALE	0.581107	0.163816	3.547312	0.0004

What is the probability that a male with a GPA = 3.2 is a binge drinker? Show your calculations.

$$\ln(\frac{BINGE_i}{1 - BINGE_i}) = 2.174010 - 0.552753(3.2) + 0.581107(1) = 0.9863074$$

$$(\frac{BINGE_i}{1 - BINGE_i}) = 2.6813; \quad BINGE = 72.84\%$$

7. Label each statement below TRUE or FALSE. (3 pts. each)

A) **T** In a regression through the origin, $\hat{\beta}_1 = \dfrac{\Sigma X_i Y_i}{\Sigma X_i^2}$.

B) **T** Altering the units that the variables in a regression are measured in may alter the values of the structural parameters, but never their t-ratios.

C) **F** If two models have the exact same dependent variable, then the one with the better fit is the better model.

D) **T** R-squared is not a good measure of fit for a linear probability model.

E) **T** The magnitude of a coefficient by itself says nothing about its significance.

F) **F** A logistic model can yield a predicted value for the dependent variable that is equal to one, but never greater than one.

G) **F** A linear probability model can yield a predicted value for the dependent variable that is equal to one, but never greater than one.

H) **F** R-squared is invalid in regressions including dummy independent variables.

I) **T** Regressions in the wrong functional form are biased.

J) **T** Ramsey's Reset test can help to determine if a regression is in the correct functional form.

Solutions to Test Yourself on Chapters 8 and 9

1. Is a study that uses "experimental" data superior to a similar study that uses "nonexperimental" data? Explain. **Not necessarily. Experimental data has the advantage of controlling for other factors that can affect the results. However, a regression using nonexperimental data can control for other factors affecting the dependent variable by including them in the specification.**

A regression using nonexperimental data will have independent variables that are not predetermined. However, the regression may still be linear if the error terms are not correlated with the independent variables.

2. Prove that $E[\hat{\beta}_1] = \beta_1$.

Assume $\hat{\beta}_1$ is a linear estimator of β_1.

$$\hat{\beta}_1 = \frac{\Sigma(X_i - \overline{X})Y_i}{\Sigma(X_i - \overline{X})^2} = \Sigma w_i Y_i \; ; \quad \text{where } w_i = \frac{(X_i - \overline{X})}{\Sigma(X_i - \overline{X})^2}$$

$$\hat{\beta}_1 = \Sigma w_i Y_i = \Sigma w_i(\beta_0 + \beta_1 X_i + u_i) = \beta_0 \Sigma w_i + \beta_1 \Sigma w_i X_i + \Sigma w_i u_i$$

$$\hat{\beta}_1 = \beta_1 + \Sigma w_i u_i \text{ since } \Sigma w_i = 0 \text{ and } \Sigma w_i X_i = 1$$

Then $E[\hat{\beta}_1] = E[\beta_1 + \Sigma w_i u_i] = \beta_1$ **only if** $E[\Sigma w_i u_i] = 0$

3. Assume $\hat{\beta}_1$ is linear and unbiased. Use that information to argue that $\hat{\beta}_0 (= \overline{Y} - \hat{\beta}_1 \overline{X})$ is unbiased as well. **If $\hat{\beta}_1$ is linear and unbiased then so is the constant term because the constant term is a linear function of $\hat{\beta}_1$.**

4. Defend the process known as "data mining." Does this process not violate the theories of inference?
Data mining does indeed violate the theories of inference. By running several specifications, variables are given more than one chance to be significant. This is an invalid form of hypothesis testing. However, as long as hypothesis tests are carried out with this precaution in mind, data mining can be a very useful activity. Often economic theory is not specific enough to dictate functional form or even which independent variables to include. Data mining can help make determinations of functional form and model specification.

5. Discuss the pros and cons of the following remedies for multicollinearity:
   A) drop a variable – **this remedy is worse than the disease if it results in an underspecified model.**
   B) try first-differences – **this is not possible with cross-sectional data; it often lowers r-squared; there should be a theoretical reason for using this form as well.**
   C) try an alternate functional form such as the reciprocal form – **this remedy is worse than the disease if it results in a misspecified model.**
   D) do nothing – **is a valid response since the consequences of multicollinearity can be mild. Still, hypothesis tests should be conducted with caution.**

6. Use the following equation to argue that the SE($\hat{\beta}_1$) is undefined under perfect

multicollinearity: $SE(\hat{\beta}_1) = \sqrt{\dfrac{\Sigma e_i^2 / (n-k)}{\Sigma(X_{i1} - \overline{X}_1)^2 (1 - r_{12}^2)}}$; where r_{12}^2 is the square of

the correlation coefficient bewteen X1 and X2. **The square of the correlation coefficient bewteen X1 and X2 will equal 1 under perfect multicollinearity. This makes the denominator of the formula above equal to zero, which makes the SE($\hat{\beta}_1$) undefined.**

Mark each of the following statements TRUE or FALSE.

1. **F** $\hat{\beta}_1$ is BLUE in the presence of serial correlation.

2. **F** In order to show that $\hat{\beta}_1$ is best, it must be assumed that the e_i's are not correlated with each other.

3. **F** In order to show that $\hat{\beta}_1$ is unbiased, it must be assumed that the true error terms are not correlated with each other.

4. **T** One of the conditions necessary for hypothesis testing is that the u_i's are normally distributed.

5. **F** One of the conditions necessary to prove that the OLS estimators are BLUE is that the u_i's are normally distributed.

6. **F** A regression in the incorrect functional form violates assumption 4 of the Classical Linear Regression Model (CLRM).

7. **F** In the presence of multicollinearity, the estimate of R-squared will be biased.

8. **T** $VAR(\hat{\beta}_1) = E\left[(\hat{\beta}_1 - \beta_1)^2\right] = E\left[(\beta_1 + \Sigma w_i u_i - \beta_1)^2\right] = \sigma^2 \Sigma w_i^2$

9. **T** It is possible, although unlikely, that the structural parameters in an underspecified regression are unbiased.

10. **T** With perfect multicollinearity, the OLS estimators are undefined.

11. **F** Consider $Y_i = \hat{\beta}_0 + \hat{\beta}_1 X1_i + \hat{\beta}_2 X2_i + \hat{\beta}_3 X3_i + \hat{\beta}_4 X4_i + e_i$. If X1 and X2 are highly collinear, then the standard errors of $\hat{\beta}_1$ and $\hat{\beta}_2$ will be bloated, but not those of $\hat{\beta}_3$ and $\hat{\beta}_4$.

12. **F** $\Sigma w_i X_i = 0$; where $w_i = \dfrac{(X_i - \overline{X})}{\Sigma(X_i - \overline{X})^2}$

13. **F** A predetermined explanatory variable is stochastic.

14. **F** A VIF (variance inflation factor) less than 5 means multicollinearity is nonexistent.

15. **T** $u_i \sim N(0, \sigma^2)$ indicates that the true error terms are normally distributed with an expected value of 0 and each true error term has a variance equal to some constant, σ^2.

16. **F** Assumptions 1 and 2 of the Classical Linear Regression Model (CLRM) are necessary to prove that the OLS estimators are linear.

17. **T** Assumptions 1 and 2 of the (CLRM) are necessary to prove that the OLS estimators are unbiased.

18. **F** Assumptions 3 and 4 of the (CLRM) are necessary to prove that the OLS estimators are linear.

19. **F** Assumptions 3 and 4 of the (CLRM) are necessary to prove that the OLS estimators are unbiased.

20. **T** Assumptions 3 and 4 of the (CLRM) are necessary to prove that the OLS estimators are best.

Solutions to Test Yourself on Chapters 10 and 11

1. Describe the following procedures:
   A) Park test

   To test if $Y_i = \hat{\beta}_0 + \hat{\beta}_1 X_i + e_i$ suffers from heteroskedasticity, square the residuals and regress them on the explanatory variable giving rise to the heteroskedasticity. Use the double-log form if possible; if that is not possible, the semi-log form will do:

   $$\ln(e_i^2) = \alpha_0 + \alpha_1 \ln(X_i) + \varepsilon_i$$

   If α_1 is statistically significant, then heteroskedasticity is present.

   B) Weighted least-squares

   Suppose the error terms from $SAVING_i = \beta_0 + \beta_1 INCOME_i + u_i$ are heteroskedastic in that the variance of the error terms varies with INCOME. Multiply through the original regression by 1/INCOME.

   $$\frac{SAVING_i}{INCOME_i} = \beta_0 \frac{1}{INCOME_i} + \beta_1 \frac{INCOME_i}{INCOME_i} + \frac{u_i}{INCOME_i}$$

   Or
   multiplying through by $1/\sqrt{INCOME_i}$

   $$\frac{SAVING_i}{\sqrt{INCOME_i}} = \beta_0 \left[\frac{1}{\sqrt{INCOME_i}} \right] + \beta_1 \left[\frac{INCOME_i}{\sqrt{INCOME_i}} \right] + \frac{u_i}{\sqrt{INCOME_i}}$$

   C) Generalized least-squares

   $$Y_t - \rho Y_{t-1} = \beta_0 (1-\rho) + \beta_1 (X_t - \rho X_{t-1}) + u_t - \rho u_{t-1}$$

   D) Cochrane-Orcutt iterative procedure

---

(1)   Estimate ρ with this formula → $\rho = \dfrac{\Sigma e_t e_{t-1}}{\Sigma e_{t-1}^{\,2}}$

(2)   Run GLS and obtain the new e_t's

(3)   Go back to (A)

(4)   Stop when sequential estimates of ρ do not vary by much.

E) Hildreth-Lu scanning procedure

    Since ρ is expected to lie between plus and minus unity, a computer can easily check to see which value of ρ gives the best results in a GLS regression.

        Assume ρ = –1. Run GLS. Assume ρ = –.9. Run GLS. Assume ρ = –.8. Run GLS. Assume ρ = +.9. Run GLS. Assume ρ = +1. Run GLS. Of all these GLS regressions, use the one that has the best fit according to the R² or SER.

F) Maximum likelihood procedure

    This procedure assigns initial values to $\hat{\beta}_0$, $\hat{\beta}_1$, and ρ, then considers the residuals from this GLS model. The pattern of the residuals indicates adjustments to the initial values of $\hat{\beta}_0$, $\hat{\beta}_1$, and ρ. The residuals from the new GLS model are again considered and used to make further adjustments to $\hat{\beta}_0$, $\hat{\beta}_1$, and ρ. The process stops when sequential estimates of $\hat{\beta}_0$, $\hat{\beta}_1$, and ρ do not vary significantly.

2. Draw a diagram indicative of heteroskedasticity. Label the horizontal axis "culprit" and be sure to correctly label the vertical axis. Draw a diagram indicative of negative serial correlation. Be sure to label the axes of your diagram.

Time

3. Describe the pros and cons of any 3 remedies for heteroskedasticity.
   Use alternate functional form – simple; often effective, but may lead to biased results.
   Do nothing – unbiased estimators good for forecasting, but hypothesis testing is invalid.
   Form ratios – simple; often effective, but not always possible.
   Newey-West – fixes standard errors and t-ratios, but not biased residual stats.
   Weighted Least-Squares – the appropriate remedy, but what weights to use?

4. What is a first-order Markov scheme? What is second-order serial correlation? What is "white noise"?
   A first-order Markov scheme is when the error terms from a regression are related to one another by: $e_t = \rho\, e_{t-1} + \varepsilon_t$ where $-1 < \rho < +1$ and ε_t is white noise. (i.e., $\varepsilon_t \sim N(0, \sigma^2)$) for all t. Second-order serial correlation is when the error terms from a regression are related to one another by: $e_t = \rho_1\, e_{t-1} + \rho_2\, e_{t-2}\, \varepsilon_t$

5. Does the White test below indicate heteroskedasticity? Show the 5-step procedure.

White Heteroskedasticity Test:

F-statistic	0.491592	Probability	0.780723
Obs*R-squared	2.645362	Probability	0.754462

Test Equation:
Dependent Variable: RESID^2
Method: Least Squares
Sample: 1 50
Included observations: 50

Variable	Coefficient	Std. Error	t-Statistic	Prob.
C	–275.2148	329.0460	–0.836402	0.4074
ED	18.22919	33.65147	0.541706	0.5908
ED^2	–0.211078	0.952250	–0.221662	0.8256
ED*EXPER	–0.453429	0.645192	–0.702781	0.4859
EXPER	16.12281	15.23650	1.058170	0.2958
EXPER^2	–0.236866	0.208270	–1.137306	0.2616

R-squared	0.052907	Mean dependent var	19.62276

Adjusted R-squared	−0.054717	S.D. dependent var	66.54024
S.E. of regression	68.33644	Akaike info criterion	11.39893
Sum squared resid	205474.2	Schwarz criterion	11.62837
Log likelihood	−278.9733	F-statistic	0.491592
Durbin-Watson stat	2.086374	Prob(F-statistic)	0.780723

1) Ho: no hetero   Ha: hetero exists
2) 5%
3) If $nR^2 > \chi c$, then reject Ho
4) 50(0.052907) = 2.645362; χc = 11.07 (d.f. = k − 1 from the auxiliary regr = 5)
5) Do Not Reject Ho: heteroskedasticity is not present in the original regression

6. Does the regression featured in the Eviews printout below suffer from autocorrelation according to a Durbin-Watson test at the 5% critical level? Show the 5-step procedure.

Dependent Variable: WHY
Method: Least Squares
Sample: 1956 1980
Included observations: 25

Variable	Coefficient	Std. Error	t-Statistic	Prob.
C	−0.325482	8.371100	−0.038882	0.9693
EX1	0.913309	0.032584	28.02956	0.0000
EX2	−0.558162	2.745564	−0.203296	0.8408

R-squared	0.997461	Mean dependent var	640.6560
Adjusted R-squared	0.997230	S.D. dependent var	173.4284
S.E. of regression	9.127571	Akaike info criterion	7.372643
Sum squared resid	1832.876	Schwarz criterion	7.518908
Log likelihood	−89.15804	F-statistic	4321.229
Durbin-Watson stat	1.655326	Prob(F-statistic)	0.000000

----

1) Ho: no positive auto   Ha: positive auto
2) 5%
3) If $0 < d < d_L$, then reject Ho
   If $d_L < d < d_U$, then inconclusive
4) get the numbers
5) reject or do not reject Ho

1) Ho: no negative auto   Ha: negative auto
2) 5%
3) If $4 - d_L < d < 4$, then reject Ho
   If $4 - d_U < d < 4 - d_L$, then inconclusive
4) get the numbers
5) reject or do not reject Ho

1) Ho: no positive auto   Ha: positive auto
2) 5%
3) If $0 < d < d_L$, then reject Ho
   If $d_L < d < d_U$, then inconclusive
4) d = 1.65 d_L = 1.21 d_U = 1.55 (n = 25; k = 3)
5) Do Not Reject Ho → no auto present

Mark each of the following statements TRUE or FALSE.

1. F The "culprit variable" is the dependent variable in a heteroskedastic regression.
2. F Application of Newey-West technique will alter the estimate of the SER.

3. **F** The standard error of the regression (SER) is biased downward in a regression suffering from heteroskedasticity.
4. **T** $E[u_i^2] = E[u_j^2] = \sigma^2$ for all $i \neq j$ is the definition of homoskedasticity.
5. **T** In the presence of heteroskedasticity, tests of significance must be carried out with caution since the T-ratios of the structural parameters are biased.
6. **T** The standard error of $\hat{\beta}_1$ is biased downward in the presence of serial correlation.
7. **T** The R-squared from a GLS regression is not directly comparable to the R-squared from the same regression run using OLS.
8. **T** The standard error of the regression (SER) is biased downward in a regression suffering from serial correlation.
9. **T** After correcting for autocorrelation, one would expect the standard errors of the structural parameters to increase.
10. **F** After correcting for heteroskedasticity, one would expect the standard errors of the structural parameters to increase.

Solutions to Test Yourself on Chapter 12

1. Given:

Dependent Variable: WHY
Method: Least Squares
Date: 02/26/03   Time: 15:28
Sample(adjusted): 1960 2001
Included observations: 42 after adjusting endpoints

Variable	Coefficient	Std. Error	t-Statistic	Prob.
C	−179.2567	163.7257	−1.094860	0.2803
EX	0.259430	0.091487	2.835696	0.0072
WHY(−1)	0.739760	0.198066	3.734916	0.0034

R-squared	0.997038	Mean dependent var	14665.26
Adjusted R-squared	0.996886	S.D. dependent var	4023.018
S.E. of regression	224.5044	Akaike info criterion	13.73442
Sum squared resid	1965686.	Schwarz criterion	13.85854
Log likelihood	−285.4227	F-statistic	6563.263
Durbin-Watson stat	0.866017	Prob(F-statistic)	0.000000

A) What is the short-run impact of EX on WHY? **.259430**

B) What is the long-run impact of Ex on WHY? **.259430/(1−.739760)=.99688**

C) Does this regression suffer from serial correlation according to Durbin's h-test? Show the 5-step procedure.
   1) **Ho: no autocorrelation Ha: auto present**
   2) **5%**
   3) **If $|h| > t^c$, then reject Ho (d.f. = n − k)**
   4) **h = undefined; t^c = 2.042 (d.f. = 42 − 3; using d.f. = 30)**
   5) **Do not reject Ho → no auto present**

$$h = (1 - \frac{d}{2})\sqrt{\frac{n}{1 - n(\text{var}(\hat{\beta}))}} \qquad h = (1 - \frac{0.866017}{2})\sqrt{\frac{42}{1 - 42(0.198066^2)}} = undefined$$

D) Does this regression suffer from serial correlation according to the Lagrange multiplier test? Show the 5-step procedure.
  1) **Ho: no serial correlation   Ha: serial correlation exists**
  2) **5%**
  3) **If $nR^2 > \chi c$, then reject Ho (d.f. = k (from the auxiliary regression) – 1)**
  4) **14.75185 > 7.81**
  5) **Reject Ho $\rightarrow$ serial correlation is present**

$$h = (1 - \frac{d}{2})\sqrt{\frac{n}{1 - n(\text{var}(\hat{\beta}))}}$$

Breusch-Godfrey Serial Correlation LM Test:

F-statistic	20.57279	Probability	0.000056
Obs*R-squared	14.75185	Probability	0.000123

Test Equation:
Dependent Variable: RESID
Method: Least Squares
Date: 02/26/03 Time: 15:29
Presample missing value lagged residuals set to zero.

Variable	Coefficient	Std. Error	t-Statistic	Prob.
C	-93.87846	135.1921	-0.694408	0.4917
EX	0.104824	0.078148	1.341348	0.1878
WHY(-1)	-0.113005	0.083810	-1.348355	0.1855
RESID(-1)	0.622442	0.137231	4.535724	0.0001

E) Suppose the regression does suffer from serial correlation. What is the major consequence? **Biased estimators (and residual statistics).**

2. A) Using lags of two periods on both independent variables, write the Granger equation to test if the chicken came before the egg.
  $EGG_t = b_0 + b_1\ EGG_{t-1} + b_2\ EGG_{t-2} + b_3\ CHICK_{t-1} + b_4\ CHICK_{t-2} + e_t$

B) Given the Eviews printout on page 204, did the chicken come before the egg? Explain how you know. **Yes, because we can reject the hypothesis that CHICK does not precede EGG at the 5% critical level, but we cannot reject the hypothesis that EGG does not precede CHICK.**

```
Pairwise Granger Causality Tests
Date: 04/14/05  Time: 10:37
Sample: 1951 1994
Lags: 2
```

Null Hypothesis:	Obs	F-Statistic	Probability
CHICK does not Granger Cause EGG	42	0.09849	0.04644
EGG does not Granger Cause CHICK		12.55461	0.17900

3. Are the first differences of M1 (FDM1) stationary? Using the Eviews printout below, show the 5-step procedure.

ADF Test Statistic	−0.615077	1% Critical Value*	−3.7667
		5% Critical Value	−3.0038
		10% Critical Value	−2.6417

Unit root test on FDM1.

1) **Ho: B1 = 0 (FDM1 is nonstationary)   Ha: B1 < 0 (FDM1 is stationary)**
2) **5%**
3) **If t-ratio < −tc*, reject Ho**
4) **−.615077 > −3.0038**
5) **Do not reject Ho: FDM1 is nonstationary**

4. A) List the three conditions for a variable to be stationary.
   1. **the mean of X is constant over time**
   2. **the variance of X is constant over time**
   3. **the correlation between Xt and Xt–k (for all k) is constant**

   B) What is spurious correlation? **A strong relationship between variables that is the result of a statistical fluke, not by an underlying causal relationship.**

5. A) What is "Granger causality"? **When changes in one times series precede the changes in another.**
   B) What is the consequence of a dependent variable "Granger causing" an independent variable in the regression? **The estimators are biased.**

6. A) What is the permanent income hypothesis? **Consumption depends most heavily expected future income.**
   B) Write the Koyck model that was used to test the permanent income hypothesis and explain why this regression is a test of the hypothesis.

$$CONt = Bo + B1DPIt + B2CONt–1$$

If B2 is positive and significant it implies that CONt depends on DPI lagged with geometrically declining weights which is a measure (albeit poor) of permanent income.

7. A) Explain why two nonstationary time series are likely to be spuriously correlated. **Assume time series A does not cause time series B. However, if both A and B have upward trends they will have a positive correlation coefficient.**

   B) What is the consequence of using nonstationary variables in a regression? **The estimators and residual statistics are biased.**

8. A) Write the Granger regression to determine if changes in A precede changes in B. Assume lags of 2 periods. $\mathbf{B_t = b_1 + b2\ B_{t-1} + b3\ B_{t-2} + b4\ A_{t-1} + b5\ A_{t-2} + e_t}$

   B) Why is it important to do the reverse Granger test before concluding that changes in A precede changes in B. **Because if B precedes A, then we cannot unequivocally conclude that A precedes B despite a Granger test that says so. The precedence in this case is inconclusive.**

9. A) Draw the correlogram (autocorrelation function) of a stationary variable. (Be sure to label the axes of your drawing.)

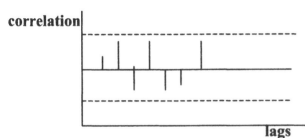

   B) Draw the correlogram (autocorrelation function) of a nonstationary variable.

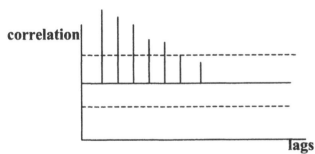

10. A) What is cointegration? **variables that are nonstationary to the same degree**

    B) Given $Y_t = B0 + B1\ X_t + e_t$ describe how to determine if Y and X are cointegrated. Spell out the Dickey-Fuller regression involved.

    • **Run the regression: $Y_t = B0 + B1\ X_t + e_t$**
    • **Run the Dickey-Fuller regression: $(e_t - e_{t-1}) = B0 + B1e_{t-1} + z_t$**
    • **Perform a negative sign test on B1**
    1) Ho: B1 = 0 (e is nonstationary)   Ha: B1 < 0 (e is stationary)
         (X and Y are not cointegrated)   (X and Y are cointegrated)
    2) 5%
    3) If t-ratio < –tc*, reject Ho
    4) The t-ratio is the usual one, but tc* is about 60% higher than tc from the usual t-table. As n approaches infinity tc* approaches 2.86 from higher levels.
    5) state the results of the test

Critical Values Tables

Critical Values of the t-Distribution

As indicated by the chart below, the areas given at the top of this table are the right tail areas for the t-value inside the table. For a one-tailed test at the 5% critical level with 6 degrees of freedom, look in the 5% column at the 6 row to get $t^c = 1.943$. For a two-tailed test at the 5% critical level with 6 degrees of freedom, look in the 2.5% column at the 6 row to get $t^c = 2.447$.

df	10%	5%	2.5%	1%
1	3.078	6.314	12.71	31.82
2	1.886	2.920	4.303	6.965
3	1.638	2.353	3.182	4.541
4	1.533	2.132	2.776	3.747
5	1.476	2.015	2.571	3.365
6	1.440	1.943	2.447	3.143
7	1.415	1.895	2.365	2.998
8	1.397	1.860	2.306	2.896
9	1.383	1.833	2.262	2.821
10	1.372	1.812	2.228	2.764
11	1.363	1.796	2.201	2.718
12	1.356	1.782	2.179	2.681
13	1.350	1.771	2.160	2.650
14	1.345	1.761	2.145	2.624
15	1.341	1.753	2.131	2.602
16	1.337	1.746	2.120	2.583
17	1.333	1.740	2.110	2.567
18	1.330	1.734	2.101	2.552
19	1.328	1.729	2.093	2.539
20	1.325	1.725	2.086	2.528
21	1.323	1.721	2.080	2.518
22	1.321	1.717	2.074	2.508
23	1.319	1.714	2.069	2.500
24	1.318	1.711	2.064	2.492
25	1.316	1.708	2.060	2.485
26	1.315	1.706	2.056	2.479
27	1.314	1.703	2.052	2.473
28	1.313	1.701	2.048	2.467
29	1.311	1.699	2.045	2.462
30	1.310	1.697	2.042	2.457
40	1.303	1.684	2.021	2.423
50	1.295	1.676	2.009	2.403
60	1.296	1.671	2.000	2.390
80	1.292	1.664	1.990	2.374
100	1.290	1.660	1.984	2.364
1000	1.282	1.646	1.962	2.330
∞	1.282	1.640	1.960	2.326

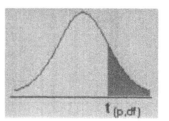

Critical Values of the F-Distribution (5%)

The table below shows critical values of the F-distribution at the 5% level of significance. For example, the critical F (Fc) for 3 degrees of freedom in the numerator and 25 degrees of freedom in the denominator is 2.99.

df denom	df numerator										
	1	2	3	4	5	6	7	8	12	24	∞
5	6.61	5.79	5.41	5.19	5.05	4.95	4.88	4.82	4.68	4.53	4.37
6	5.99	5.14	4.76	4.53	4.39	4.28	4.21	4.15	4.00	3.84	3.67
7	5.59	4.74	4.35	4.12	3.97	3.87	3.79	3.73	3.57	3.41	3.23
8	5.32	4.46	4.07	3.84	3.69	3.58	3.50	3.44	3.28	3.12	2.93
9	5.12	4.26	3.86	3.63	3.48	3.37	3.29	3.23	3.07	2.90	2.71
10	4.96	4.10	3.71	3.48	3.33	3.22	3.14	3.07	2.91	2.74	2.54
11	4.84	3.98	3.59	3.36	3.20	3.09	3.01	2.95	2.79	2.61	2.41
12	4.75	3.89	3.49	3.26	3.11	3.00	2.91	2.85	2.69	2.51	2.30
13	4.67	3.81	3.41	3.18	3.03	2.92	2.83	2.77	2.60	2.42	2.21
14	4.60	3.74	3.34	3.11	2.96	2.85	2.76	2.70	2.53	2.35	2.13
15	4.54	3.68	3.29	3.06	2.90	2.79	2.71	2.64	2.48	2.29	2.07
16	4.49	3.63	3.24	3.01	2.85	2.74	2.66	2.59	2.42	2.24	2.01
17	4.45	3.59	3.20	2.96	2.81	2.70	2.61	2.55	2.38	2.19	1.96
18	4.41	3.55	3.16	2.93	2.77	2.66	2.58	2.51	2.34	2.15	1.92
19	4.38	3.52	3.13	2.90	2.74	2.63	2.54	2.48	2.31	2.11	1.88
20	4.35	3.49	3.10	2.87	2.71	2.60	2.51	2.45	2.28	2.08	1.84
21	4.32	3.47	3.07	2.84	2.68	2.57	2.49	2.42	2.25	2.05	1.81
22	4.30	3.44	3.05	2.82	2.66	2.55	2.46	2.40	2.23	2.03	1.78
23	4.28	3.42	3.03	2.80	2.64	2.53	2.44	2.37	2.20	2.01	1.76
24	4.26	3.40	3.01	2.78	2.62	2.51	2.42	2.36	2.18	1.98	1.73
25	4.24	3.39	2.99	2.76	2.60	2.49	2.40	2.34	2.16	1.96	1.71
26	4.23	3.37	2.98	2.74	2.59	2.47	2.39	2.32	2.15	1.95	1.69
27	4.21	3.35	2.96	2.73	2.57	2.46	2.37	2.31	2.13	1.93	1.67
28	4.20	3.34	2.95	2.71	2.56	2.45	2.36	2.29	2.12	1.91	1.66
29	4.18	3.33	2.93	2.70	2.55	2.43	2.35	2.28	2.10	1.90	1.64
30	4.17	3.32	2.92	2.69	2.53	2.42	2.33	2.27	2.09	1.89	1.62
40	4.08	3.23	2.84	2.61	2.45	2.34	2.25	2.18	2.00	1.79	1.51
60	4.00	3.15	2.76	2.53	2.37	2.25	2.17	2.10	1.92	1.70	1.39
80	3.96	3.11	2.72	2.49	2.33	2.21	2.13	2.06	1.88	1.65	1.33
100	3.94	3.09	2.70	2.46	2.31	2.19	2.10	2.03	1.85	1.63	1.28
120	3.92	3.07	2.68	2.45	2.29	2.18	2.09	2.02	1.83	1.61	1.26
∞	3.84	3.00	2.61	2.37	2.22	2.10	2.01	1.94	1.75	1.52	1.00

Critical Values of the χ2-Distribution

d.f.	10%	5%	1%
1	2.71	3.84	6.63
2	4.61	5.99	9.21
3	6.25	7.81	11.34
4	7.78	9.49	13.23
5	9.24	11.07	15.09
6	10.64	12.53	16.81
7	12.02	14.07	18.48
8	13.36	15.51	20.09
9	14.68	16.92	21.67
10	15.99	18.31	23.21
11	17.29	19.68	24.72
12	18.55	21.03	26.22
13	19.81	22.36	27.69
14	21.06	23.68	29.14
15	22.31	25.00	30.58
16	23.54	26.30	32.00
17	24.77	27.59	33.41
18	25.99	28.87	34.81
19	27.20	30.14	36.19
20	28.41	31.41	37.57
21	29.62	39.67	38.93
22	30.81	33.92	40.29
23	32.01	35.17	41.64
24	33.20	36.42	42.98
25	34.38	37.65	44.31
26	35.56	38.89	45.64
27	36.74	40.11	46.96
28	37.92	41.34	48.28
29	39.09	42.56	49.59
30	40.26	43.77	50.89
40	51.81	55.76	63.69
50	63.17	67.50	76.15
60	74.40	79.08	88.38
80	96.58	101.90	112.30
100	118.50	124.30	135.80

Critical Values for the Durbin-Watson-Statistic

Level of Significance = 5 percent

k = # of structural parameters

n	k = 2 d_L	k = 2 d_U	k = 3 d_L	k = 3 d_U	k = 4 d_L	k = 4 d_U	k = 5 d_L	k = 5 d_U	k = 6 d_L	k = 6 d_U
15	1.08	1.36	0.95	1.54	0.82	1.75	0.69	1.97	0.56	2.21
16	1.1	1.37	0.98	1.54	0.86	1.73	0.74	1.93	0.62	2.15
17	1.13	1.38	1.02	1.54	0.9	1.71	0.78	1.9	0.67	2.1
18	1.16	1.39	1.05	1.53	0.93	1.69	0.92	1.87	0.71	2.06
19	1.18	1.4	1.08	1.53	0.97	1.68	0.86	1.85	0.75	2.02
20	1.2	1.41	1.1	1.54	1	1.68	0.9	1.83	0.79	1.99
21	1.22	1.42	1.13	1.54	1.03	1.67	0.93	1.81	0.83	1.96
22	1.24	1.43	1.15	1.54	1.05	1.66	0.96	1.8	0.96	1.94
23	1.26	1.44	1.17	1.54	1.08	1.66	0.99	1.79	0.9	1.92
24	1.27	1.45	1.19	1.55	1.1	1.66	1.01	1.78	0.93	1.9
25	1.29	1.45	1.21	1.55	1.12	1.66	1.04	1.77	0.95	1.89
26	1.3	1.46	1.22	1.55	1.14	1.65	1.06	1.76	0.98	1.88
27	1.32	1.47	1.24	1.56	1.16	1.65	1.08	1.76	1.01	1.86
28	1.33	1.48	1.26	1.56	1.18	1.65	1.1	1.75	1.03	1.85
29	1.34	1.48	1.27	1.56	1.2	1.65	1.12	1.74	1.05	1.84
30	1.35	1.49	1.28	1.57	1.21	1.65	1.14	1.74	1.07	1.83
31	1.36	1.5	1.3	1.57	1.23	1.65	1.16	1.74	1.09	1.83
32	1.37	1.5	1.31	1.57	1.24	1.65	1.18	1.73	1.11	1.82
33	1.38	1.51	1.32	1.58	1.26	1.65	1.19	1.73	1.13	1.81
34	1.39	1.51	1.33	1.58	1.27	1.65	1.21	1.73	1.15	1.81
35	1.4	1.52	1.34	1.58	1.28	1.65	1.22	1.73	1.16	1.8
36	1.41	1.52	1.35	1.59	1.29	1.65	1.24	1.73	1.18	1.8
37	1.42	1.53	1.36	1.59	1.31	1.66	1.25	1.72	1.19	1.8
38	1.43	1.54	1.37	1.59	1.32	1.66	1.26	1.72	1.21	1.79
39	1.43	1.54	1.38	1.6	1.33	1.66	1.27	1.72	1.22	1.79
40	1.44	1.54	1.39	1.6	1.34	1.66	1.29	1.72	1.23	1.79
45	1.48	1.57	1,43	1.62	1.38	1.67	1.34	1.72	1.29	1.78
50	1.5	1.59	1.46	1.63	1.42	1.67	1.38	1.72	1.34	1.77
55	1.53	1.6	1.49	1.64	1.45	1.68	1.41	1.72	1.38	1.77
60	1.55	1.62	1.51	1.65	1.48	1.69	1.44	1.73	1.41	1.77
65	1.57	1.63	1.54	1.66	1.5	1.7	1.47	1.73	1.44	1.77
70	1.58	1.64	1.55	1.67	1.52	1.7	1.49	1.74	1.46	1.77
75	1.6	1.65	1.57	1.68	1.54	1.71	1.51	1.74	1.49	1.77
80	1.61	1.66	1.59	1.69	1.56	1.72	1.53	1.74	1.51	1.77
85	1.62	1.67	1.6	1.7	1.57	1.72	1.55	1.75	1.52	1.77
90	1.63	1.68	1.61	1.7	1.59	1.73	1.57	1.75	1.54	1.78
95	1.64	1.69	1.62	1.71	1.6	1.73	1.58	1.75	1.56	1.78
100	1.65	1.69	1.63	1.72	1.61	1.74	1.59	1.76	1.57	1.78
150	1.72	1.75	1.71	1.76	1.69	1.77	1.68	1.79	1.66	1.8
200	1.76	1.78	1.75	1.79	1.74	1.8	1.73	1.81	1.72	1.82

CRITICAL VALUES TABLES

Critical Values for the Durbin-Watson Statistic

Level of Significance = 5 percent

k = # of structural parameters

n	k = 7 d_L	k = 7 d_U	k = 8 d_L	k = 8 d_U	k = 9 d_L	k = 9 d_U	k = 10 d_L	k = 10 d_U	k = 11 d_L	k = 11 d_U
15	0.45	2.47	0.34	2.73	0.25	2.98	0.18	3.22	0.11	3.44
16	0.5	2.39	0.4	2.62	0.3	2.86	0.22	3.09	0.16	3.3
17	0.55	2.32	0.45	2.54	0.36	2.76	0.27	2.98	0.2	3.18
18	0.6	2.26	0.5	2.47	0.41	2.67	0.32	2.87	0.24	3.07
19	0.65	2.21	0.55	2.4	0.46	2.59	0.37	2.78	0.29	2.97
20	0.69	2.16	0.6	2.34	0.5	2.52	0.42	2.7	0.34	2.89
21	0.73	2.12	0.64	2.3	0.55	2.46	0.46	2.63	0.38	2.81
22	0.77	2.09	0.68	2.25	0.59	2.41	0.51	2.57	0.42	2.73
23	0.8	2.06	0.72	2.21	0.63	2.36	0.55	2.51	0.47	2.67
24	0.84	2.04	0.75	2.17	0.67	2.32	0.58	2.46	0.51	2.61
25	0.87	2.01	0.78	2.14	0.7	2.28	0.62	2.42	0.54	2.56
26	0.9	1.99	0.82	2.12	0.74	2.24	0.66	2.38	0.58	2.51
27	0.93	1.97	0.85	2.09	0.77	2.22	0.69	2.34	0.62	2.47
28	0.95	1.96	0.87	2.07	0.8	2.19	0.72	2.31	0.65	2.43
29	0.98	1.94	0.9	2.05	0.83	2.16	0.75	2.28	0.68	2.4
30	1	1.93	0.93	2.03	0.85	2.14	0.78	2.25	0.71	2.36
31	1.02	1.92	0.95	2.02	0.88	2.12	0.81	2.23	74	2.33
32	1.04	1.91	0.97	2	0.9	2.1	0.84	2.2	0.77	2.31
33	1.06	1.9	0.99	1.99	0.93	2.09	0.86	2.18	0.8	2.28
34	1.08	1.89	1.02	1.98	0.95	2.07	0.89	2.16	0.82	2.26
35	1.1	1.88	1.03	1.97	0.97	2.05	0.91	2.14	0.85	2.24
36	1.11	1.88	1.05	1.96	0.99	2.04	0.93	2.13	0.87	2.22
37	1.13	1.87	1.07	1.95	1.01	2.03	0.95	2.11	0.89	2.2
38	1.5	1.86	1.09	1.94	1.03	2.02	0.97	2.1	0.91	2.18
39	1.16	1.86	1.1	1.93	1.05	2.01	0.99	2.09	0.93	2.16
40	1.18	1.85	1.12	1.92	1.06	2	1.01	2.07	0.95	2.15
45	1.24	1.84	1.19	1.9	1.14	1.96	1.09	2.02	1.04	2.09
50	1.29	1.82	1.25	1.88	1.2	1.93	1.16	1.99	1.11	2.04
55	1.33	1.81	1.29	1.86	1.25	1.91	1.21	1.96	1.17	2.01
60	1.37	1.81	1.34	1.85	1.3	1.89	1.26	1.94	1.22	1.98
65	1.4	1.81	1.37	1.84	1.34	1.88	1.3	1.92	1.27	1.96
70	1.43	1.8	1.4	1.84	1.37	1.87	1.34	1.91	1.31	1.95
75	1.46	1.8	1.43	1.83	1.4	1.87	1.37	1.9	1.34	1.94
80	1.48	1.8	1.45	1.83	1.43	1.86	1.4	1.89	1.37	1.93
85	1.5	1.8	1.47	1.83	1.49	1.86	1.42	1.89	1.4	1.92
90	1.52	1.8	1.49	1.83	1.47	1.85	1.45	1.88	1.42	1.91
95	1.54	1.8	1.51	1.83	1.49	1.85	1.46	1.88	1.44	1.9
100	1.55	1.8	1.53	1.83	1.5	1.85	1.48	1.87	1.46	1.9
150	1.65	1.82	1.64	1.83	1.62	1.85	1.6	1.86	1.59	1.88
200	1.71	1.83	1.7	1.84	1.69	1.85	1.68	1.86	1.67	1.87

Subject and Name Index

nonlinear, 163
normal distribution, 95
normal equation
defined, 19, 187
derived, 14–15, 44–45, 161, 191
notation, 10–11, 95

Okun, A. M., 59, 121–122, 145
ordinary least-squares
BLUE, 99
defined, 5, 19
method, 11–13
Newey-West, 109–111
properties of, 88–95, 152

panel data, 6
Park, R.E., 145
Park test, 108, 112–113, 124
polynomial model, 65
population regression function, 11, 19, 187
predetermined variable, 89
probability value, 39, 57, 189–190
pseudoautocorrelation, 121, 122, 130
psychometrics, 5

Ramsey, J.B., 145
Ramsey's reset test, 50–57, 67, 87
reciprocal model, 65
regression
multiple, 43–52, 66, 98, 109
through the origin, 59–61, 67, 87
regression function
population, 11, 19, 187
sample, 11, 19, 187
repeated sampling, 26–27, 46, 52–53, 92, 95, 99, 153–155, 158, 187, 190
residual, 2, 19
statistics, 23, 45, 52, 74, 99, 109, 116, 120–122, 130, 202–203
See also error term

r-squared. *See* coefficient of determination
retail sales, 75–76

sabermetrics, 5
sample regression function, 11, 19, 187, scattergram, 4, 6, 10–11, 30, 53, 61, 63, 65, 67, 79, 158, 162–163, 187
Schwarz criterion, 50–53, 55, 60, 160
seasonal adjustment, 75–76
second-differences, 135, 137–138
semi-log model, 64, 69–70, 108–109, 162, 197
SER. *See* standard error of the regression
serial correlation
and Classical Linear Regression Model, 94, 103
consequences of, 109, 116
defined, 116, 122
detection of, 116–120, 129, 139–142, 173–177
remedies, 120–121, 130
second-order, 116, 120, 122, 125, 199
See also autocorrelation
sociometrics, 5
Spector, L. C., 77, 80, 146
specification
model, 49–53, 100
over, 52–53
under, 51–53, 122
spurious correlation, 131–133, 137–138, 143, 203
standard error
of an estimator, 27–29, 46, 52, 92, 99–100, 104, 107, 109, 111–116, 121–126, 139, 153–155, 172, 176
of the regression, 27, 116, 126
stationary, 131–138, 141, 143, 180–183, 203–204
structural parameter
defined, 11, 19

test
for r = 0, 37–38
for r² = 0, 38–39
negative sign, 36
positive sign, 36–37
of significance, 33–35
specific value, 37
Theil, H., 2, 146
time series, 6, 29, 100, 138, 143, 145, 187
t-ratio, 34–39, 47–48, 50–52, 57, 61, 67–68, 87, 92, 100, 107–108, 112, 116, 124, 126, 136–137, 155–158, 161, 170–171, 175, 181–183, 189, 191, 194, 199–202, 205
trend variable, 64, 66
t-statistic, 38–39, 56
See also t-ratio
two-stage least squares, 130
type I error, 33–34, 40
type II error, 33–34, 40

unbiased estimator, 57, 89–92, 95, 190, 200
unit root, 135–137, 145

variable
independent variable, 11, 19
predetermined, 89
stochastic, 19
See also dependent variable
variance inflation factor, 100–101, 104, 197

Wang, H., 145
Watson, G.S., 118, 145
weighted least-squares, 109–113, 124, 170, 172, 197, 199
West, K.D., 109, 145
Wheeler, D., 145
White, H., 108, 146
white noise, 116, 120–122, 125, 199
White test, 109, 112

For Product Safety Concerns and Information please contact our EU
representative GPSR@taylorandfrancis.com Taylor & Francis Verlag GmbH,
Kaufingerstraße 24, 80331 München, Germany

Printed and bound by CPI Group (UK) Ltd, Croydon, CR0 4YY
08/05/2025
01864543-0001